NORTH CAROLINA
STATE BOARD OF COMMUNITY COLLEGES
LIBRARIES
FORSYTH TECHNICAL COMMUNITY COLLEGE

D1259018

NO ANGELS

NO ANGELS

Women Who Commit Violence

Edited by Alice Myers and Sarah Wight

LIBRARY
FORSYTH TECHNICAL COMMUNITY COLLEGE
2100 SILAS CREEK PARKWAY
WINSTON-SALEM, NC 27103-5197

An Imprint of HarperCollins*Publishers*

Pandora
An Imprint of HarperCollins*Publishers*
77–85 Fulham Palace Road,
Hammersmith, London W6 8JB
1160 Battery Street,
San Francisco, California 94111-1213

Published by Pandora 1996

10 9 8 7 6 5 4 3 2 1

© Anette Ballinger, Sean French,
Laura Grindstaff, Emily Hamer,
Tracy Hargreaves, Rachel Holmes,
Cindy Jenefsky, Martha McCaughey,
Alice Myers, Patricia J. Priest,
Stephanie Savage, Anne Scully,
Elizabeth Stanko, Jill D. Swenson,
Sarah Wight and Helen Yeates 1996

The contributors to this work
assert the moral right to be
identified as the authors of this work

A catalogue record for this book
is available from the British Library

ISBN 0 04 440957 5

Printed and bound in Great Britain by
Caledonian International Book Manufacturing Ltd, Glasgow

All rights reserved. No part of this publication may be
reproduced, stored in a retrieval system, or transmitted,
in any form or by any means, electronic, mechanical,
photocopying, recording or otherwise, without the prior
permission of the publishers.

CONTENTS

ACKNOWLEDGEMENTS

We would like to thank the contributors for the thought, energy and time they gave to this book with their chapters. Mandy Merck encouraged us throughout this project and gave us much useful advice. Sara Dunn also provided encouragement and guidance. Thanks are due to Matthew Lockwood for all his practical help, to Belinda Budge at Pandora for her support, to the faculty and staff of the media studies programme at the University of Sussex for their aid and advice, and to Jeremy Gavron for suggesting the title. We are also grateful to the family, friends, colleagues, and many others encountered in the course of this project who have been enthusiastic, helpful and supportive.

CONTRIBUTORS

Anette Ballinger is a Ph.D. student in the Faculty of Law at the University of Sheffield. She is currently completing her thesis 'Dead Woman Walking: Executed Women in England and Wales 1900–1955'.

Sean French is a columnist for *New Statesman and Society*. He has also written biographies and fiction. His British Film Institute monograph on *The Terminator* was published in the autumn of 1996. A new novel, *The Memory Game*, co-written with his wife Nicci Gerrard, will be published in January 1997.

Laura Grindstaff is assistant professor in the Annenberg School for Communication at the University of Pennsylvania. She teaches courses in Field Work, Media, and Popular Culture, and is currently writing a book on daytime television talk shows.

Emily Hamer is the author of *Britannia's Glory: A History of Twentieth-Century Lesbians*. She lives in London.

Tracy Hargreaves lectures in Modern Literature at the University of Leeds. She is currently working on a biography of Dame Ethel Smyth.

Rachel Holmes lectures in Lesbian Studies at the University of Sussex and teaches on the Sexual Dissidence MA. She specializes in the history, politics and culture of sexuality in South Africa.

Cindy Jenefsky is an assistant professor at the University of Georgia, where she teaches courses in both communications and women's studies.

Martha McCaughey is assistant professor of Women's Studies at the Center for Interdisciplinary Studies at Virginia Polytechnic Institute and State University. She recently completed a book on the women's self-defense movement (New York University Press, 1997).

Alice Myers has an MA in media studies from the University of Sussex. She is a writer and lives in London.

Patricia J. Priest is a rape crisis advocate and media critic who teaches part-time at the University of Georgia. She is the author of *Public Intimacies: Talk Show Participants and Tell-All TV* (Hampton Press, 1995).

Stephanie Savage is a Ph.D. candidate at the University of Iowa. She lives and works in Los Angeles, where she is completing her dissertation 'Been Around: The Star Body in the Studio Era'. Other topics of interest include true-crime narratives, scandal and pornography.

Anne Scully received her L.L.M. from University College London. She is a lecturer at Brunel University, where she teaches Jurisprudence, particularly feminist legal theory, Public Law Legal Method, and Law, State and Gender.

Elizabeth Stanko, Reader in Criminology, Brunel University, has explored gender and justice for the past 15 years. Recent publications include *Everyday Violence: How Women and Men Experience Physical and Sexual Danger* (Pandora, 1990); *Intimate Intrusions* (Routledge, 1985) and *Just Boys Doing Business: Men, Masculinities and Crime* (co-editor with Tim Newburn; Routledge, 1994).

Jill D. Swenson is an assistant professor of Media Studies and Journalism at Ithaca College in Ithaca, New York.

Sarah Wight is a freelance editor living in Montreal. She received an MA in media studies from the University of Sussex.

Helen Yeates teaches Film, Media and Feminist Studies at the School of Media and Journalism, Queensland University of Technology, Australia. She has published extensively on issues relating to women, crime and the media, and more recently on competing formations of masculinity in the media.

INTRODUCTION

Sarah Wight and Alice Myers

When Lorena Bobbitt cut off her husband's penis in 1993 after four years of domestic abuse, everyone heard about it. News agencies initially reported the case for its novelty value; female violence, after all, is rare. But in the months leading up to Lorena Bobbitt's trial, articles, dramatizations, interviews and opinion pieces proliferated in all forms of the media. Today, after a best-selling pornographic video starring John Bobbitt as hero of his own life, a 'true crime' book, and numerous jokes, the original events have been so over-written they have been virtually obscured. The instant celebrity of Lorena Bobbitt and the extraordinary energy devoted to examining and reworking the details of her crime were the starting-off points for this collection. Why are violent women like Lorena Bobbitt the object of such fascination? And why, in spite of this seemingly powerful drive to understand and explain their actions, are the explanations offered so inadequate? The essays in this book raise a series of related questions about how modern society reacts to violence done by women, how such violence threatens the social order, and how society tries to contain such threats through the way it represents and analyses their crimes.

The women in these studies were charged with many different acts of violence, from murder to terrorism. Each is unique and complex – yet the public representations of these women are strikingly similar regardless of the nature of their acts. As the essays in this collection show, when a

woman commits an act of criminal violence her sex is the lens through
which all her actions are seen and understood; her sex is the primary
'explanation' or mitigating factor offered up in any attempt to understand
her crime. Consequently this book is less about violence than about
gender. The title *No Angels* alludes to the many contradictory and
stereotypical notions of 'woman' that are evoked in the explanations of and
judgements on female violence. As Patricia Priest, Cindy Jenefsky and Jill
Swenson demonstrate in their chapter, the press coverage of the Bobbitts
glossed over John's lengthy history of domestic violence, choosing instead
to emphasize and condemn Lorena's single act against him. Male violence
as such does not attract mass attention; it is not an anomaly to be dissected
in popular representations.

The chapters that follow analyse the legal defences used in the cases of
real women, fictional representations of real crimes, and purely fictional
depictions of female violence. However, there is an intimate dialogue
between reality and how it is presented. Fiction borrows from real life, and
'facts' can easily be compromised in the very process of reporting them.
Even the legal system shapes the stories which are told: murder defences,
for example, must stress those facts that will fulfil the legal definitions of
mitigating factors, such as self-defence or temporary insanity.

Ultimately, the cultural meaning of stories of women's violence lies
somewhere between reality and representation. As we write this, Rosemary
West is seeking leave to appeal against her conviction for ten murders; her
defence lawyer is blaming the media for having 'exercised [a] malign
influence on the proceedings such as to deprive the applicant of a fair trial'.
Every major witness at the trial had a contract with the media, thus opening
up the way for evidence to be exaggerated or pre-rehearsed to the point
where it became distorted.[1] How can the facts of the case be determined
once exclusive contracts, book deals and other inducements are allowed to
play a part in the legal narrative?

Mad or Bad?
The proliferation of stories told about violent women is out of all proportion to their actual numbers. For instance, in Britain in 1991, 43,300 men
were charged with violence against the person, compared with just 3,900
women.[2] The excessive storytelling about women's violence – in court, in
the press, and in docu-drama and fiction – can be seen as a symptom of
social anxiety about women's roles and the perceived abandonment of

traditional femininity. When a woman transgresses the bounds of her prescribed gender role, her actions are translated in less threatening terms. The 'abnormality' of her 'unwomanly' behaviour is explained away: she is either mad (hysterical, suffering from pre-menstrual tension or Battered Woman Syndrome) or bad (the inadequate mother, the lesbian, the just plain evil). These 'justifications' recur in representations of women who commit violence, from Myra Hindley to Lindy Chamberlain.[3] While the hysteric suffers from an excess of femininity, the 'bad' woman is unnatural in her lack of it. As Anette Ballinger and Sean French show in their contributions, a woman's conformity (or otherwise) to the stereotype of femininity crucially affects how she fares in the courts. Violent women are treated more leniently by the courts if they can be represented as mad, since their alleged pathology separates them safely from ordinary womanhood. Madness relieves women of responsibility for their actions, denying them moral agency. As for those violent women who are dubbed evil and unnatural, they are doubly vilified since their transgression doesn't just threaten individuals, but the whole edifice of 'womanhood'. Here the extreme again serves to define and police the boundaries of the normal: society writes these women off as 'abnormal' while protecting itself from their pernicious influence.

Anette Ballinger addresses the question of how notions of femininity filter legal and public perceptions of female killers. She contrasts the trials of Marie Fahmy and Ruth Ellis to show how different models of feminine behaviour led to opposing judgments of their very similar crimes. Why was Marie Fahmy, who played the consummate victim – taking advantage of her biological claim to innocence – released, while Ruth Ellis, who refused such a role, was hanged? Elizabeth Stanko and Anne Scully examine Emma Humphreys' successful appeal of her murder conviction and show that there are no legal absolutes. Without any fresh evidence, Humphreys established a new legal version of her crime: manslaughter on the grounds of provocation. How did the changed political climate allow her crime to be understood differently? The Humphreys case shows that dominant myths about gender can shift, and Stanko and Scully applaud the role of feminist campaign groups such as Justice for Women in Britain in effecting change.

Sean French looks at the various defence strategies of women accused of crimes with their partners, such as Rosemary West and Hedda Nussbaum – what stories can be told when there is a man to share the blame? The case of Hedda Nussbaum and Joel Steinberg, who were accused of the murder of their adopted daughter in 1987, is a striking example of society's reluctance to admit women's capacity for committing heinous crimes. Nussbaum had all charges against her dropped providing she testified against her husband. This preference or choice of men's criminality over women's illustrates a hierarchy of imperatives. Apparently, it is more important that women's traditional role as moral cornerstone of society remains intact than it is to punish them. If the criminal justice system can shift the burden of responsibility on to men, or excuse women's violence through allegations of madness, it will. Helena Kennedy writes in *Eve Was Framed* that our reluctance to criminalize women is 'a profound expression of our worst fears about the social fabric falling apart. Women are still the glue that cements the family unit, providing cohesion and continuity.'[4] If women embody all that is innocent and good in society, if they are to remain 'the angel in the house', then assigning them responsibility for criminal (and especially violent) acts is deeply uncomfortable, problematic and contradictory. For how can women secure culture in its present form, as agents of stability, if they are also the agents of violent crime, of anarchy?

True Stories?
Outside the constraints of legal discourse, representations of women's violence multiply in numerous forms and media. Stephanie Savage looks at how the story of Betty Broderick, who killed her ex-husband and his second wife, emerged in multiple versions in news reports, women's magazines and a made-for-TV movie, and traces the differences among them. Is it possible, she asks, to imagine an undistorted 'true' story? Fiction raises similar questions: Tracy Hargreaves examines the interaction between public debates on women who murder abusive husbands and the storyline of the soap opera *Brookside*. She demonstrates soap opera's capacity to make private worlds public, and analyses why the fiction of *Brookside* aroused as much public indignation as the actual British murder case on which it was based.

This need to tell and re-tell stories of women's violence is further evidence that this behaviour threatens the social order in a way that men's violence does not. Laura Grindstaff and Martha McCaughey look at Lorena Bobbitt's assault on her husband's penis and argue that the general uproar around the case is linked to hysterical anxiety about the phallus, symbolic of male privilege in society. The enormous effort which went into putting John Bobbitt back together and 'restoring his masculinity' (both literally and figuratively) parallels the way in which society tries to 'reconstruct' female violence to make it more palatable (and, perhaps, easier to dismiss).

Emily Hamer's paper looks back at the UK suffragette campaign, which often used extreme tactics to attract public attention to the cause of votes for women. The suffragettes mounted a direct attack on the male-dominated political order, and were in turn denounced as unnatural women. Rachel Holmes offers an account of the changing political status of Winnie Mandela in South Africa. She shows how Winnie Mandela's complex relationship to legitimate and illegitimate violence in the context of a violent national liberation struggle transformed her from 'mother of the country' to deviant mother. She outlines the inherently conflicting roles of loyal wife, mother, and political activist within that struggle, raising questions about women's problematic relationship with political authority.

Equal Representation?

The varied analyses of women's violence in this anthology are all concerned with how this violence is represented – by whom, for whom, and to what purpose. Although the authors have diverse concerns and raise different issues, they share a dissatisfaction with the limited avenues open for this representation, including any stories violent women might tell for themselves. Helen Yeates contends that even innocent women can have difficulty being portrayed as credible in the media, examining the double-edged celebrity of Lindy Chamberlain, still burdened with perceptions of guilt for a crime she did not commit, and Fairlie Arrow, perpetrator of a hoax kidnapping. Sara Thornton, who was tried for killing her allegedly abusive husband in 1990, articulates this problem of violent women being silenced or misinterpreted: 'Is there any reason … why I cannot speak for myself at the Court of Appeal?' she asks. 'I am fighting for myself and I wish to be heard.'[5] Similarly, Betty Broderick protests the appropriation of her story for a TV movie. 'They're using my name, pretending it's my voice, leading people to believe it was my story. Hah! I don't think so.'[6]

The female of the species is neither deadlier than the male, nor incapable of aggression. However, if every act of female aggression must be explained first and foremost by looking at gender, then adequate explanations will never be possible. A climate must be created in which women's violence can be seen for what it is: as complicated and dependent on individual circumstances as men's, in which being a woman is neither an asset nor a liability in the courts. As long as women are on trial for crimes against their gender as well as against their victims, miscarriages of justice and misunderstanding in the public mind will continue. We hope that the feminist analyses in this collection further encourage the development of alternative conceptions of violence by women.

THE GUILT
OF THE INNOCENT
AND THE INNOCENCE
OF THE GUILTY:

The Cases of Marie Fahmy and Ruth Ellis

Anette Ballinger

> *Prosecutor:* What did you do intentionally?
> *Madame Fahmy:* I never did anything intentionally. I just moved my arm when I saw he wanted to come to me. It was done instinctively … I never wanted to do him any harm. I never did.[1]

> *Prosecutor:* Mrs Ellis, when you fired that revolver at close range into the body of David Blakely, what did you intend to do?
> *Ruth Ellis:* It is obvious. When I shot him, I intended to kill him.[2]

Throughout history, women who kill have been portrayed as 'mad' – victims of 'raging hormones' and related biological functions which make them unaware of what they are doing – or 'bad', their evilness making them an aberration and setting them apart from 'normal' women and 'true' feminine behaviour. By denying the rationality behind women's murderous acts, traditional ideas about women's nature – their 'supposed passivity, submissiveness, asexuality and gentleness' are allowed to remain unchallenged; such violent women are not 'real' women after all.[3]

So far, the only alternative to this 'mad or bad' dichotomy has been yet another stereotype – that of 'woman as victim', or as the 'victim of a tragedy', a model within which the offender is 'presented as a *generally* harmless or pathetic or tragic individual' who is not considered a danger to the community at large, and who consequently, despite having committed a serious offence, may receive a relatively light sentence.[4] This model is therefore no more than a variation on the 'mad' model, because it removes moral responsibility and agency for the crime and thereby allows traditional and idealised beliefs around women's virtuousness and passivity to remain firmly in place.

Within our culture women's conduct and sexual morality are intimately linked to the 'mad or bad' dichotomy surrounding violent women. The mere fact that a woman has broken the law ensures she will be regarded as someone who has failed to fulfil gender role expectations, and if this is compounded by a refusal to demonstrate her commitment to conventional female roles in her personal life, especially in the areas around respectability, domesticity and motherhood, she can expect to find herself at the receiving end of what Pat Carlen has termed 'judicial misogyny'.[5] In short, those who fall within the 'bad' category because they are assertive, unemotional, promiscuous, divorced or have children in care can expect to be judged more severely than defendants who, 'at the time of their court appearances, are living at home with their husbands and children,' and who are prepared to '"soften" … [their image] to conform with the judge's stereotype of appropriate womanhood by presenting an image of docility'.[6] On the other hand, women who can trace their murderous act to acceptable female pathological causes such as PMT, post-natal depression, or indeed any other form of mental illness, fall into the 'mad' category, any rationality or agency on their part is ignored as they are deemed 'sick' and hence not responsible for their behaviour.[7] Subsequently such women may receive a lighter sentence than those within the 'bad' category. In particular, women found guilty of infanticide may avoid a custodial sentence altogether providing they agree to receive medical and/or psychiatric treatment.[8]

Compared to the vast array of research now available concerning other areas of women's lives, feminism has shown a marked reluctance to deal with female violence, perhaps concerned that the subject will harm the feminist cause. Yet to deny that women are capable of experiencing the full range of human emotion and experience is to argue on the same terrain as men who have perpetuated sexist myths regarding women's 'nature' throughout history.[9] When feminists have addressed the issue of violent women, they too have been inclined to portray the perpetrators as victimised individuals reacting to a particular set of circumstances, although unlike the victim category described above, feminists seek to avoid employing this concept for the purpose of rendering women pathetic or harmless. Instead it is used to explain female violence as when the abused strike back at their abusers. Those who do not fit into this category are usually presented as individuals who are engaged in the act of challenging dominant ideologies and prejudices regarding female behaviour.[10] Both these portrayals are valid and relevant and I shall draw from these traditions in the case-study analyses of Marie Fahmy and Ruth Ellis. Yet I shall also be arguing for the creation of new discourses through which we may begin to understand and subsequently analyse the actions of women who kill.[11] These new discourses can be created by exposing, exploring and analysing the differences between how such women view themselves and the circumstances which led up to their crimes, and the way in which their accounts are mediated and 'translated' in the court-room, the media and the public mind. A crucial aspect of the creation of new discourses is therefore *listening to and taking seriously* what these women are telling us, thus creating feminist research which is both located in and proceeding from 'the grounded analysis of women's material realities'.[12] This will enable us to present alternative accounts of their violence compared to those articulated by judicial personnel and the mass media.

In considering the case-studies it is essential that we understand how perceptions of female murderers are produced and how these perceptions come to be regarded and accepted as 'true' at the expense of other versions of the 'truth' about violent women and their crimes. Thus, when women attempt to resist the mad/bad categories by presenting their own logical and rational explanations of their violent crimes, they are disqualified as speakers – their accounts become 'muted' by dominant 'expert' (and common-sensical) knowledge constructions around violent women. Having become members of a muted group they will only be 'heard' again if and when they communicate through dominant modes of expression.[13] A failure to follow this rule will ensure their continued disqualification as speakers – their accounts will not be *listened to*.

In this chapter I intend to illustrate, through the case-studies, how these theoretical contentions operate in practice when violent women are standing in the dock. First, in the case of Madame Fahmy we meet a woman who communicated through the dominant modes of expression with great expertise – that is – Madame utilised and exploited her ability to express herself in an ultra-feminine manner, adhering closely to highly conventional expectations of female behaviour, for which, as we shall see, she was greatly rewarded.

Second, in my case-study of Ruth Ellis – the last woman to be hanged in England – I analyse her failure to conform to appropriate standards of female conduct both before and after her arrest. This failure assured her of a position within a 'muted' group – her account was not 'heard' because there were no channels open to receive what she had to say. Thus, although Ellis was by all accounts well-mannered, polite and extremely co-operative towards every one of the state servants who came into contact with her, she was nevertheless classified within the 'bad' category.[14] Her account of her crime appeared to be grounded in matter-of-fact logic and coherent rationality which ensured her exclusion from either the 'mad' or the 'victim' category. Yet Ellis was not someone who had made a deliberate or conscious decision to challenge and defy dominant ideologies around female behaviour. On the contrary, in her appearance, for example, Ellis paid almost exaggerated attention to feminine conventions, and some of her views can be seen to represent the epitome of conventionality, as illustrated by her response to her punishment: 'An eye for an eye, a life for a life.'[15] Yet despite such conformity she became regarded as a 'bad' woman – unruly and subversive – because there were no other discourses available through which she could be 'heard'. Following the work of Anne Worrall, this case-study therefore highlights the struggle which takes place 'between those who claim to know the "truth" and those about whom they claim to know it.'[16]

Third, in my conclusion I intend to illustrate how, 40 years after Ellis's execution and despite the very different natures of their crimes, Myra Hindley finds herself in exactly the same position as Ellis, as a member of the muted group who cannot be understood outside the mad or bad categories. Despite her vociferous and ongoing attempts to be 'listened to' and 'heard', and thus (even if unintentionally) become part of the process towards creating and establishing new discourses and a new language around women's violent and murderous behaviour, Hindley is responded to in much the same manner today as at the time of her arrest in 1965. This is largely due to the sheer hostility and opposition facing anyone attempt-ing to open up new discourses around the representation of female murderers such as Hindley, since such action is invariably (mis)interpreted as condoning the violent nature of the crimes. Four decades have passed since the hanging of Ruth Ellis, while, after 30 years of imprisonment, Myra Hindley has become Britain's longest-serving female prisoner.[17] I therefore argue that there is a need for feminist theorists to ask ourselves what lessons we can learn from the treatment by the legal system and the mass media of the women discussed in this chapter. Feminist writers must acknowledge and confront the issue of violent women in order to facilitate the process of establishing a new language which will allow us to analyse women's violence outside the 'mad versus bad' framework, and thus challenge the imposition of silence which has dominated women's experiences of the legal system in England and Wales.

Murder at the Savoy Hotel: The Case of Madame Fahmy

The trial of Marie Marguerite Fahmy, a 32-year-old Frenchwoman, opened at the Old Bailey on 10 September, 1923. She was accused of having murdered her husband Ali Kamel Fahmy Bey, a 23-year-old Egyptian millionaire, who through charitable works had received the honorary title of 'prince'. The couple had been married for just over six months when Madame shot her husband in the early hours of 10 July, 1923. According to Madame Fahmy she had endured much suffering during this period at the hands of Ali Fahmy, including frequent threats, imprisonment, beatings and 'unnatural sexual acts'.[18]

While there can be no doubt that Ali had frequently abused and mistreated his wife, evidence suggests that Marie's behaviour did not always fit the description of the innocent, fragile and helpless victim which she consistently presented herself as in court, but that she instead often traded insult with insult and violence with violence, to which the dead body of Ali was the ultimate testament.[19] Marie was a so-called 'woman of the world' with a plethora of life experiences behind her who had been able to leave her humble background behind as the result of a large personal allowance granted to her by an ex-husband. Moreover, long before pre-nuptial agreements had become commonplace amongst the wealthy, Marie had the foresight to hire a lawyer prior to her wedding, whose task it was to secure her the right to divorce should she so choose, a condition which Ali refused to agree to, as it was in conflict with Muslim law. She subsequently agreed to 'sell' this right for the sum of £2,000.[20] Once the trial was over, Marie instigated a six-year court battle against Ali's family over his fortune estimated at over £3 million which, according to one writer, involved a faked pregnancy in order to increase her chances of the inheritance.[21] She eventually lost this case in a Cairo court in 1930. However, Marie's strong personality and sense of independence, as well as her shrewd business mind, were not to be the main discourses through which her case would be conducted, as I shall now illustrate.

The Trial of Madame Fahmy

Due to her wealthy circumstances, Madame Fahmy was able to buy herself the services of the man considered to be the best defence counsel available at the time, Sir Edward Marshall Hall. Sir Edward constructed her defence around the contention that the shooting had been accidental. The exact circumstances surrounding the shooting can, in the absence of eye-witnesses, only remain speculative, but the careful preparation of letters and statements by Madame, which were later to become vital evidence in court, together with a very public row between the Fahmys on the eve of the shooting, make it difficult to ignore the possibility that at least the thought of releasing herself from a dominant and violent husband had been an option Mme Fahmy had considered.[22] The only witness who saw the couple around the time of the shooting was John Beattie, a porter who, moments before hearing the shots, saw Ali Fahmy in the hallway, very agitated and shouting: 'Look at my face! Look what she has done!' Beattie attempted to calm the couple down before leaving them, but within minutes he heard gun-shots and upon returning found Madame Fahmy on her knees by her dying husband's side, repeatedly crying 'What have I done!' and 'Speak to me, speak to me!'[23] She was described as being 'excited one moment, distressed the next, and dazed'. By the time the hotel manager arrived on the scene, Mme Fahmy exclaimed: 'Oh, Sir, I have been married six months, which has been torture to me. I have suffered terribly … What will they do? My poor children!'[24] When she phoned Ali's personal secretary, her words were: 'Come quickly, come quickly; I have shot Ali … I do not know how I did it.'[25] Once at the police station she exclaimed:

> 'I cannot understand what I have done.' She was thoroughly dazed. She said, 'They say I have shot my husband. How many shots did I fire?' When told that her husband was dead she broke down and wept.[26]

The following day, 'the accused looking very pale and ill was escorted into court by the matron and was at once given a seat in the dock' where she was to hear the charges against her.[27]

The murder of Ali Fahmy became a high-profile case and media interest in the trial was intense. Madame Fahmy behaved impeccably, casting herself in the role of the grieving widow by appearing in court 'attired in deep mourning' as she pleaded 'Not Guilty' to the charge of murder.[28] In her statement she expressed surprise that the pistol had gone off, claiming to have fired the first shot out of a window to frighten her husband off. When she pulled the trigger the second and third time she assumed the gun was unloaded and was apparently taken by deep surprise when Fahmy collapsed:

'I lifted my arm, and without looking pulled the trigger. The next moment I saw him on the ground before me without realising what had happened. I do not know how many times the pistol went off. I did not know what had happened, and I saw my husband on the floor, and I fell on my knees beside him. I caught hold of his hand and said, "Sweetheart, it is nothing. Speak, oh please speak to me." While I was on my knees the porter came up, but I was so touched that I understood nothing.'

Sir Edward: 'When that pistol went off had you any idea that it was in a condition to be fired?'

'None. I thought there was no cartridge when you had pulled the barrel and that it could not be used.'

Mme Fahmy was frequently in tears as she told her story. On one occasion she was so overcome that Mr Justice Swift asked if she would like time to compose herself.[29]

Already we can discern the mobilisation of several discourses around female behaviour and conduct. First, Mme Fahmy's apparent incompetence and lack of knowledge of the technical aspects of guns is only to be expected. From the time of the 17th-century scientific revolution, women's supposed 'irrationality' came to be regarded as being in direct conflict with scientific practices and principles.[30] In particular, women would not be expected to display expert knowledge in the ultra-masculine area of armoury and weaponry. Thus, despite having committed the very masculine act of firing three bullets into her husband's body, Mme Fahmy preserved her femininity when, in response to a request to examine the murder weapon whilst in the dock she replied that 'she did not understand automatics.'[31]

Second, Mme Fahmy's dazed and confused state of mind during and after the shooting ensures that her act of violence appears uncalculated and unpremeditated, implying that she was in a highly emotional state, even hysterical – 'ruled by her emotions' and acting on the 'spur of the moment' – characteristics strongly associated with women's 'irrationality' and lack of self-control, which in turn were thought to spring from their inherent biological instability. Early legal, medical and criminological experts considered women to be 'emotional and irrational' by *nature*, their hormones and reproductive role inexorably determining 'their emotionality, unreliability, childishness, deviousness etc.'[32] Such views were to have a profound impact upon what was to become defined as normal conduct and behaviour for women in decades to come, and as late as 1970, doctors who took part in a study in which they were asked to list typical characteristics associated with a 'normal, healthy adult' saw virtually no difference between such a person's characteristics and that of a 'normal, healthy male'. However, 'typical traits for normal healthy women … included being conceited about their appearance, being "excitable in minor crises", being highly emotional, being submissive and unaggressive and being uninterested in science.'[33] The discourse of a nervous, excitable child-like woman is further reiterated when Counsel asks Mme Fahmy if she is afraid of thunder and lightning (a violent storm had raged on the night of the shooting), she replies: 'I am very much afraid, and I was very nervous and very tired besides.'[34]

Third, Mme Fahmy is immediately *very sorry* for her rash action. She cannot believe what she has done and regrets it the instant she realises what has happened. She is someone who seeks redemption as soon as she is made fully aware of the severity of her crime. Remorseful, she activates 'appropriate' discourses around femininity by breaking down and crying – apparently unable to *cope* or function normally – such is the extent of her regret, grief and sorrow. Thus, as the speech for the prosecution ended, 'Mme. Fahmy sobbed violently. She seemed nervous and unable to keep still.'[35] The Victorian (middle-class) idealised female traits of frailty, delicacy and helplessness were still current and would therefore have been part of the image which members of the legal profession and jury alike would have been brought up to expect from a 'lady'.[36] Madame Fahmy never missed an opportunity to display her delicate femininity as for example when Judge Swift decided to adjourn for the day although the trial was near its conclusion, 'she seemed to be almost overcome by it, and had to be assisted from the dock.'[37]

Fourth, Madame Fahmy's first thought is for her children. Once more, she acts according to women's supposed nature, utilising discourses around motherhood by prioritising concern for her children rather than for herself. A 'normal' mother is altruistic, serving the needs of her children before her own.[38] A good wife and mother sacrifices her own interests for those of her family.[39]

Those who examined Madame Fahmy's past might conclude that she fell somewhat short of the criteria usually required for respectable, innocent and helpless femininity. She had become a single parent at the age of 16, she had been married twice before her marriage to Fahmy with whom she had co-habited prior to their marriage, and there were rumours that she had lived with several other rich foreign businessmen, including another Egyptian.[40] These rumours led the prosecutor Percival Clarke to request permission from the judge to question her about her past: 'I want to prove that she associated with men from an early age, and that she is a woman of the world in the widest sense.'[41]

Her past behaviour was not dissected in court, however, as Judge Swift refused permission for this line of inquiry. Even if it had been, the defence might well have succeeded in sustaining her image as a wretched, helpless and hapless victim, exploited by, and at the mercy of, a foreign – or rather, dark-skinned – man, for running through the trial was a powerful sense of racism against so-called 'Orientals' which worked in Mme Fahmy's favour to a high degree. Thus, while 'Madame Fahmy had, on the face of it, killed with a lethal weapon an unarmed and defenceless man', the defence was able to turn the case around to one where Mme Fahmy 'was a butterfly on the wheel'.[42] Marshall Hall achieved this by juxtaposing this 'Western woman' – a citizen 'of the most cultured city of the Western world' – and afflicted with a 'nervous temperament', with an 'Oriental' whose civilisation may well be 'one of the oldest and most wonderful … in the world.[43] But if you strip off the external civilisation of the Oriental you get the real Oriental underneath.'[44] Referring to the murder Marshall Hall stated:

I submit … that this poor wretch of a woman, suffering the tortures of the damned, driven to desperation by the brutality and beastliness of this man, whose will she had dared to oppose, thought that he … was about to kill her.[45]

He further stated:

In sheer desperation – as he crouched for the last time, crouched like an animal, like an Oriental, retired for the last time to get a bound forward – she turned the pistol and put it to his face and to her horror the thing went off.'[46]

Here was a delicate, cultured and helpless woman who had been 'outraged, abused, beaten, degraded' by an Oriental with an 'Eastern feeling of possession of the woman, the Turk in his harem … that is something almost unintelligible, something we cannot deal with…' Bearing these factors in mind Marshall Hall made the following plea:

Members of the jury, I want you to open the gates where this Western woman can go out, not into the *dark* night of the *desert* but back to her friends … and her child who will be waiting for her with open arms. You will open the gate, and let this woman go back into the *light of God's great Western sun*.[47]

This juxtaposition of East and West, of a 'cultured Western woman' and a 'crouching, beast-like Oriental', stands as a powerful and blatant example of 'Orientalism' – the body of literature created at the turn of the century by '"us" (the Colonial Powers) to develop a systematic and practical knowledge about "them" … so-called "Orientals".' [48]This literature reduced a vast and diverse population living in Asia, India and the Middle East to a limited set 'of racial traits and cultural stereotypes':

The 'Oriental' is depicted as a problematic 'other', an exotic alien who is difficult to classify and troublesome to control but who can nevertheless be spoken of – by Western experts – with authority and scientific understanding.[49]

Marshall Hall was one such expert and was by all accounts a very persuasive speaker.[50] In this particular case it took the jury just over an hour to find Madame Fahmy 'not guilty' of all charges, a popular decision judging by the cheers and clapping from the public gallery which was so raucous that the judge cleared the court-room. Right to the very end Mme Fahmy did not disappoint: when the judge discharged her she 'bowed, and as her strength seemed to fail, she was assisted out of the dock by the wardresses.'[51]

The case-study of Mme Fahmy provides an example of a woman who displayed 'true' and appropriate feminine behaviour during her trial. There was no conflict between expected and actual female conduct; at no point did Madame challenge dominant modes of expression. Moreover, the racist discourses which were mobilised not only justified her disobedience to her husband, but legitimated her attempts at resisting him which subsequently were portrayed in positive terms – as acts of bravery: the innocent and beautiful white woman versus the atavistic, brutish dark-skinned Oriental.

The sheer level of hostility and racism towards another nation displayed in the course of this trial resulted in the Egyptian bar filing a complaint against Marshall Hall. It is also a clear example of the way discourses around racism can in certain circumstances override those surrounding women's conduct and behaviour.[52] For example, Madame Fahmy may not have found it quite so easy to avoid a focus upon her own conduct if Prince Fahmy had been a member of the English aristocracy, a scenario in which *she* would have become the 'uncontrollable and passionate foreigner'. Thus the case provides an insight into the complex relationships between the various factors and discourses of race and gender which interact and have an impact upon the final outcome of a trial. Madame Fahmy's account was not muted because it fell well within the parameters of established framework of female conduct and behaviour. An alternative account of the events surrounding the murder was not sought despite various unexplained factors such as a) Beattie's observation that immediately before the shooting he had heard Fahmy whistling to his dog in the hallway, which would seem to throw into doubt the accuracy of Mme Fahmy's statement that Ali was shot during a violent row; b) Fahmy's body was found 'lying in the corridor near his suite' which might well indicate he was running away from his wife when she shot him and which, at the very least, stands in strong contrast to Marshall Hall's version of events which had Fahmy 'crouched like an animal' ready to pounce; and c) Mme Fahmy's letter to her doctor written on the morning of the murder, which was subsequently regarded as 'strong corroboration of her story' but which could equally well be interpreted as having been deliberately written for this purpose.[53] Yet the jury took only 68 minutes to find Madame Fahmy not guilty on all counts, and must therefore have found her account both plausible and convincing. Judicial misogyny was not an issue in this case; Mme Fahmy was a woman who understood the art of 'softening' herself to fit in with judicial stereotypes of appropriate womanhood.

A Shooting in Hampstead: The Case of Ruth Ellis

There were many similarities between the lives of Marie Fahmy and Ruth Ellis. Like Marie, Ruth was at the age of 16 already a girl with a 'reputation', a 'good-time' girl, although rather than associating with rich men, Ruth enjoyed the company of Allied soldiers in London nightclubs. Also like Marie, Ruth was to become a teenage single parent when in 1944, aged 17, she had her first child. Within the next year she worked as a nude model before taking up a position as a nightclub hostess where she was soon earning eight times as much as when she had been employed in a factory. Working in the nightclub did nothing to improve Ruth's reputation, especially in the light of the activities of the club's owner Maury Conley, who was involved in both fraud and vice-rackets.[54] By 1950 Ruth had married a dentist, George Ellis, who, it emerged, was not only an alcoholic but also violent towards her. The marriage subsequently lasted less than a year, leaving Ruth with a second child, whom it was agreed the father should take custody of following the couple's divorce.[55] Ruth was thus a single parent, separated, soon-to-be divorcee when she met David Blakely in 1953, just the sort of woman to fuel the moral panic around immoral and criminal behaviour in austere, button-lipped postwar Britain.[56]

The similarities between the life-experiences of Marie and Ruth continue – Blakely was several years younger than Ruth, a member of the upper-middle class with plenty of charm, good looks and breeding. By all accounts, however, he was also a shallow and immature human being whose main interests were alcohol, women and racing-cars.[57] Moreover, he was living proof that the mistreatment of women was not confined to Marshall Hall's 'Orientals' – the chivalry Marshall Hall had attributed to Western males was notable for its absence from Blakely's repertoire. Incapable of holding down a permanent job, David soon moved in with

Ruth and let her support him. The next 19 months were taken up with their extremely complex, stormy and intense love/hate relationship, in which Ruth initially appeared to be the dominant partner 'confident and self-possessed while [David] was weak and ineffectual'.[58] This power balance shifted towards the end of their relationship when David intensified his use of both physical and psychological cruelty towards Ruth – repeatedly leaving her guessing and uncertain about their future together as he see-sawed from promising her marriage to ignoring her for days, even weeks, during which he would be involved in other sexual relationships.[59] Ruth, mentally drained from these uncertainties, and taking medication for her nerves, as well as physically exhausted from a miscarriage only ten days earlier – brought on by one of David's beatings – finally shot him on Easter Sunday in 1955. It is important to place the shooting within the context of yet another prolonged episode of provocative and contradictory behaviour by David, which had left Ruth in mental agony, seething and furious for three days. David had left Ruth on Good Friday morning in a loving and attentive frame of mind – hinting at marriage and promising to pick her up in the evening so they could spend the Easter weekend together. When he failed to appear, Ruth attempted to contact him on numerous occasions throughout that weekend by telephone. She also tried to gain entry to the house where he was staying. David however, refused all contact and would not even come out for the purpose of returning Ruth's key.[60]

Thus, like the Fahmy case 32 years earlier, the Ellis case was set to become a *cause célèbre* due to its various intriguing and scandalous features. That is to say, the discourses which were to guarantee Ruth a place within the 'bad' category were immediately activated. Hence by the time the case opened the media had already portrayed Ellis as a particular 'type' of woman – 'young, blonde, sexually attractive and immoral'.[61] In particular, she was constantly referred to as 'the platinum blonde' a description which, as writer Helen Birch has noted, conjures up a powerful image of the *femme fatale* – 'the blonde with perverse sexuality and social aberration'.[62] She was also repeatedly described as a 'model', despite the fact that she had worked as a club manageress for several years, and her one modelling job had taken place almost a decade earlier.[63] Edgar Lustgarten in *The News of the World* described her thus:

Ruth Ellis was an attractive young woman. Of her kind. But what was her kind? Experienced. Worldly. Sexually provocative. The kind of woman you would expect to find in places like The Little Club.[64]

The implication was unmistakable – there was something immoral, even smutty about her. Taken together, newspaper reports played a fundamental role in the construction of Ruth's image, not only as provocative and promiscuous, but also as someone whose behaviour and attitude combined to make her a dangerous, even lethal *femme fatale*:

Her crime was not that of a sexual innocent suddenly discovering man's inhumanity to woman. It seemed like the vengeance of a cool sophisticate, proud of her lone act of savagery.[65]

These descriptions mobilised discourses of dangerous femininity; an 'unknowable' and unpredictable element within Ruth's personality and femininity had come about as a result of her rejection of established codes of female conduct and behaviour. Her femininity was seen as dangerous because it was both contradictory and insidious: on the one hand Ruth was an attractive woman who took an almost exaggerated amount of care over her appearance – make-up, dyed hair, smart clothes and stilettos. On the other hand, and unlike Marie Fahmy, her behaviour and actions did not match her ultra-feminine image, but seemed to have more in common with qualities usually associated with men: cool, ruthless, unemotional, violent, and above all else, *very capable* and *rational*. As author Jacqueline Rose has explained, because Ruth's femininity failed to limit her violence it 'could appear only as an outrage, as something inappropriate and out of place – the peroxide she insisted on for her hair for her appearance in court, for example. If not essence, femininity can be only trapping or mere show.'[66] In short, unlike Marie, Ruth consistently and systematically refused to communicate through dominant modes of expression.

The Trial of Ruth Ellis

The manner in which Ruth had 'thwarted social expectations' and conventions prior to the shooting ensured that she was represented as the stereotypical 'bad' woman before the trial had even started.[67] Ruth's presentation of herself during the trial did nothing to alter this perception but did everything to reinforce her 'dangerousness'. Unlike Marie, Ruth did not wear 'deep mourning' for her court appearances but was instead described as looking 'like a film-star':[68]

> All eyes turned to the wooden dock as she entered. Many of the public were surprised at what they saw. Instead of a dejected young woman, tired-looking, sombre, and about to stand trial for her life, she looked like she was attending the premiere of a West End show.[69]

Not only did her physical appearance 'not match the line of her defence' [of provocation], her calmness and composure during the trial were overwhelmingly interpreted in negative terms – further evidence of her dangerousness as a cold, calculating and ruthless killer who refused to be sorry for what she had done[70]: 'Ruth describes the shooting of the man with whom she had been living, like a male motorist reporting the running down of a stray dog.'[71]

Ruth's failure to seek redemption and show 'appropriate' feminine feelings and emotions became an endless source of fascination for the media, both at the time and during years to come when it was still considered headline material: 'Ruth displayed no remorse as she emptied the gun point blank into her lover' ran an article written in 1971, some 16 years after her trial.[72] In short, Ruth's self-presentation ensured from the very start that unlike Marie before her, and despite having suffered similar abuse, she would not be regarded as a victim by either judge or jury. Moreover, her determination to prove the rationality behind her act ensured she would not fall within the 'mad' category. When her mother tried to persuade her to plead insanity, Ruth's response was: 'It's no use Mother. I *was* sane when I did it. And I *meant* to do it …'[73]

Where Marie Fahmy had said: 'What have I done!', 'I do not know how I did it,' 'I cannot understand what I have done' and 'How many shots did I fire?' Ruth said:

> 'I was feeling just a little – in a peculiar mood then: rather a nasty mood …' 'I had an idea I wanted to kill him,' 'When I put the gun in my bag I intended to find David and shoot him' and 'I thought I had missed him, so I fired again. He was still running, and I fired the third shot.'[74]

This apparently ruthless and determined approach to the killing did
not endear her to the jury nor did it earn her any favour with the media:
'It [the murder] was committed by a woman certainly; but a woman
capable of such a crime can hardly expect the leniency traditionally
given to her sex.'[75] 'She shot him not once but six times: she meant him
to die.'[76]

   This was a woman who, instead of being sorry for having committed the
ultimate violent act, did exactly the opposite – and set out 'to prove that
she had been morally justified in killing David'.[77] She was a woman who
refused to seek redemption, just as she refused to plead for mercy. She
simply would not humble herself, and in so blatantly rejecting the role of
the 'downtrodden mistress' who begs for sympathy and understanding, she
almost certainly sealed her fate:

> Ruth Ellis was hanged not just because of her act of killing David
> Blakely, but also and more particularly because of how that killing
> was constructed and how she was constructed by the popular press,
> and then by both the prosecution and the defence at her trial.[78]

Taken together, these agencies all played a part in constructing Ruth as
'too rational', 'calm and unemotional in court', someone who, prior to her
court appearance had been 'a possessive, domineering and determined
woman' whose crime was that 'of a cold and calculating woman rather
than the uncontrollable passion of a heart-broken mistress'.[79] This portrayal
was made possible because unlike Marie Fahmy, Ruth was not prepared to
modify her behaviour and attitude in an attempt to save her life – unlike
Marie, she refused to articulate her femininity through dominant and
accepted modes of expression. Where Marie had become hysterical after
the shooting, Ruth turned to the nearest bystander (who coincidentally was
a police officer) and said: 'Please take this gun and arrest me.'[80] Where
Marie had been so overcome in court that she had to be assisted from the
dock, Ruth was 'standing in the dock "firm, erect and unafraid"'.[81] Where
Marie's 'strength seemed to fail' and she once more had to be assisted out
of the dock upon hearing the verdict, Ruth 'seemed to shrug her shoulders.
She turned towards the woman prison officer at her side and smiled.'[82] 'As
two warders moved to take her arms, she gently and calmly brushed them
aside and made her own way down to the cells in readiness for her last
journey on earth…'[83]

Ruth's failure to fulfil gender-role expectations inside the court-room fitted only too well with her refusal to demonstrate commitment to conventional female roles in her personal life, especially within the areas most likely to give rise to judicial misogyny – those of respectability, domesticity and motherhood. During the trial, Ruth's attitude to these issues repeatedly reinforced her image as an immoral woman and callous mother. First, when asked if she was 'very much in love with' David, her response was: 'Not really.' When asked to confirm that she was aware David was already engaged to another woman, she replied: 'Yes. I didn't take our affair seriously…'[84] In other words, Ruth was a woman who casually entered into a sexual relationship with a man whom she did not love, who was already engaged, and whom, after only two weeks of acquaintance she allowed to move in with her, all while she herself was still married.

Second, when asked about her pregnancy by David and his subsequent offer to marry her, she replied:

> I was not really in love with him at the time, and it was quite unnecessary to marry me. I thought I could get out of the mess quite easily.
> [Counsel]: What mess?
> I decided I could get out of the mess quite easily.
> [Mr Justice Havers]: You mean the child?
> Yes.
> [Mr Justice Havers]: Without him marrying you?
> Yes.
> …
> [Mr Justice Havers]: You had an abortion?
> Yes.[85]

Here Ruth had been offered the chance to become 'respectable' by marrying David, an offer which, given the moral climate in Britain in the 1950s, both judge and jury may well have thought she was lucky to receive. But her comment that marriage was 'quite unnecessary' does not indicate an eagerness to become 'respectable'.

Third, her choice to have an abortion as well as her description of her pregnancy as 'the mess' does not demonstrate great commitment to motherhood and would hardly have endeared her to those within the court-room. In fact Ruth failed to display any of the characteristics associated with good mothering during her trial. Her young son was left alone while she was pursuing David late at night and she had given up custody of her two-year-old daughter without a struggle.[86] Furthermore, where Marie Fahmy's first thoughts had been for her children after the shooting, Ruth when asked by her counsel 'if she thought about her children' replied that 'she did not think about them at all.'[87]

Fourth, where Marie's case had benefited from racist discourses against her husband, Ruth's case suffered further detriment due to discourses around snobbery and social class. For while David had been a member of the upper middle class with a private income, Ruth was described by one jury member as a 'typical West End tart'.[88] A police inspector investigating the case was more subtle but no less condemnatory:

> The two people, Blakely and Ellis, are of completely different stations in life. … On meeting Blakely and realising that his class was much above her own, and finding he was sufficiently interested in her to live with her, and, if we are to believe Cussen, to promise her marriage, it seems she was prepared to go to any lengths to keep him. Finding this impossible, she appears to have decided to wreak her vengeance upon him.[89]

This statement indicates disbelief that Blakely was seriously considering marrying someone 'below his station'. This confirms the view 'that people "never understood why an upper middle-class man and a lower middle-class woman should fall so obsessively in love"'.[90] For Carol Smart, this view can best be understood within the context of class-ridden and austere 1950s Britain with its concern about the destabilisation of family life and moral decay. Within this atmosphere the prostitute had become the new folk-devil:

> The prostitute could no longer be held as a class apart from respectable women, the separate spheres were merging and in this way the prostitute became more of a threat to respectable family lifestyles. Her proximity, both socially and spatially, presented a challenge to all the values embodied in ideologies of family life and motherhood prevalent in the 1950s.[91]

Even though Ruth supported David financially, she nevertheless fitted the image of a lower-class 'brassy tart' who had fallen in love with 'a young gentleman way "above" her class' – someone more suitable as a mistress for a man of David's breeding, than for marrying.[92] Indeed he was engaged to someone from a similar background to his own, and in an earlier era this situation may have been resolved by David marrying his fiancee from his own social class, with Ruth, a lower-class woman, remaining his mistress.[93] However, Ruth was not prepared to accept this Victorian way of resolving an 'unsuitable' relationship; instead she demanded to become fully acknowledged, and thus fully 'visible' as David's wife. As such, she can be seen to exemplify the shift in visibility of 'the immoral woman' described by Smart. Thus, having already disobeyed the gender code of conduct, Ruth now also disobeyed the code relating to social class, that of 'knowing your place': it was 'the eternal class struggle expressed in sexual terms – blonde tart chases refined upper-middle-class, ex-public school boy'.[94] Such conduct was met with disapproval from many quarters including the *Daily Mail* which seized the opportunity to undermine Ruth's attempts to improve herself by taking French and elocution lessons:

> Her hair was short, stylish, her dress exclusive, but she failed to rid herself of a Manchester accent … She felt it a barrier to Mayfair … every turn failed, for Blakely was still ashamed of her.[95]

Where Marie had found the complex inter-relationship between race and gender could be mobilised in her favour, Ruth found that the dialectic relationships around discourses of class and gender operated to her detriment by reinforcing an already hostile attitude, not only towards her lower-class background, but also in the ways she thwarted social expectations in pursuing her desire to 'improve' herself. This hostility and snobbery was further reiterated in the common-sensical belief that intimate relationships which cut across social class are doomed to failure: 'The law, so apparently impartial, takes vengeance when the lower classes refuse to humble themselves, or acknowledge their place.'[96]

In sum, the lives and crimes of Marie Fahmy and Ruth Ellis were unusually similar. Both women had come from humble backgrounds and shared a determination to 'better' their social standing. They both became single mothers while teenagers, they were both divorcees and they were both trapped within abusive and violent relationships with men several years younger than themselves who enjoyed higher social status than the two women. Finally, they both brought an end to their disastrous relationships by shooting dead their partners, a murder method very rarely utilised by women in England and Wales. This, however, is where the similarities ended, for where Ruth had no interest in a future without David and faced death without resistance, Marie remained ambitious for herself. Furthermore, while Marie had managed to escape her past Ruth was never allowed to forget hers.

The cases of Fahmy and Ellis illustrate how essentially similar crimes came to be 'heard' very differently according to the discourses utilised by the defendant. As noted above, Marie Fahmy conformed to expectations of female conduct and behaviour. Within a patriarchal legal system, she played the role of ultra-feminine, technically inept, helpless and highly strung victim. Her violent crime came to be seen as an aberration from her otherwise passive and submissive nature, a crime which only came about as a result of extreme provocation from a man who was little more than a 'beast' – an 'Oriental'. As such Marie's crime was not considered 'rational' in a premeditated sense. Instead the act had been carried out by someone with a 'nervous temperament' who suffered repeated victimisation by a 'brute', and who on this occasion, in self-defence, tried to frighten him off by pointing a gun at him which subsequently went off 'by accident'. As I have shown in this chapter, the plausibility of this version of events depended more upon Marie's conduct and behaviour (taken together with the conduct and origin of Ali Fahmy) than on the available evidence at the murder scene.

Ruth Ellis, on the other hand, failed to mobilise this stereotypical image of emotional, hysterical and out-of-control femininity in her defence.[97] Instead she activated another stereotype: the glamorous but brittle, jealous and vengeful, immoral woman. Her appearance and demeanour, coupled with her life-style and attitude towards sex, marriage, motherhood and domesticity ensured that both prosecution and defence perceived her in a negative, condemnatory manner. Her trial was perceived as an 'open and shut' case – in its stark simplicity her guilt was a foregone conclusion – neither the prosecution nor defence appeared to have any doubt about how to interpret her crime. Thus Humphreys, opening the case for the Crown, after a very short outline already felt able to make this confident assessment:

That, in a very few words, is the case for the Crown, and nothing else I say to you, however much detail, will add to the *stark simplicity* of that story.[98]

Ending his opening speech Humphreys again emphasised the 'obvious-ness' of the case:

Members of the jury, there in its *stark simplicity* is the case for the Crown, and whatever be the background and whatever may have been in her mind, when she took that gun, if you have no doubt that she took that gun with the sole purpose of finding and shooting David Blakely and that she then shot him dead, in my submission to you, subject to his Lordship's ruling in law, the only verdict is wilful murder.[99]

The defence made no attempt to complicate this 'stark simplicity' by producing character witnesses in support of Ellis. For example, noted for their absence were first, her friends and work colleagues 'who would have seen ... Blakely's boorish, drunken and latterly violent behaviour ... and could have indicated the stresses and strains endemic in the relationship as well as in his general attitude and behaviour'.[100] Second, hospital staff who had treated Ruth's injuries after a beating by David, and hospital staff who had treated her after her miscarriage, also after a beating; and third, Dr T. P. Rees, a psychiatrist who had treated her for several months prior to the shooting.[101] Even Desmond Cussen, possibly Ellis's closest friend at the time of the shooting, appeared for the prosecution.[102] Finally, her Counsel, Mr Stevenson, declined to give a closing speech for the defence.[103] Unsurpris-ingly, the jury took only 23 minutes to find Ellis guilty.[104] As with the Fahmy case, no-one perceived a need for an alternative account of Ellis's crime. Like Fahmy before her, Ellis fitted equally well into the role of a stereotypi-cal woman – albeit a very different stereotype to that of Fahmy – for she was the type most likely to experience judicial misogyny. Thus, while her guilt was established beyond doubt by herself, the manner in which the trial was conducted nevertheless ensured that she was considered less deserving of a reprieve than a woman like Marie Fahmy whose court-room conduct affirmed conventional femininity.

Conclusion – A Comparison with Myra Hindley

The case-studies of Fahmy and Ellis illustrate the gap between those who claim to know the 'truth' and those about whom they claim to know it. In each case those who held power reconstructed the women's actions and statements into an 'interpretive schema' through which their cases were subsequently heard.[105] While the outcome of the two trials was very different, both cases nonetheless illustrate how various sexist discourses operate within the court-room. Madame Fahmy's acceptance of, and adherence to, women's supposed nature ensured that she quickly ceased to be a threat and was instead responded to with chivalrous attitudes, as the 'truth' about this case came to seem obvious to court personnel. The Ellis case, on the other hand, precipitated 'a crisis of sexual difference' because every one of her acts disrupted established assumptions about women.[106] Intentionally or unintentionally, Ellis – by her refusal to conform to conventional female standards – was 'demonstrating the existence of heterogeneity and contradiction', and in doing so – albeit unconsciously – was 'helping to keep open the space within which knowledge is produced'.[107] Her rationality and her calm demeanour throughout the trial and during her detention in prison as well as her extraordinary bravery in facing death were characteristics usually associated with male conduct and stood in sharp contrast to expected female behaviour.[108] When found in Ellis they denoted further deviance, with her presence in the court-room becoming increasingly threatening, constantly disrupting and challenging what was 'known' about women. The threat she represented could only be removed by muting her, which was achieved by situating her within a 'known' female category – that of the cold, calculating, vengeful, blonde tart/killer. Categorising her thus ensured that she would subsequently be heard, if not only, at least predominantly, through the interpretive schema of the 'evil woman'.[109] In this way the space for creating new discourses, new knowledge, and thus new 'truths' about violent women was closed down and equilibrium was restored to the court-room in particular, and to public consciousness and common-sense in general.

Forty years after the Ellis trial, and despite the very different nature of her crime, Myra Hindley finds herself in a similar space to that which Ellis occupied – that is her account cannot be heard outside the 'evil woman' category. As had been the case with Ellis, Hindley's appearance, composure and attitude during her trial became sources of fascination. Her newly bleached hair, heavy make-up and smart suits were commented upon as were her antagonistic attitudes towards marriage, motherhood and religion.[110] Thus, her refusal to take an oath on the Bible when she entered the witness box as well as her 'cool and calm' demeanour during the trial were widely publicised.[111] Today, whatever Hindley has to say appears almost irrelevant, the response is always the same. For example, while it was regarded as cruel and heartless to withhold her confession to the murders of Pauline Reade and Keith Bennett for over 20 years, when Hindley did confess in 1987, her motives were regarded as equally evil – the actions of a 'calculating killer … exploiting an opportunity for her own advantage'.[112] Furthermore, Hindley has, like Ellis before her, consistently refused to excuse her crimes by claiming to be mad. On the contrary, she has emphasised her sanity:

> In my 30 years in prison I have met, spoken with and been examined by psychiatrists and, in particular, a senior psychologist with whom I did a series of tests, the results of which ruled out psychopathy, schizophrenia, manic depression, episodic dyscontrol and any form of psychosis or neurosis. In a word, there was no evidence of a mentally disordered mind. And my EEGs revealed no abnormalities or dysfunctions. Nor was I ever, as a child or teenager, cruel to animals or children.[113]

This statement indicates not only that she accepts personal responsibility for her crimes, but also that otherwise 'normal', sane women are, under certain circumstances, capable of heinous violent acts, a possibility which is too much to bear for those who can only make sense of Hindley's crimes by regarding her 'evilness' as her *only* characteristic – immutable and unchanging – thus situating her in a category which stands apart from the rest of the world:

> The tone of her letter would seem to indicate her belief that these crimes were committed by another Myra Hindley and that she, the letter-writing Myra Hindley, need bear no responsibility. Myra Hindley's salvation must come from within herself, by her reaching a true understanding of the enormity of her crimes, with no excuses. When she reaches that state, from which she seems a million light years away, how will she even wish to be released into the community? Neither we, the public, nor the families of her victims are eligible

to offer her forgiveness. Her continued self-propulsion into public awareness only causes distress to those she has harmed – hardly the action of the truly repentant. She should keep her head down, as does Ian Brady, and wait for death to release her.[114]

We note that the response to Hindley's letter bears little or no relationship to its contents, which is unsurprising because the respondent has not *listened to* what Hindley has to say, but is instead responding to the stereotypical evil image of Hindley, as so many have done before her during the past 30 years. Hindley has not 'gone mad' like Ian Brady, nor has she 'broken down' from the unimaginable burden of seeking redemption for what she has done. Instead she appears so utterly 'normal' – with hopes and aspirations that we all recognise which is precisely why we are so outraged by them. She is simply not *different enough* from 'us'. It is within this context that Hindley is constantly challenging our 'mad versus bad' explanation of women's violence – every time she speaks she is reopening the space within which new knowledge can be produced about women who kill. And every time – regardless of what she has to say – we observe vociferous and swift attempts to close that space – to 'mute' her account. To do otherwise would challenge idealised and traditional beliefs about women's 'nature' – their supposed passivity, gentleness and submissiveness as well as their caring, nurturing maternal instincts. It would mean facing up to the reality that the propensity to commit violent acts affects both men *and* women. It would mean moving beyond 'mad or bad' stereotypes, and instead examining the extremely complex set of relations and interactions which eventually lead to murderous crimes. It would therefore also mean an end to the comfort we gain from the 'them and us' categories in operation outside court-rooms particularly in relation to abhorrent murders such as that of James Bulger, where shouting obscenities at the murderers serves to cleanse ourselves of responsibility and to emphasise how different *we* are from *them*. We cannot explain murderous acts in clear-cut and simplistic language which simply places the perpetrator in a category apart from ordinary people. Hindley already started the creation of new discourses around women who kill when she attempted to explain her crimes thus:

> I knew what we were doing was wrong. But I can't explain it.
> When we were arrested it was a relief, although I couldn't admit it to
> myself at the time. I was so terrified, and what we'd done was so
> terrible. For years I just blocked it; I couldn't talk about it or even
> admit it to myself.[115]

Like us, Hindley does not have appropriate discourses at hand which can
neatly explain her crimes. But she *does* know that current discourses are
not adequate. This is why she 'can't explain it'. Hindley's counselling in the
1980s resulted in her confessing to two other murders. After the confes-
sions counselling was terminated, many believe, because of Home Office
fears of being seen to have gone 'soft' on one of the most hated and reviled
criminals in this country. Another (unconscious) reason for the termination
might also be that an insight into Hindley's criminal behaviour would once
again challenge our comfortable 'mad versus bad' classificatory system
and might just make it more clear that she is not all that different from us.[116]
This system, however, is coming under increasing pressure from several
other quarters, not least in the form of Josie O'Dwyer, a woman with a
reputation for violent behaviour who has been in and out of borstals and
prisons since the age of 14.[117] O'Dwyer was 'set up' by two prison officers
to attack Myra Hindley while in Holloway prison.[118] The officers presented
O'Dwyer with a copy of *The News of the World* which detailed the
Brady–Hindley case. O'Dwyer consequently 'snapped':

> I battered her and cracked her head off the railings and wall. I
> broke her fingers stamping on her hands trying to make her let go of
> the floors so she'd fall off down to the bottom and be killed. I wanted
> to kill her. I saw bone show through her face when I bashed her.
> When I'd finished with her, her teeth were all loosened at the front,
> her nose crossed to the left side of her face, two black eyes, split lip,
> ear, knees. She had to eat through a straw for the next six weeks and
> needed cosmetic surgery.[119]

After inflicting these appalling injuries upon Hindley, O'Dwyer was treated
'like a celebrity'.[120] There was no need to reconstruct O'Dwyer's violence
(or that of the prison officers whose desire to see Hindley beaten up led
them to instigate this incident) and situate her self-confessed murderous
desire into the 'mad' or 'bad' category because it seemed perfectly *rational*

25

within the framework of existing sexist assumptions regarding women's nature and instincts. That is to say, if women's violence appears to spring from a desire to protect children or as an outrage against cruelty towards children, it will be regarded not only as *rational* but as *normal* and *natural*. O'Dwyer's violence thus stands in sharp contrast to Hindley's which cannot be rationalised because it disrupts and 'unhinges our assumptions about women'.[121] Two decades later O'Dwyer received a life-sentence for the murder of Peter Sutherland, a crime for which she 'had no apparent motive'.[122] Although O'Dwyer's violence resulted in death on this occasion, in other aspects, this was simply one of many violent attacks carried out by her over a number of years, and in contrast to the Hindley attack, this could not be neatly rationalised, since battering to death what appeared to be a defenceless man does not fall within the category of 'appropriate and expected' female behaviour.[123] I have chosen to focus on only two of O'Dwyer's attacks in order to illustrate the shortcomings of an ideological system which allows us to pick and choose which acts of violence to rationalise, even when carried out by the same person, which in turn places on the agenda the whole issue of our inadequate under-standing of violent women.

While the crimes of Hindley and O'Dwyer are as different from each other as they each are from the crimes of Fahmy and Ellis, it becomes increasingly apparent that we need new discourses and alternative 'truths' – not just in explaining women's violence against men, but in *all* types of violence carried out by women. Thus, although – after having examined the available evidence – Fahmy's crime could well be construed as being 'more' calculated and premeditated than Ellis's, the point of this chapter has not been to argue that Marie Fahmy should have received a life-sentence for murder, nor that Ruth Ellis should have been released immediately after her trial. Rather, it has been to question why – when both women suffered appalling levels of abuse and violence from their partners – why then did Marie's victimisation and emphasis upon her femininity increase her chances of being understood as 'innocent', while Ruth appeared 'even more' guilty as a result of the presentation of herself? The answer must lie in the limited subject positions available within the discourses of femininity and sexuality.

When Ruth Ellis was executed the feminist movement was at a low, almost non-existent ebb. At the height of Second Wave feminism in 1977, the American cases of Inez Garcia and Yvonne Wanrow were at the centre of a legal landmark, when, after being granted re-trials, their cases were 'argued successfully on the basis of self-defence'.[124] This victory for battered women was to be short-lived. The trial of Francine Hughes which took place only months later, could equally well have been argued in terms of self-defence. Her lawyers however, chose what they considered to be a safer route, and succeeded in having her acquitted on the grounds of 'temporary insanity',[125] yet another reminder of the precariousness and fragility of newly opened discourses around violent women. In 1991 Sara Thornton made a spirited attempt at keeping such discourses open when she wrote to the Registrar of Criminal Appeals:

> ... I am not bad, I am not mad, I was subjected to intolerable pressure, enhanced by a society that for reasons of its own, did not want to care ... I do not wish to be freed under the banner of diminished responsibility ... I want and demand justice ... I am a modern woman and I ask for modern justice. Is there any reason ... why I cannot speak for myself at the Court of Appeal? I will do so firmly, and above all, with dignity ... I don't want to be squabbled over like a piece of meat, by grown men who have ... no feeling for truth. I'd rather stay in prison and work towards a better understanding of women ... I am not really interested in rules, regulations and precedents. I am fighting for myself and I wish to be *heard*.[126]

Today, as this is written, the second appeal of Sara Thornton has been heard, an event which – apart from Thornton's own campaign – has largely come about as the result of the hard work of feminist activists. Her original defence of diminished responsibility was to become a case of 'the face that doesn't fit' – that is – Thornton's 'stroppiness' and confidence meant that she was quickly labelled an 'uppity' woman and, taken together with other aspects of her life such as drug-taking and abortions, she failed to fulfil the required criteria for the role of 'victim'.[127] Like Ellis before her, Thornton did not appear to be in pursuit of redemption – she was neither humble nor sorry enough. Her first appeal in 1991 was fought on the grounds that the conviction should be reduced to manslaughter as a result of provocation.[128] It was dismissed. Since then legal landmarks have been reached in Britain in the cases of Kiranjit Ahluwalia and Emma Humphreys, with a widening of the definition of provocation from 'sudden and temporary loss of self-control' to 'cumulative abuse as possible provocation'.[129] Thornton's defence during her second appeal has been that of provocation together with so-called 'Battered Woman Syndrome' – a term which ultimately ensures that violent women remain within the mad and/or victimised category. Hence, we can only truly claim to have added to the language around violent women when we are able to argue in court that 'they are not mentally unbalanced when they kill; they are not suffering from diminished responsibility. On the contrary, they are attempting to save their lives: "they are reacting in a normal [and *rational*] way to abnormal and dangerous circumstances."'[130] At the same time it is perfectly understand-able that Thornton's lawyers, like Francine Hughes' before her, have attempted to 'play safe' by utilising traditional and conventional discourses around femininity, since their priority must be to ensure her freedom. Like the Hughes case, the Thornton case therefore also exemplifies the precariousness of newly won terrain on which a discussion of violent women can take place. If her appeal is won,* a new definition of provoca-tion potentially could be established which, despite including 'Battered Woman Syndrome', signals a momentary opening of a space in which new 'truths' about women who kill can be created. As feminist activists we must not falter in our tenacious struggle to keep such spaces upon which new knowledge and discourses can be created and thus add to our understand-ing of women's violence.

* On 30 May 1996, Thornton's second trial ended with a verdict of manslaughter on the grounds of diminished responsibility. – Eds

PARTNERS
IN CRIME:

Defending the Female of the Species

Sean French

In British legal history, at least, there has never been a murder trial like that of Rosemary West. When her husband, Frederick West, committed suicide on the first day of 1995, it was difficult to see how the case against her could continue. The only other witness to the murders of ten young women of which she was accused was dead. There was no evidence directly linking Rosemary with any of the killings.

Much of the forensic and circumstantial evidence was appalling in what it suggested of the victims' last hours, or even days. For example, Lucy Partington was abducted on the evening of 27 December, 1973. Seven days later (just after midnight on 3 January, 1974), Frederick West was treated in Gloucester hospital for a severe cut to his hand. There are two plausible inferences that can be made from this: first, that he was dismembering her body; second, that she had been kept alive for six days. (On another occasion, Rosemary West was also treated in hospital for a badly cut hand, claiming both that she had been playing with knives and that she had been chopping wood.) The body of Shirley Hubbard was found in the Wests' cellar (where five victims had been buried clockwise in a circle, in the order in which they had been killed). As with the other skeletons there was no surviving evidence about the actual cause of death, but Hubbard's skull was still swathed in adhesive tape up to eye level, and penetrated by a plastic tube which had been inserted into her nostril. Obviously the tape had been to stop her screaming and the tube had been inserted to allow her to breathe. Once again, this suggested an ordeal of days rather than hours. At least something of what these young women must have suffered was suggested by the curious absence of some skeletal remains: knee-caps, fingers, a shoulder blade. After 20 years, however, there was no hope that any evidence would survive which could identify the murderer, whether Frederick or Rosemary West or, for that matter, anybody else. There was, indeed, no evidence that Rosemary had even met three of her alleged victims.

The prosecution relied on a range of evidence, of which both the admissibility and the relevance were highly controversial. An ex-nanny of the family, Caroline Owens, testified about a sexual assault made on her by both Wests in 1972, before the first of the joint murders. Her testimony depicted the couple acting together as violent sexual predators, with Rosemary helping to pick up a woman who might not have accepted a lift from a car driven by a lone man. Other witnesses described Rosemary's violence towards her children, her prostitution and the climate of brutal sexuality at their Gloucester home. It was suggested that Rosemary's step-daughter, Charmaine, had been murdered by her alone, because Frederick had been in prison at the time. There was no doubt that Rosemary had lied about the disappearance of several of the vanished girls, most notably about her own daughter, Heather, who was 16 when she was last seen. At various times Rosemary told different people that Heather had absconded with a lesbian friend, that she had given her £600 to help her leave, that she had subsequently spoken to Heather on the phone and that Frederick had actually seen her. It was suggested that the only explanation for these lies was Rosemary's involvement in the murder. There was also the question of simple common sense: was it credible that in this small terraced house Frederick could have kidnapped women, brought them to the house, tortured them to death over days, dismembered their bodies and disposed of them in the cellar and elsewhere without Rosemary suspecting anything?

The nebulous nature of the evidence against her created problems for the defence as well. As the prosecution presented its case against Rosemary West in the trial at Winchester Crown Court, there was much speculation, both in the courtroom and beyond, about what the defence strategy would be. Whatever it was, and whatever the truth of the accusations, it would surely touch on deep-seated notions about female criminality. But would these notions count for or against Rosemary West?

One possibility was that West would admit to participating in at least some of the murders, but deny responsibility for her actions. The absolving circumstances virtually spoke for themselves. She was only 15 years old – and a victim of physical abuse from her own father – when she first met Frederick West. He had already committed at least two murders by himself. The defence could argue that an immature, traumatized young girl had fallen into the hands of a manipulative psychopath. Would not a jury of ordinary people be more willing to believe that a girl had been bewitched into participation in these atrocious crimes than that the two worst serial killers in British history happened to meet and marry?

Precedents

There are two well-known examples of this defence being successfully mounted. In New York City in 1987, Joel Steinberg and Hedda Nussbaum were charged with the murder of their six-year-old adopted daughter, Lisa. The couple had been freebasing cocaine together while Lisa lay in a coma for 12 hours on the kitchen floor of their apartment. When the police broke in they found Lisa – and her 16-month-old brother, Mitchell (also adopted), who was tied to his cot. He was so dirty and neglected that his hair had to be washed three times before it was revealed to be blond. This case received a great deal of coverage in the media, not least because these atrocities had occurred in an apparently respectable middle-class family: Steinberg was a lawyer, Nussbaum a well-known editor of children's books at the publishers Random House.

From a feminist perspective, two directly conflicting analyses of the case were possible: there was the argument that Nussbaum was as much a victim of Steinberg's violence as Lisa. Her failure to help her daughter was itself evidence of how she had been brainwashed and terrorized. In opposition to this it could be argued that such a view merely reworked a traditional perception of women as irrational, instinctual creatures, unable to take responsibility for their own actions. Was the former analysis reduced to the assertion that men are violent, women are not violent, so if a woman *is* violent, it must be because she is in thrall to a man? Was it not, in its way, more a sign of respect to assume that both Steinberg and Nussbaum were individually responsible for their actions?

No objective evidence could prove either side's case – but Hedda Nussbaum's defence evidently benefited from the stereotype of the violent man and the passive, helpless woman. Her lawyer, Barry Scheck, negotiated a deal with the prosecution according to which all charges against her would be dropped if she testified against her husband. Scheck spoke of Nussbaum as a woman whose will was destroyed by the violence she suffered at Steinberg's hands. Steinberg was found guilty of murder and is currently in prison. Nussbaum was charged with no offence, though she did not retain custody of Mitchell, who was fostered elsewhere.

A similar legal strategy was employed in Canada a few years later. Karla Homolka and Paul Bernardo, a strikingly attractive young couple, both from comfortable backgrounds, married in 1991. In fact, Bernardo's public personality was a sham. He was, it would later emerge, the perpetrator of a series of rapes which had terrorized Scarborough, a suburb of Toronto. Soon after their first meeting in 1987, by which time they were living in St Catharines, a small town near Niagara Falls, Homolka was colluding with Bernardo's violent sexual tastes. She was especially useful in helping him to find young girls. On 23 December, 1990, the couple drugged Homolka's sister, Tammy, with an animal tranquillizer. Bernardo and Homolka then videotaped each other having sex with the unconscious Tammy. Tammy then began vomiting and the couple called an ambulance, without saying anything of the drug she had been given. She died on the following day, but no foul play was suspected by the doctors who attended her.

On 15 June, 1991, two weeks before their wedding, Homolka and Bernardo abducted 14-year-old Leslie Mahaffy. After days of imprisonment she was murdered. On 16 April, 1992, 15-year-old Kristen French was snatched while walking home from school. A witness saw a car stop and a blonde woman ask the girl for directions before she was overpowered and driven away. French was subjected to 13 days of rape and sexual torture, much of it videotaped (she was also shown the tapes of Mahaffy's torture); she was then murdered. In January 1993 Homolka left Bernardo because of his violence (to her). On 17 February Bernardo was arrested, not because of Homolka's allegations of violence against him, or, indeed, because of any connection with the murder, but because of a DNA test result received after an extraordinary two-year laboratory delay that identified Bernardo as the Scarborough rapist.

The police quickly found the soundproofed room in their house where they had tortured Mahaffy and French. Bernardo was charged with murder, kidnapping and a string of other offences. After some delay, Homolka agreed to testify against her husband. Though the tapes later showed her to be a full participant in the tortures and sexual assaults, she was assumed to be in the power of her violent partner and allowed to plead guilty to two charges of manslaughter. She was tried in 1993, two years before Bernardo, and sentenced to 12 years in prison, of which she is unlikely to serve more than half. Bernardo's 1995 trial featured the videos, which had been excluded from his wife's proceedings. He was convicted of murder, kidnapping, forcible confinement, aggravated sexual assault and even the unusual offence of 'doing an indignity to a human body' (the dismemberment of Leslie Mahaffy). He was also declared a dangerous offender, a technicality in Canadian law which can be used to forestall any release.

Pleading Innocence

The alternative strategy for the West defence was simply to deny everything. In muddled fashion, Myra Hindley attempted this when she was tried at Chester Assizes in northwest England alongside her lover, Ian Brady, in April 1966 for what came to be called the Moors murders. They were charged with the murders of two children, Lesley Ann Downey and John Kilbride, and that of a teenage boy, Edward Evans. Hindley grew up in 'a tough working-class district' (her phrase) of Manchester. At the age of 18, working as a typist and already engaged to be married, she fell in love with Brady, who worked in the same office and was five years older than she. Much about their relationship and the balance of responsibility is still disputed, but at the time they met, Brady was a petty criminal who had assimilated a confused Nazism to his own paranoid sense of grievance. By contrast, Hindley seemed to be an unremarkable teenager.

The couple planned and then enacted criminal and sexual fantasies. They made plans for robberies, of which the only practical result was that Hindley passed her driving test (Brady never learned to drive). They took pornographic photographs of themselves, with the aim of selling them. Then, on 12 July, 1963, Hindley picked up 16-year-old Pauline Reade in her mini-van. Pauline was murdered and buried on Saddleworth Moor. On 23 November, 1963, Hindley approached 12-year-old John Kilbride at the market in Ashton-under-Lyne. He too was murdered and buried in the remote moorland. On 16 June, 1964, 12-year-old Keith Bennett set off alone to visit his grandmother in the Longsight district of Manchester and never arrived. On 15 August, 1964, Hindley and Brady were married at a registry office.

All the murders required painstaking planning; indeed, the organization of these murderous scenarios was evidently part of their attraction for Hindley and Brady. The two were living with Hindley's grandmother. On 26 December, 1964, having arranged for her grandmother to stay with her uncle, Hindley picked up ten-year-old Lesley Ann Downey at a Christmas Fair and took her back to the house. Lesley was photographed in various pornographic poses. Her piteous pleas to be allowed home, and Hindley's threats, were tape-recorded. Then she was strangled and buried on the moor.

Their sadistic career might have continued for much longer had it not been for their bizarre recruitment of Myra Hindley's 16-year-old brother-in-law, David Smith, as a potential partner in crime. The trio discussed the possibility of various robberies and even the murder of a man whom Smith disliked, though nothing came of these schemes. Brady and Hindley decided to force the issue. Towards midnight on 6 October, 1964, Hindley asked Smith to walk her home. The apparent plan was to win his allegiance by forcing his complicity in a murder. On his arrival, Hindley summoned Smith from the kitchen to the sitting room where Ian Brady was beating 17-year-old Edward Evans to death with an axe. Smith, deeply shocked, helped clean up the flat. On returning home he told his wife (who was also Hindley's sister), Maureen, what had happened; she made him phone the police early next morning.

Hindley and Brady were immediately arrested. Brady claimed that Evans had been killed in self-defence. Hindley made no admissions and refused to distance herself in any way from Brady: 'Wherever he has gone, I have gone,' she famously told the police. 'He has never been anywhere without me.'

At first, the case against the couple was far from clear-cut. But the police made skilful use of photographs of Hindley on Saddleworth Moor to identify the resting places of Lesley Ann Downey and John Kilbride. (She had posed directly over where they had been buried.) In Hindley's prayer book the police found the ticket to a luggage locker at Central Station, Manchester. This contained shotgun cartridges, a cosh, pornographic books, a woman's wig, several tapes and nine photographs of Lesley Ann Downey, naked and gagged with a scarf. There were no adults visible. One of the tapes featured 17 minutes of Lesley's torment. This was played in open court during the trial. It featured the child pleading for help. Hindley is heard whispering to the child to shut up and then saying: 'Shut up or I'll forget myself and hit you one.'

There was no evidence to link the couple with the disappearances of Pauline Reade or Keith Bennett, so they were not charged with these murders. During the trial Brady and Hindley continued to protest their innocence with an absurd explanation for the tapes and photographs. (They said that two men, whose names they didn't know, had brought her to the house to be photographed and then taken her away again.)

The result of the trial was never seriously in question: Ian Brady was found guilty of all three murders; Hindley was found guilty of the murders of Edward Evans and Lesley Ann Downey. She was found not guilty of the murder of John Kilbride, but guilty of being an accessory after the fact (when the body was transported to Saddleworth Moor, she must have driven the car). The two were sentenced to life imprisonment (capital punishment had been abolished just a few weeks earlier). It wasn't until 1987 that Hindley actually confessed to the crimes, however, as well as to the murders of Pauline Reade and Keith Bennett, giving information that helped locate Pauline's body. Keith Bennett's body has still not been found. The most that Hindley has ever confessed to is her involvement in the planning and the abductions, but she has continued to insist that it was Brady who committed the actual sexual assaults and murders. Brady, who also confessed in 1987, said that Hindley was fully involved and that she strangled Lesley Ann Downey herself. Ian Brady has never sought release, while Hindley has repeatedly sought parole.

On 18 December 1995, the *Guardian* published a long article by Myra Hindley in response to an earlier article they had published about whether violent criminals can be cured. She revealed, plausibly enough, that her barrister had told her that the only way he could defend her was to prosecute Brady, but she refused. Such a defence might well have succeeded. The particular public horror was partly a response to Hindley's stubborn failure in court and in later years to confess. Her sullen, intractable demeanour was remarked on both by police interrogators and those who attended the trial.

The psychological and social function of a public trial is to restore a feeling of order, to make the public feel that chaos has been held at bay. If Hindley had been abjectly remorseful, disclaiming all culpability, blaming everything on Brady, emotionally asserting that she had been in his power and deprived of all free will, this might well have allayed public disquiet. That, after all, would have been the way that a woman might be expected to behave. The Lesley Ann Downey tape was horrific, but no more so than the videotapes that were shown to the jury at the Paul Bernardo trial. If Hindley had agreed to testify against Brady, she might have escaped with a lesser charge or no charge at all. Of course, her supporters claim that her refusal to do so makes for further evidence of the degree to which she *was* in thrall to Brady.

Pleading Ignorance

The Rosemary West defence was both easy and difficult. It was certainly arguable, in strictly legal terms, that the case should never have been brought, or that if it were brought, most of the prosecution evidence should be excluded. Rosemary West was not on trial for assault, so what did it matter what Caroline Owens had to say? The judge decided, surely correctly, that since the murder victims could never be heard, common sense and humanity dictated that the jury hear from surviving victims of the Wests. The result, inevitably, was a mass of prejudicial evidence against Rosemary West – prejudicial against her as a woman, I would argue.

Paradoxically, the case for the defence was also hampered by the lack of direct evidence against Rosemary. If she had been specifically linked to the murders, she would have been forced into the defence that worked for Hedda Nussbaum and Karla Homolka. The problem was that, in order to adopt this tactic, the defence would have had to volunteer a detailed series of admissions about Rosemary's involvement which might have aided the prosecution.

Even the defence never seriously disputed that Rosemary West was savagely violent to her own children, that she colluded in their sexual abuse in a variety of forms, that she was a violent sexual aggressor, that she was a prostitute. Whether she was guilty or not, her children had been murdered while under her care. Many witnesses, including her own mother, testified to Rosemary West's motherliness and her love of children, but Rosemary couldn't deny that one stepdaughter and one natural daughter in her care had been murdered. She might have pleaded weakness, loss of will. Instead, she simply denied everything, constantly responding to the prosecuting cross-examination with the (obviously prepared) refrain, 'I don't remember, sir,' even when questioned about the details of her daughter's disappearance. The defence argued that it didn't matter if she was habitually violent, a prostitute, a sexual criminal, an abuser of her own children. All that mattered was that there was no specific evidence linking her to the murders. The jury disagreed, finding her guilty of all ten murders. The law lords evidently concurred with the sentence when they refused to grant her leave to appeal in March 1996. She is no more likely than Myra Hindley ever to be released.

The decisive reason why the defence employed the strategy it did was that Rosemary West resolutely asserted that she was innocent. Nor should it be thought that her legal team were cynically trying to obtain her release on a technicality. Those who were present during the six weeks of the trial were struck by the obvious sincerity of her solicitor's belief in her innocence. When the verdict was delivered, West's junior defence counsel (a woman) was seen to be in tears: she really believed that her client was innocent.

But what if the alternative defence strategy had been attempted? Would she, should she, have been found not guilty? Or, perhaps, did she have to be found guilty because, in the absence of Frederick, a scapegoat was necessary? There are significant differences between the case of Rosemary West and those of Karla Homolka and Hedda Nussbaum. The West murders took place over a much longer period. To be a truly prolific serial killer, the psychopathic impulse is not enough. Hindley and Brady showed considerable ability in organizing their crimes. Homolka and Bernardo re-constructed a part of their house to facilitate the torture of their victims. Both couples snatched, or lured, their victims off the street, producing major police hunts in each case. It is doubtful whether they could have got away with this for long, even if they had not been apprehended for other reasons. The Wests snatched girls off the streets as well, but in general they drew their victims from a floating population of runaways, vagrants, orphans. Most of their victims were not missed or seriously looked for. The Wests would almost certainly have escaped detection were it not for the murder of their own daughter, Heather, which may well have been unplanned, if not accidental.

If the Homolka/Nussbaum defence would not have worked for Rosemary West, then that is not because she was obviously more guilty than they were. She allowed her daughter to be brutally murdered, but then so did Nussbaum. The inconceivable sufferings of Lucy Partington and Shirley Hubbard are unlikely to have been more obscene than the torture of Leslie Mahaffy and Kristen French. If anything, the extenuating circumstances for Rosemary West are more striking: she was still a minor when she met Frederick, and he was already a multiple murderer.

But the Wests were members of the unrespectable working class, existing in a milieu quite different from that of Hedda Nussbaum and Karla Homolka. The disparity between Nussbaum's appalling neglect of her children and what might have been expected of a woman in her position was so great that factors were found that might explain it away. It may have been thought that a children's publisher would only behave in such a way when in the grip of madness. For the Wests there seemed to have been no barriers between work, family, sex, crime, murder, money, drugs, pornography. Fatefully, the couple found their niche in a squalid, dispossessed world in which lost children came and went, unseen and unremembered by other lost children. Screams were heard, and not exactly forgotten (because they were later recalled under oath), but they were not responded to. Close friends suddenly disappeared and nothing was said or, apparently, even thought of. Professional, middle-class people would be able to identify with the situations of Homolka and Nussbaum in a way they could perhaps not with Rosemary West.

That the Moors Murder case can be considered a major event in post-war British culture is largely because, in the words of one popular account of the case, 'it changed our ideas about what women are capable of'. The police photograph of Hindley, dyed blonde hair and impassive stare, what she herself has called 'that awful mugshot', has become an icon of modern, affectless evil in a way that the contemporary photograph of Brady never has. Over the years, public figures such as Lord Longford and David Astor have claimed that this visceral horror about a woman coldly killing children has made Hindley a scapegoat. While other murderers have reformed, served their time and been quietly released, she has remained a focus of a public hatred that has been repeatedly stirred up by the popular press. It has been argued that the belief that women don't commit murder has resulted in especially harsh treatment of Hindley – for being 'unnatural'.

There is no doubt that this particular horror of the female murderer lies deep in the grain of our culture. When Lady Macbeth decides to become a murderer she rebels against her own biology, calling on spirits to 'unsex' her, to turn her milk to gall.

The 'true crime' section of any bookshop will contain at least a couple of examples of books that show the same fascination with female evil. A typical current example is called *Deadlier Than the Male: Stories of*

Female Serial Killers by Terry Manners, an associate editor of the *Daily Express*. The cover features a grainy photograph of Karla Homolka, monotone except for the eyes, which have been coloured yellow, giving her an air of unearthly evil. It is worth recalling the source of Manners' title. It is, of course, from Kipling's poem, *The Female of the Species* (a tellingly biological title), of which the following is just a part:

She who faces Death by torture for each life beneath her breast
May not deal in doubt or pity – must not swerve for fact or jest.
These be purely male diversions – not in these her honour dwells.
She the Other Law we live by, is that Law and nothing else.

She can bring no more to living than the powers that make her great
As the Mother of the Infant and the Mistress of the Mate.
And when Babe and Man are lacking and she strikes unclaimed
   to claim
Her right as femme (and baron), her equipment is the same.

She is wedded to convictions – (in default of grosser ties);
Her contentions are her children, Heaven help him who denies! –
He will meet no suave discussion, but the instant, white-hot, wild,
Wakened female of the species warring as for spouse and child...

So it comes that Man, the coward, when he gathers to confer
With his fellow-braves in council, dare not leave a place for her
Where, at war with Life and Conscience, he uplifts his erring hands
To some God of Abstract Justice – which no woman understands.

And Man knows it! Knows, moreover, that the Woman that God
   gave him
Must command but may not govern – shall enthral but not
   enslave him.
And She knows, because She warns him, and Her instincts never fail,
That the Female of Her Species is more deadly than the Male.

Notice how this ultra-Conservative polemic (written in 1911, when women were starting to demand the vote) resembles the feminist argument that womanly values are more profound than the relatively trivial activities of men. Kipling (perhaps, for both better and worse, the most skilled rhetorician in the English language) uses apparent praise as a means of keeping women in their place. There is no doubt that many use a professed reverence for femaleness to indict those women who seem to violate it.

Any candid discussion about female murderousness must make clear that it is a marginal subject and that any suggestions about females being 'deadlier than the male' are absurd. A representative statistic (from the U.S. Department of Justice) is that, in 1989, of people arrested for violent crime, 88.6 per cent were men. As Myriam Miedzian puts it in her study of male violence, *Boys Will Be Boys*, 'whatever the future might reveal with respect to the male potential for violence, at present it is overwhelmingly male violence that leads many men and women in our country to live in fear of murder, rape, and assault.'[1] The victims of Myra Hindley and Rosemary West acted rationally when, reassured by the presence of a woman, they accepted lifts from them. To that extent, the horror of crimes, especially murders, committed by women is also understandable, if not rational. We react more strongly to rare events.

It should also be said that this horror cuts both ways. The arguable leniency shown towards Karla Homolka and Hedda Nussbaum is not typical of the treatment received by women convicted in Britain of lesser offences. Though women commit a small minority of crimes, they are substantially more likely to be imprisoned for minor offences such as shoplifting or the non-payment of television licences.[2]

In this climate of bias, is David Astor correct when he says, as he did in a television documentary, that Myra Hindley is the victim of a witchhunt? This is a term that should be used with some care. It is now widely accepted that women burned at the stake in, for example, seventeenth-century Salem, Massachusetts, were both excessively punished and innocent of the charges against them. Some of Hindley's more vociferous supporters speak as if she weren't really a murderer.

Campaigners for Hindley's parole, including Catholic priests who have been her spiritual advisors (she has been a practising Catholic for many years), speak of her liveliness, her intelligence, her affable manner, her professions of repentance, as if any of this were evidence for or against her case. Similarly, there can have been few readers of her *Guardian* article who were not impressed by her obvious fluency and intelligence. Yet it was unsettling as well. Though it had the air of frankness, on closer inspection it was not entirely clear what she was being frank about. The following passage is an example of her pseudo-confessional style:

When the judge wrote to the then Home Secretary two days after the trial he said: 'Though I believe Brady is wicked beyond belief without hope of redemption (short of a miracle) I cannot feel that the same is necessarily true of Hindley once she is removed from his influence. At present she is as deeply corrupted as Brady but it is not so long ago that she was taking instruction in the Roman Catholic Church and was a communicant and a normal sort of girl.'

And it is true that by then I was corrupt; I was wicked and evil and had behaved monstrously.

Without me, those crimes could probably not have been committed. It was I who was instrumental in procuring the children, children who would more readily accompany strangers if they were a woman and a man than they would a man on his own.

My greatest regret is that Ian Brady and I ever met each other. If we hadn't, speaking for myself, there would have been no murders, no crime at all. I would have probably got married, had children and by now be a grandmother.[3]

Has Hindley been reformed, or has she merely learned the modern language of victimhood? The extravagance of her self-mortification obscures her evasiveness about what is being admitted: without her, the crimes 'could probably not have been committed'. She cannot even bring herself to say that she procured the children; instead, she was 'instrumental in procuring' them, as if she were on a par with the car or the tape recorder. Perhaps most disturbing is her 'greatest regret'. The reader sees her point while wondering whether her greatest regret oughtn't to be that she killed five children. As phrased, it suggests a chilling detachment from her own actions, as if she was thrust into her role of childkiller by a chain of events. This is re-enforced by another of her 'admissions': 'the crimes were committed by the person I was then, between the ages of 20 and 23, for which I bear full responsibility and always will do, but the person I am now, aged 53, bears little resemblance to the creature involved in the crimes.' Isn't this akin to saying, 'I bear full responsibility, except that it wasn't really me who did it'?

Contemporary and subsequent reports of these cases are frequently said to show something about what women are capable of. Given that such female killers are exceedingly rare, it is doubtful whether their stories establish anything surprising or new, except for those with a naïve view of the difference between men and women. We could give credit to Rosemary West's autonomy as a woman, as a person, by saying that she collaborated in torture and murder because she liked it. She killed her children, or allowed her children to be killed, because other things mattered to her more. Probably much the same could be said of Myra Hindley, Karla Homolka and Hedda Nussbaum. They murdered because they wanted to.

The notion of free will is as contentious as ever, even among philosophers, and many people, both psychologists and lay people, find it intolerable when applied to sexual psychopaths. After Myra Hindley's article, there was a furious debate on the letters page of *The Guardian*. The following letter (from 21 December, 1995), reproduced in its entirety, was written by a Dr James Hemming. I cite it not as an example of academic analysis but of the problems that occur in the area where medical expertise, the law and public opinion collide:

> In my experience as a psychologist, some young women between the ages of 15 and 20 become fascinated by male arrogance. They are totally dominated by such a man. Ten years later, they are amazed at their naiveté and despise him. This cycle accounts for a number of divorces.
>
> The effect of an attractive girl's adulation on a vain, selfish man is to make him want to prove he is even tougher than she supposed. Killing gives some men a sense of power; it is the ultimate manifestation of distorted masculinity. Once his partner has become involved with him in his cruelties she is trapped. To inform on her husband is to inform on herself. The Myra Hindley of those subservient years is not to be confused with the mature Myra Hindley.[4]

The method put forward here is to establish a context or structure for the murder, which then becomes a form of absolution. This is what person *X* does in context *Y*. If she (or he) had not been in context *Y*, she would not have done it, so she cannot be held genuinely responsible. Furthermore, once removed from context *Y*, she will never do it again. It is a doctrine that goes beyond 'understanding is forgiving' because it holds that true understanding dispenses with any need for forgiveness because no wrong has been committed.

To say that each of these cases was a *folie à deux* is to concede nothing. As an extenuating argument, it is a psychological version of the English common-law doctrine that the husband and wife are one person, namely the husband. It was according to the logic of this that for centuries the wife gave the husband her property in exchange for his name, and in public, legal terms, her will was subsumed in his. A re-reading of Kipling's *The Female of the Species* shows that, on its own terms, a woman cannot do evil any more than, say, a dog or a tree can do evil. She can only act according to or against her own nature. Whatever else they may have been in legal terms, the trials of Karla Homolka and Hedda Nussbaum were retrograde in what they implied about women as free persons, rather than mere human beings. The distinction is itself complex and contentious, but it might be said that the human being is a part of nature, while the person is part of society; the human being is subject to the laws of nature, the person has rights and duties as a citizen; the human being has instincts, the person has free will. The human being acts without volition, the person kills and tortures because that is what he or she wants to do. Women can be people too.

TRYING
THE
BROOKSIDE
TWO:

Domestic Violence, Soap Opera, and Real Life

Tracy Hargreaves

> In the absence of rules of the game, things become caught up in
> their own game; images become more real than the real…
> JEAN BAUDRILLARD

Mother and daughter Mandy and Beth Jordache have been systematically
physically and sexually abused over many years by Mandy's husband
Trevor, but feel powerless to stop the abuse. After a particularly violent
assault, which results in Mandy's hospitalization, Trevor is imprisoned and
Mandy, Beth, and the youngest daughter, Rachel, are moved to a 'safe
house' on Brookside Close, in Liverpool. On his release, Trevor Jordache
tracks them down and inveigles his way into their home, only to resume
his violent attacks and transfer his incestuous attention to Rachel. Beth
discovers her father in bed with Rachel, and forms a plan to poison the
man who has terrorized them, raped them and persistently beaten her
mother.[1] As he slowly dies from the poison she has administered, he realizes
what has been done to him. He threatens to kill Mandy, Beth and Rachel,
but as he begins to beat Beth, Mandy fatally stabs him in the back with
a kitchen knife.

Mandy and Beth conceal the body in refuse sacks – like so much
rubbish – and, with the help of a friend, Sinbad, build a patio and conceal
the body under it. And there it lies, until a leaking underground pipe in the

44

garden next door prompts neighbours to dig up the patio to locate the source of the problem. They find much more than they bargained for – cutting open the refuse sack, what they think is a swag bag turns out to be a makeshift coffin as a badly decomposed hand flops out. Mandy, Beth and Sinbad embark on a desperate week on the run, taking a mystified Rachel with them. Rachel's mystification turns to anger when she discovers what her mother and sister have done. From then on, she is something of a loose cannon. The four are caught and Mandy and Beth are tried, found guilty of murder and conspiracy to murder, and sentenced to life and five years' imprisonment respectively.

These events took place between 1993 and 1995 on the British soap opera *Brookside*. The murder was welcomed with a sigh of relief: 'An action surely approved by at least 99.9 per cent of the millions who follow *Brookside*,' enthused one critic.[2] There is always one exception, however; Lady Olga Maitland, Tory MP for Sutton and Cheam, teetered across the dizzy heights of the moral high ground as she icily observed: 'they plotted to do something that was every bit as barbaric as that [*sic*] Trevor had been doing to them, and when they did it, they lost the right to our sympathy.'[3] Julie Bindel, of Justice for Women, was pleased with the verdict, but for quite different reasons: 'We like the verdicts because they show the audience how dreadful the law is.'[4] *Brookside* appeared to have achieved its aims: it provided a popular forum to expose a law that could, did – and does – sentence women who strike back in self-defence; a law that was – and is – in need of revision.

After the murder, *Brookside* received 17 complaints, and five phone calls and 40 letters in praise of the drama. After the verdict, Channel 4 was inundated with an unprecedented 70 calls from viewers complaining about the outcome. Phil Redmond, the executive producer of the soap, invited groups of irate protesters into the Mersey television studios in order to justify his decision. But all this was not, argued the *Independent's* television critic Allison Pearson, 'evidence that some viewers cannot tell the difference between fiction and reality, but proof that popular drama can reach the parts complex legal cases cannot'.[5] At issue was a plea for a change in the legal system mediated through a sustained (two-year) dramatic representation that pitted itself against the apparently stern intractability of The Law. Indeed, this is where soap comes into its own, as 'it open[s] up for public discussion emotional and domestic issues which are normally deemed to be private.'[6] Phil Redmond, defending his decision to send Mandy and Beth down, found remarkable the way in which the 'fictional story has become entwined with the perceived shortcomings of Britain's legal system'.[7]

This article looks at both 'real life' cases and at the representation of domestic violence, murder, and the laws which deal with women who murder their violent partners. Phil Redmond exercised the power of serial fiction, but he also expressed an unease which strikes an important chord: 'there is something disturbing about the capacity of a television story to provoke a debate which seems entirely to have passed by politicians and other pundits who remain so Westminster-focused that they often appear no longer to notice the really big questions facing people on a daily basis.'[8] What was remarkable in the light of *Brookside*'s dramatization of domestic violence was the wave of popular outrage that swept the nation after the verdict. Both domestic violence and the laws of provocation became issues of popular national concern rather than the concern of women's pressure groups or of the actual victims of domestic violence.

'Free the *Brookside* Two' was a slogan that appeared across the country, echoing other, earlier demands for the quashing of unsafe convictions in the case of political prisoners – the Guildford Four, the Birmingham Six. On screen, protesters in Liverpool walked through the city carrying banners which demanded that the courts should 'Free the Jordaches', whilst members of the pressure group Women Against Violence stormed the headquarters of Mersey Television studios, where the soap is filmed. Even Sandra Maitland, the actor who plays Mandy Jordache, admitted, 'One morning I woke up and for a few seconds I thought, "Oh my God, I don't know how I'm going to get away with it." Then I remembered that I hadn't really killed anybody.'[9]

What was astonishing about all of this fracas and public appeal was that Mandy and Beth were fictional characters in a soap opera. Although *Brookside* is committed to mimetic or realistic presentations of contemporary cultural issues, it is also fictional, dramatic representation. What had *Brookside* managed to achieve in its portrayal of two women who, driven to an unbelievable point of desperation, stood up for themselves, and ended years of bullying, beating, and incestuous rape? How, and why, did their story strike such a resonance?

Regina v Thornton

The case of Sara Thornton, imprisoned for the murder of her allegedly violent and alcoholic husband in 1990, was the ostensible foundation for the *Brookside* story.[10] The *Today* newspaper reported that *Brookside* had 'pinched the plot wholesale from newspaper reports of a real case', although quite which real case it is difficult to tell in the unhappy flotsam of the late twentieth century.[11] Thornton's story had already inspired one play, *Manslaughter*, performed at the Battersea Arts Centre in 1992, and hers was one of three high-profile cases which, at that time, exposed the inequities in the law surrounding the issue of provocation. There were certainly parallels between the cases: Sara Thornton had previously put sleeping tablets into Malcolm Thornton's food, then telephoned a doctor and reported that Malcolm had taken an overdose. Her plan was foiled when he awoke before the arrival of the ambulance, apparently 'incensed and violent at what the defendant had done'.[12] Returning from the pub one night, Sara Thornton arrived home to find Malcolm sleeping on the sofa. After several unsuccessful attempts to wake him, she went into the kitchen, sharpened a knife and stabbed him once in the stomach. The wound was fatal. When the ambulance service tried to revive him, Sara Thornton apparently told them not to bother, and to let him die: 'I know exactly what I am saying,' she told them, 'I sharpened the knife so I could kill him. Do you know what he has done to me in the past?'[13] At the time, Malcolm Thornton was facing trial for an assault on Sara – she had been knocked unconscious and hospitalized.

Thornton unsuccessfully appealed against her sentence twice before she was finally released on bail on 28 July, 1995. She launched her first appeal against her conviction on the grounds of extreme and persistent provocation. Although the Court of Appeal rejected Thornton's plea that her sentence should be reduced to one of manslaughter on the grounds of provocation, her high-profile case provoked debates about the laws surrounding provocation and the ways in which provocation was narrowly defined. The Criminal Division of the Court of Appeal ruled on 20 July, 1991, that the defence of provocation is only available to an accused person who kills in 'hot blood' during a sudden and temporary loss of self-control. But sudden rage is more typical of men than of women. What was ironic and particularly galling for Sara Thornton's supporters was that husbands are more likely to kill their wives in a surrender to a momentary loss of control. Women are either too terrified to fight back in the heat of the moment – or simply too powerless to do so. British law was seen to fail battered women because it took no account of the different ways in which men and women react to provocation. Thornton had accrued a 'slow-burning emotion' which had driven her 'to the end of her tether'.[14] Murder carries a mandatory life sentence; provocation is one successful defence against this, leading to the lesser verdict of manslaughter – for which the judge can fix the sentence. The Court of Appeal and Kenneth Baker, then Home Secretary, who 'reacted stonily' to Thornton's appeal. were to push Sara Thornton even beyond the end of her tether.[15] Two days after Thornton's plea for provocation was turned down, Joseph McGrail, who had murdered his wife, had his plea for provocation accepted. His wife had been that most abusive of women: she had 'nagged' him. Thornton's only means of protest against the crude disparity of their cases was to go on hungerstrike, a protest which she kept up for almost three weeks before she issued this statement: 'My solicitor has told me that people are weeping over my predicament, crying for me to stop my hungerstrike so I can live to see justice done. I cannot ignore such love and compassion.'[16]

Regina v Jordache

This issue of cumulative provocation was at stake in *Brookside*'s dramatization of the case of *Regina v Jordache*. Traces of poison in Trevor's body indicated that Mandy and Beth's actions were premeditated rather than the result of 'a sudden and temporary loss of control'. The perpetrators were consequently found guilty of murder and conspiracy to murder, rather than of manslaughter. Phil Redmond argued that he had wanted to raise the issue of provocation and ask 'whether judges should have the discretion not to put a character like Mandy Jordache in the same bracket as an armed villain who robs a post office'.[17] As Beth Jordache reflected in her 'journal':

> The trouble is they can just lock us up. It's happened to women before, even when there's been heaps of protests. There's this group – Women for Justice – who've been campaigning to get a woman released that killed her husband. He'd tortured and beaten and raped her for years and years and years. She was so terrified of him, she killed him. Only, because she used a weapon, the police said it was premeditated and she was banged up for life.[18]

That Trevor Jordache – who had incessantly brutalized and traumatized his wife and daughter – served only two years of a custodial sentence for the beating of Mandy only underscores the unfairness of the lengths of the sentences meted out to Mandy and her daughter Beth. Notoriously, Bisla Rajinder Singh, who had strangled his wife, was given a one-year suspended sentence for manslaughter in January 1992; like Joseph McGrail, he was deemed to have already suffered enough from 'nagging'.[19]

The *Brookside* plot had a profound and very real relevance for women in Mandy Jordache's situation. Two nights after it was set up, the helpline run by *Brookside* for victims of domestic violence had received 260 calls. After Mandy and Beth were sentenced and sent down, Sandra Horley, the director of Refuge, the charity that gives accommodation to battered women, said that 'even the word "inundated" failed to reflect the number of calls the organization had received since the TV jury returned its majority verdict on Tuesday evening.'[20]

The sympathy and anxieties that had been evoked for Mandy and Beth partly evolved from the fact that the spectator of the drama was party to all sides of the action; we were the real witnesses who saw everything, gaining in the process a particular empathy which enabled an understanding of why Mandy did not just get up and leave the violent Trevor, or why she didn't just call the social services or the police. Sandra Maitland, who played Mandy, researched her role by talking to women who had been battered – in part because she couldn't understand why Mandy would allow Trevor home again. She commented:

> It's such a behind-closed-doors issue. The women feel shame, that it's their fault, and that they can't change their partners. So they believe him when he says he's sorry with the chocs and the flowers and that he won't do it again. On average, a woman leaves seven times before she finally leaves for good.[21]

The soap opera spectator enjoys an omniscience ordinarily denied outside of narrative, where knowledge is only partial or solipsistic. But the omniscience that comes with watching drama is limited, since the spectator is powerless to predict the outcome. The popular outcry at the guilty verdicts was due to a feeling of disempowerment they exposed that feeling of omniscience to be a fantasy. But the outcry was not just about powerlessness; it was also about a realization that the law failed women.

DISCARDED

LIBRARY
FORSYTH TECHNICAL COMMUNITY COLLEGE
2100 SILAS CREEK PARKWAY

Mandy and Beth were victims of violence and, like Thelma and Louise, they were punished for fighting back in self-defence, as every justifiable act of retaliation signifies yet another transgression. As Pragna Patel of Southall Black Sisters commented, women who stand up for themselves are treated harshly by the law because a woman who fights back has upset the applecart of a rotten version of family values.[22]

Brookside worked closely and carefully with women's groups and with legal specialists in the construction of the Jordache story line. Two versions of the verdict were made – one in which they would be found innocent, and the other in which they would be found guilty; one was a kind of wish-fulfilment, the other more realistically representative of the draconian measure of the law on the issue of provocation. If there was a popular fantasy that Mandy and Beth would be found innocent – the triumph of good over evil, victim over victimizer – Brookside resisted succumbing to it in its transmission of the verdict. In the other world outside of soap, women who have committed acts of violent retaliation against their violent partners have been sent to prison – Kiranjit Ahluwalia, Janet Gardner, Georgina Gee, Emma Humphreys, Carol Peters, Sara Thornton, Amelia Rossiter, Violet Walton. Like Mandy Jordache, all of these women were released on appeal; Brookside both reflected and anticipated a turning tide of feeling about the often arbitrary laws of provocation and the discrimination that women endure under the law: some women are charged with manslaughter, some with murder, with a less than casual regard for the similarities in their shared histories of abuse. Mandy Jordache was released shortly after Sara Thornton and Emma Humphreys – the timing of the programme was allegedly scheduled to coincide roughly with Thornton's release.

Phil Redmond's aims were manifold – from wanting to explore domestic violence, he moved on to the state of the law surrounding provocation, exploring sexual abuse (Beth's and Rachel's), lesbianism (Beth's) and general teenage delinquency (Rachel's) along the way. 'What we can do through television drama,' he argued, 'is create a climate, however fleeting, that pushes the issue to the forefront of public consciousness and therefore hopefully provides a more sympathetic climate for campaigners.'[23] Apart from the odd bit of carping from David Thomas in the Sunday Express and the ubiquitous Lady Olga Maitland in the Daily Mail, Redmond did precisely that. The high-profile campaigning of the Southall Black Sisters had preceded Brookside's dramatization of the Jordache trial, and had successfully won the release of Kiranjit Ahluwalia (who had set fire to her husband after a decade of horrific abuse) on 25 September, 1992. The Court of Appeal's decision to grant Ahluwalia a retrial was seen by lawyers as a significant turning point for battered women, although Lord Chief Justice Taylor stressed that the case would not set a precedent for other cases arising from domestic violence. In April of the same year, 71-year-old Amelia Rossiter, who had served four years of a life sentence for killing her violent husband, was released by the Court of Appeal. And in February of that year, Elizabeth Line was acquitted of murder and manslaughter in connection with the stabbing of her abusive husband.[24] Both decisions were welcomed by groups campaigning for a change in the law on provocation. Emma Humphreys was also released after serving ten years of her sentence, in June, 1995. The Court of Appeal were told that the jury should have considered the cumulative effects of her violent lover's treatment of her, in a case which may well have set a precedent. Sara Thornton was released a month later, on 28 July, 1995, amidst calls to reform the law on the sentencing of women who had endured long-term provocation. In August, 1995, Hilary Kingsley, writing in *Today*, paid tribute to the power of soap opera: 'Amazing to think that both Emma Humphreys and Sara Thornton have been released after serving long sentences in the few months that actress Sandra Maitland has pretended to be in jail.'[25] Amazing, too, that a month later Kingsley complained about 'the soap that can rightly claim to have treated domestic violence responsibly, [has] thrown away all the credibility with *Dynasty*-style nonsense.'[26] If it was not *Dynasty*-style nonsense, *Brookside* was honouring 'a time-honoured theatrical form: the lurid melodrama'.[27] What brought these critiques on is another twist in the plot: on the night before their appeal date, Beth is killed in prison at the hands of a shocking *deus ex machina*, in a rather tragic if ironic twist. She has inherited a congenital heart defect, a legacy from her father, and in this neat thematic turn of events, a kind of punishment or revenge is enacted as the daughter is killed by this awful, if not wholly plausible, genetic legacy. It *is* soap, after all.

Mandy, meanwhile, is released on appeal, but after returning home, Trevor's loyal and vengeful sister Brenna returns and wheedles her way back into the Jordache home. Once settled there, she begins to poison Mandy and her unborn child (conceived whilst on the run with Sinbad). Mandy appears to die slowly before our eyes in what is, admittedly, another implausible story line, but Brenna turns out to be an even more inept poisoner than Mandy and Beth – and Mandy discovers her scheme before it's too late.

If there is a reluctant acceptance lurking in both of these comments that neither '*Dynasty*-style nonsense' nor melodrama are credible forms for negotiating an issue of any serious moral worth, there is also an exoneration of soap opera as a form which can – and did – credibly negotiate and dramatize domestic violence and the law. *Brookside* was more inventive – and successful – in its dramatization than Kingsley's comment gives it credit for.

The serious and the trivial were uncomfortable bed-fellows partly because of the harrowing nature of the story, which had its basis not in the traditionally perceived froth of soap, but in the terrible reality of a brutal and discriminatory society and legal system. Everyone had something to say, both in the soap and out, as conflict raged. Was it true to life or melodramatic fantasy? Was Mandy Jordache 'the symbolic figurehead for battered women', a new 'feminist icon' as David Thomas (even as he found it hard to drum up sympathy for 'those Jordache girls') opined in the *Sunday Express*, or was she 'one of the stupidest women ever to grace the nation's TV screens?'[28] Was the trial 'as dated as it was dramatically lame' or 'so convincing … that events in court seemed nowhere near as stage-managed as the OJ Simpson trial?'[29]

Television closes the gap between self and other, even as it defines and describes the alienation of late twentieth-century cultural identity. *Brookside* captured something of the *Zeitgeist* in its portrayal of a community at odds with itself – here in microcosm was late twentieth-century society, experiencing the rage of Caliban seeing his own face in the glass. Stuart Jefferies neatly summed up some of the distinguishing and defining features of the three main British soaps: 'Where [*Coronation*] *Street* is still presenting a vision of community that has been crumbling since the early sixties, and *East Enders* portrays the family, Kray-like, as a source of matriarchal power and tradition, *Brookside* depicts community and family as fractured things.'[30]

Trevor's violent behaviour was condemned by everyone on the Close, but it was the women, rather than the men, who attempted to help Mandy and Beth after the verdict. This was a community energized by factions rather than the collective or shared identities which we might suppose define a community. As the on-screen campaign was launched to free them, a divided local community straddled a simplified good/bad divide in their support or condemnation of the two women. At the centre of the axis that supported this fulcrum between female solidarity and an alien fraternity was the figure of Mandy Jordache and her right to defend herself and protect her children.

And what kinds of fantasies developed in the public and critical imagination, provoked by a woman and her daughter who almost get away with murder? Allison Pearson has suggested that the ordinariness (or unattractiveness) of Mandy's character is precisely where and why our sympathies lie with her – that which 'makes the Mandy Jordaches of this world the sternest test of our sense of justice'.[31] Although she was in an irrelevantly snobbish anti-Mandy mood after the verdict – 'Even as I write, you can bet that some Channel 4 costume designer is running up "Mandy Jordache is Innocent" T-shirts in our wronged heroine's preferred fabric: stretch-line velour' – she was actually half-right: the women's bookshop Silver Moon on London's Charing Cross Road had 'Free Beth Jordache' T-shirts printed (though not in stretch-line velour).[32] There was no small amount of sympathy for Beth as the lesbian icon who had been sent down with Mandy, the faint-hearted feminist, as the various implications and meanings of the drama developed.

But Mandy's story is, as it happens, the stuff of fancy – romance and gothic. Tania Modleski has drawn parallels between the genre of romance and soap as she outlines a basic plot:

> To aid her heroine in the protection of her virtue the writer ... had to disable her: e.g. to render her entirely ignorant of the most basic facts of life so that the man, finally impressed by her purity, would quit trying to destroy her and would, instead, reward and elevate her – i.e. marry her.[33]

Mandy is inept, indecisive, impulsive, desperate. As Modleski notes, just as women are categorized as virgin or whore, so women, in the tradition of the Gothic romance, divide men into two classes: 'the omnipotent, domineering, aloof male and the gentle, but passive and fairly ineffectual male'.[34] *Brookside* clearly spells out the traditional plot of the romance; but the single figure who embodies self and other as good *and* bad (like Jekyll and Hyde) is helpfully split into two discrete figures: Trevor and Sinbad. *Brookside*'s radical departure from the troubling ideologies of the traditional romance plot is that Mandy rejects both for her new role as strong protector as she absorbs into herself the strength of character of her dead daughter (thereby symbolically uniting lesbianism and feminism).

'A happy wedding in the close is just what's needed after all the tragedy of Trevor's murder, Mandy and Beth's imprisonment and then the shocking news about Beth's sudden death,' gushed the *TV Times* when Sinbad proposed to Mandy. But a happy wedding is exactly what they are not to have. Up pops Brenna, like the return of the repressed, and she almost succeeds in poisoning Mandy and her unborn child. Brenna is possibly the fictional counterpart to Malcolm Thornton's first wife Moyra, who defended the memory of Malcolm Thornton and claimed that Sara Thornton was both dangerous and devious, and that Malcolm had only ever married Sara to 'stop her nagging'.[35] Brenna was a perfect device for a vindication (if ever it was needed) of Mandy's actions. Although she lives to tell the tale, it is to other battered women that the 'new' Mandy turns. Just as we expect (or wish?) that Mandy will settle for happiness with Sinbad, their new baby and the sanctity of marriage, she goes to Bristol and performs a different kind of wish-fulfilment, where she stops her own dramatic history becoming the story of other women's lives and goes to work in a battered women's refuge.

Mandy pays for her transgression by her imprisonment and the loss of her daughter. But because *Brookside* is issue-led rather than character-based, in the case of Mandy and Beth there appeared to be difficulties of what to do with them as characters after the success of the appeal. Given that both actors wanted to leave the soap, we were, in the event, denied a happy family resolution. There was never to be a happy end for Mandy – the death of her eldest daughter (who had inverted roles and mothered her mother through much of the two-year ordeal) ensured this. Modleski argues that 'It is important to recognize that soap operas serve to affirm the family not by presenting an ideal family, but by portraying a family in constant turmoil…'[36] But if the exigencies of real life intervene (actors wishing to leave the soap), creating unexpected (and implausible) twists and turns to the plot, there is a happy end of sorts to this story: 'To the dismay of many feminist critics, the most powerful fantasy embodied in soap opera appears to be the fantasy of a fully self-sufficient family,' argues Modleski.[37] Mandy Jordache, an unlikely feminist icon, refuses this institution as a refuge and goes further afield to a refuge of a different and more radical kind.

But there is a striking parallel between the structures that shaped the plot of *Brookside* and the formulas common to the romance and gothic fiction. Modleski argues that a feature of romance is 'the transformation of the brutal (or, indeed, murderous) men into tender lovers, [and] the insistent denial of the reality of male hostility towards women'.[38] Clearly this is troubling for any but the most reactionary of readings, but *Brookside* throws this particular baby clean out with the bathwater.

A crucial part of Mandy and Beth's testimony was that Trevor was sexually abusing Rachel. Finding Trevor in bed with Rachel was the deciding moment for Mandy and Beth to kill Trevor – to protect Rachel ostensibly, but of course to protect themselves – as though Rachel were the sole remaining undamaged part of themselves. Rachel strenuously denied that Trevor had abused her, which weakened Mandy and Beth's case. The unfolding plot is a perfect exemplification of Modleski's argument that: 'Often the attempt to find an enemy and the attempt to exonerate the father are part of the same project.'[39] But when Mandy and Beth are in prison, Rachel eventually confronts what she has repressed – that her father had in fact sexually abused her. She gives fresh evidence, and the rest, as they say, is history.

Conclusion

'Soap opera', argued Christine Geraghty in her 1991 study, 'has changed … by the presence of stories which engage an audience in such a way that they become the subject for public interest and interrogation.'[40] And what an interest *Brookside* aroused between 1993 and 1995. If, as Geraghty argues, 'The relationship between mother and daughter … is central to many soaps, providing an irresistible combination of female solidarity and family intimacy,' then *Brookside* enjoyed a particularly seductive appeal in its portrayal of the unlikely feminist icon, Mandy Jordache, and her feisty lesbian daughter, Beth.[41] The symbolic axis on which this plot turned was far more radical than the critical debates allowed. At issue was not just whether *Brookside* was issue-based or character-led, lurid melodrama or the net which captured the social realities of the late twentieth-century *Zeitgeist*. The developing two-year narrative offered an often compelling dramatization of the complex psychological realities of the victims of domestic violence. If the denouement of the plot was implausible, the fantasies it portrayed are surely worth celebrating; that the bereft and traumatized figure of Mandy Jordache should develop a political consciousness and confidence in the world of the soap is fitting for a character who became 'the symbolic figurehead of battered women' in the world outside.[42] The soap raised the profile of the issues of domestic violence, incest and the laws of provocation. On 18 January 1994, Zero Tolerance, a campaign designed to raise public awareness of domestic violence, was launched by the Association of London Authorities. A recent article revealed that the Metropolitan Police show the *Brookside* murder episodes to officers as part of their training for dealing with domestic violence. Probation services show the episodes to male offenders as part of their counselling procedures.[43] After the loss of Thornton's 1991 appeal, Labour MP Jack Ashley had asked Lord Chancellor Mackay to widen the definition of provocation to include acts of violence perpetrated after control had been regained. Four years later, Lord Chancellor Mackay said that the government would reform the law on domestic violence, offering greater protection to the victim and making it easier to arrest the perpetrators. And the release of Sara Thornton in 1995 has prompted a review of 50 other similar cases.

In July, 1995, the *Daily Mail* reported on a copycat *Brookside* killing. Mary Smith, aged 18, had killed her abusive grandfather because she was afraid that he was about to start molesting her younger sister. 'Diaries seized by police revealed she had been strongly influenced by the long running storyline from the Channel 4 soap *Brookside*, which culminated with Beth Jordache [sic] murdering her abusive father Trevor because she was afraid he would molest her younger sister.'[44] She even bought a kitchen knife, like the one used by Mandy.

Mary Smith was acquitted.

RETELLING
THE TALE:

The Emma Humphreys Case

Elizabeth Stanko and Anne Scully

In July 1995, a 28-year-old woman walked through the ornately carved doors of the British Royal Courts of Justice in London, hands held high, to the cheers and embraces of her supporters outside. Emma Humphreys had just served over ten years for killing Trevor Armitage. Convicted of murder in December 1985, Humphreys had been detained at 'Her Majesty's Pleasure' as a cold-blooded murderer. But the Court of Appeal reconsidered this judgment, allowing her conviction for murder to be quashed and replaced by a conviction for manslaughter on the grounds of provocation. The law, it seemed, was now prepared to accept another story about the events of the early evening of 26 February, 1985, when Armitage was stabbed by one fatal blow which penetrated his heart and liver, leading to his immediate death.

When women are the defendants in a trial for murder, it is less likely that the 'who done it' is problematic, since women are most likely to attack and kill those closest to them. For instance, in England and Wales from 1990–1994, when women killed, 58.5 per cent killed males; of those adult men killed, ex-lovers and husbands comprised 72 per cent.[1] It is the 'why' of women's behaviour which is contested in a trial such as this. The trial is, after all, meant to be the context for making sense of the defendant's actions, and the setting of the stage for condemnation and for exacting a price for the crime. And the very fact that any woman rises up against another person – and usually the other is a man, well known to her – immediately makes her motives suspect. Indeed, women's killings were once considered treasonous acts and, as direct challenges to men's authority, especially husbands' authority, were specially punished.[2]

In this chapter we wish to consider the story-telling potential of law, particularly in situations where women kill men who have abused them. This is a story which has altered because of the direct actions of feminist campaigners who have confronted the inadequacies of English law. According to these campaigners, the law has perpetuated miscarriages of justice in situations when women kill in order to survive violence at the hands of men. What makes Humphreys' case interesting – as with the cases of the few other women who have challenged their convictions of murder in the Court of Appeal – is that a jury convicted her of murder ten years previously, a decision which meant that they collectively determined her to be a 'cool and calculating' killer.

It was Humphreys herself who initiated the challenge to her label as a 'murderer'. Publicity surrounding the cases of two women appealing against murder convictions of men who had been abusive to them alerted Humphreys to an alternate legal viewing of her conviction.[3] She contacted the campaigning group, Justice for Women, asking for help.[4]

The cumulative knowledge about men's violence against women, popularized through the campaigns of grassroots women's groups such as the British Southall Black Sisters and Justice for Women, created the context within which Humphreys' actions could be reviewed. In essence, feminist campaigners in Britain demanded that the law tell a different story about the same event and the same participants. This involved a remake of the story, casting the players in different roles, changing the public's perception so that such women are pictured not as killers but as choosing to preserve their own lives at the cost of the lives of their abusers. Characterizing women in this new way demands new legal precedents. After the successful appeal, Humphreys is no longer a 'cold-blooded murderer', but is now portrayed as a sorry soul, barely an adult woman whose unhappy childhood ultimately led her to act out of desperation and kill Armitage.

We have chosen the Humphreys' case in order to speculate whether the law is capable of seeing women's violence differently in different circumstances. Does the outcome of Humphreys' case herald a new era for women who kill after enduring years of physical and sexual abuse? Is the law able to sustain a feminist critique of women's lethal violence in situations where women are killing to live? Let us begin our explorations of the story-telling potential of law with the version of the events as summarized in the Court of Appeal in 1995.

Trevor Armitage's Killing

She [Humphreys] has a very unhappy family background. When she was about five years old her mother and father separated, her mother remarried and the appellant went to live with her [mother] and her stepfather in Canada until December 1983. Both her mother and her stepfather were alcoholics. From early adolescence she herself took drugs, drank too much alcohol, and was sexually promiscuous. She returned to England in December 1983 and went to live with her father and his second wife, and subsequently with her grandmother. However, on 30th August 1984, aged 16, she left home and went to work as a prostitute.

Shortly thereafter she was picked up by the victim, Trevor Armitage. He had a predilection for girls much younger than himself, had previous convictions for violence, was a drug addict and was known to the vice squad as somebody who was seen most evenings driving round the vice area.

Trevor Armitage took the appellant to live with him at his house in Turnbury Road, Bulwell. He was jealous and possessive, although he did not object to her continuing to work as a prostitute and, indeed, lived in part on her earnings. Their relationship began as a sexual one, but shortly after they first met he beat her up on a number of occasions and this caused her to lose interest in him.

Over Christmas and the New Year 1984/5 she appeared before the criminal courts as a result of two incidents and for some weeks she was on remand at Risley, until 21st February 1985, when she was conditionally discharged. While she was away Trevor Armitage took in another young girl.

This miserable history from August 1984 onwards was the prelude to the critical events of the 24th–26th February 1985. Before reviewing them, however, it is important to record another very important and unhappy aspect of her personal history, namely that she had a strong tendency to seek attention, exemplified in her case by frequent attempts, dating back to her residence in Canada, to cut her wrists, leaving marks and scars which were plainly visible; these were described by a doctor who examined her shortly after the killing, and who found 3 recent cuts to her right wrist, 15 well healed scars to her right forearm, 9 recent cuts running across her left wrist with fresh, dry blood over them, and 7 well healed vertical scars running up her left forearm.

On 24th February 1985 a Mrs Whitehead, who was a witness at the trial, saw the appellant in a bar and described her as very lonely, depressed and desolate. The following day two friends met up with Trevor Armitage and his son Stephen, aged 16, in a bar, where the appellant was also present. They left the bar with the appellant and Trevor Armitage told her that 'We'll be alright for a gang-bang tonight.'

The group then went on to another public house and finally to Trevor Armitage's house where he arrived drunk. The appellant went upstairs and turned on the radio. Shortly afterwards Trevor Armitage left to drive his son home.

After they had left she went down to the kitchen and took two knives from a drawer, fearing that there might be trouble when he came back and that he might give her another beating. At this juncture she cut both her wrists with one of the knives.

When Trevor Armitage returned she was sitting on the landing, listening to music with one of the knives in her hand. He came up and went past her into the bedroom, where he undressed and then came and sat near her on the landing with only his shirt on. She said she got the feeling that he wanted sex while she did not and that she was fearful that he might force himself upon her.

At this critical juncture there occurred the event which was relied upon as triggering her loss of self-control, when Trevor Armitage taunted her that she had not made a very good job of her wrist-slashing.

She reached across him as he lay on his back and stabbed him with a blow from one of the knives which penetrated his heart and went through into his liver, in a manner which expert evidence stated required a moderate degree of force.[5]

Imagining Female Killers: Criminology's Legacies

Criminology has set itself the task of explaining criminality and crime. It is a social science developed in the modernist era, where attention is focused on accounting for the differences between criminals and the rest of law-abiding folk. What does criminology offer law in the way of explanations for killing, especially when women are the perpetrators?

It has become a truism that men are largely responsible for crime and criminality. Since women's contribution to violent crime was – and still is – so rare, few criminologists have bothered to speculate about women's violence. When women offend, their actions are assessed within tradition-al notions of appropriate femininity: good girls and women, it is assumed, are law-abiding. Self-control and non-violence are assured via suitable femininity.[6] Therefore, criminology concentrates on an exploration of women's abnormality, which is found within the biological or psychologi-cal make-up of 'deviant' women. Early criminologists proposed that women's violence was indicative of *unwomanliness*: violent women, accordingly, had more body hair, a more 'primitive' physical make-up and, because they were violent, were simply more like men. In this way the violence of women was excluded from the presumed docility of woman-hood.

As feminists began to challenge criminology's logic – naming it as much a logic about conventions of gender as an explanation of crime – women's experiences of men's abuse, threats and violence began to be understood as indicative of women's place in a gender hierarchy.[7] Active campaigns by women's movements throughout the world highlighted the sexual and physical violence of men towards women.[8] This attention paid to women's experiences of men's violence brought interesting observations to light.[9] This work flowed from the actions of rape crisis centres and refuges for battered women, and successfully challenged the belief that violence was rare, or random. Research consistently demonstrates that men's violence to women is often systematic, linked to the abuse of power and the access of authority or kinship, and affects the lives of countless women and children. Feminist criminologists also began to trace a relationship between criminal offending and criminal victimization. Not only were women offenders often poor, young and disproportionately non-white, research suggested that many women serving time in prison had long histories of being abused, usually at the hands of men.[10]

In England, feminist campaign groups explicitly linked women's killing of abusive men to evidence of histories of physical and sexual violence, in an effort to make this the substance of the appeals of murder convictions. Women's autonomous acts of lethal violence, which had been adjudged in these cases as fully culpable actions under the law, were argued to be independent acts by women defending themselves against men's violence.

Feminist campaigners were now in a position to challenge one kernel of English law, the Homicide Act of 1957. Women's lethal violence in situations of sexual and physical violence connected to heterosexual intimacy must, according to the campaigners, be viewed not as 'cold-calculated killing' but as an act of self-defence. Women whose violence had lethal consequences in circumstances of self-defence, they further propose, must not be adjudged as murderers. Murder is imagined as an act that is often unpredictable, wanton, intentional and cruel (though seldom do these apply to female perpetrators). While certainly women's circumstances are taken into account when determining guilt in lethal violence, by no means do all women who face serious and repeated violence have their lethal actions understood as self-defence.

One attempt to place many women's acts of killing in a wider context of men's violence was to characterize women's potential for lethal violence as 'Battered Woman Syndrome'. Initially, Lenore Walker, the psychologist who coined the phrase, sought to explain why women often remain with violent partners.[11] While Walker's thesis about the way battered women respond to battering has many critics, it was adapted for use as a legal defence, first in North America, then around the world.

The main problem for criminology and criminal law is the explanation offered by Battered Woman Syndrome for seeming inaction: only *leaving* (not killing) violent men is seen as positive action. Research suggests that when women kill violent partners or ex-partners, death typically occurs during a confrontation or fight.[12] When applied to situations where women act with such lethal consequences, defence teams are not always successful in portraying women as incapable of escaping their violent partners. The very act of self-defence disproves one of the basic tenets of Battered Woman Syndrome: learned helplessness. Here is where such a legal defence has come under a great deal of criticism.[13] When a woman defendant is not seen as *helpless* (and as outside the image of innocence: that of being white and middle class, with documentation of the violence and abuse, and so forth), the Battered Woman Syndrome defence serves to paint many women as incapable of acting on their own behalf; perhaps most problematically, it paints women's actions as if there were a universal response for *all* battered women.[14]

R v Ahluwalia

In England in the 1990s, the case of *R v Ahluwalia* brought home the failure to link domestic terrorism with self-preservation.[15] Kiranjit Ahluwalia killed her husband, Deepak, after ten years of marriage and ten years of abuse.[16] While he slept she poured petrol on him and set him alight. He died six days later. Ahluwalia was convicted of murder.[17] Her successful appeal three years later was accepted on the grounds of her diminished responsibility at the time of the killing. The major legal *problem* was that she did not kill Deepak during a violent argument. Because she waited, and killed him when he was unable to hurt her, she could not plead that she was provoked in the heat of the moment. And because she was so devastated, she did not detail the litany of abuse she endured at his hands. It was the work of feminist activists, notably Southall Black Sisters, with their enlightened legal teams, who opened up the possibility for Ahluwalia's lethal violence to be heard by the court as an action taken not in the heat of the moment (and then eligible for a partial defence of diminished responsibility), but a planned act, deliberately designed to preserve the life of the woman whose judgment was impaired as a result of the violence she had endured.[18] The legal precedent established in Ahluwalia's case extended the concept of manslaughter to accommodate an act committed when self-control has not been suddenly lost.

R v Humphreys

Humphreys, however, was the antithesis of Ahluwalia. She was not married to Armitage. She worked as a prostitute, and had no recourse to being portrayed as a 'battered spouse'. Although Humphreys may have been judged to be in a *sorry* state, the jury ultimately came to the conclusion – by convicting her – that though her actions took place in the heat of the moment she had no *real* excuse for using lethal violence when she did.

It was another legacy of criminology's story-telling which seeped into the explanations of Emma Humphreys' violence during her appeal. The focus turned to her psychological disposition, described as her 'attention-seeking' behaviour of cutting her wrists, for an explanation of the killing.[19] The successful grounds for her appeal illustrate one of the mainstays in considering women's violence, namely 'madness'. Removed from *appropriate femininity*, violent women must be *explained* by their deviance, perhaps induced by hormonal imbalance (such as an explanation of women's violence caused by pre-menstrual tension), or by women's inability to cope with their social conditions or with motherhood. These psychological explanations, however, overshadow the part played by the violence women endure at the hands of men.

Humphreys' 'madness' is encapsulated by her so-called attention-seeking behaviour – her wrist slashing. But the *fact* of self-injury cannot determine that someone is mad – it is not a specifically recognizable mental illness. Self-injury, according to a self-injury self-help group in London, is often more a mechanism of and a release from self-loathing.[20] In the appeal, Humphreys' defence team argued that, on that fateful night of early 26 February, 1985, Armitage's mockery of Emma's self-injury triggered her self-defence. Through this logic, the act of self-preservation – defending herself against Armitage's abuse – was separated from the legal 'logic' of lethal killing. So while the wider context of Humphreys' young life is dominated by her experiences of physical and sexual abuse and the immediate circumstances of her situation with Armitage, the trigger to Humphreys' violence is 'only words'[21] (Armitage's mockery of Emma's self-injury). Men's abuse – and in the case of Humphreys, many men's abuse of her throughout her life – was not included in the immediate provocation of her ultimately lethal violence.

Why does psychopathology succeed in law where a feminist explanation for self-defence – Humphreys' endangerment and abuse at the hands of Armitage – fails? An exploration of English legal method will help us to understand both the logic of law and the popular image of homicidal women.

Constructing Legal Stories
The story told to the court in 1995 about Emma Humphreys and the death of Trevor Armitage cast the main players as very different characters to those portrayed in the original trial. Why in the first trial was legal method unequipped to allow Emma Humphreys to claim a partial defence of provocation? Furthermore, given that there was no new evidence in the appeal case, why was the prior decision (the guilty verdict), which had been based on sound legal reasoning, overturned?

It is widely stated that in English law judges interpret and apply the law: they do not make law. The two main tools which judges use to interpret and apply law are 1) the principles of statutory interpretation, and 2) the doctrine of precedent. In Humphreys' case we can consider the import of each of these tools in constructing the defendant's image as a female killer in both the initial and appeal hearings.

In the initial decision, after which Humphreys was convicted of murder, we can assess the way in which legal method aided and abetted the conviction. Equally, we can look at the decision on appeal to quash the initial conviction and the way in which the same principles, applied to the same set of facts, resulted in a significantly different result.

The English Law of Homicide

The Homicide Act 1957 requires both the act of killing the victim and the intention of so doing for the offence of murder to have been committed. Should the act of killing have been done, but the intention found to be lacking, then the 1957 Act allows for a full defence of self-defence, and the partial defences of diminished responsibility and/or provocation. Thus the law allows mitigation to murder in the form of partial defences: defendants may argue that they killed because of temporary loss of self-control caused by temporary or permanent mental disability (diminished responsibility); or that they killed because of temporary loss of self-control provoked by the words and/or actions of the victim (provocation).

The limits on the way in which a statute may be interpreted are widely accepted as a framework by which the judiciary should be guided.[22] Clearly the judiciary do not have the freedom to respond to a situation subjectively; the plight of the individual in the case at hand must not influence the manner in which the statutory provision is interpreted.

The Initial Decision

It was clear from the statute that Humphreys could not use the full defence of self-defence. Her life, at the time that she delivered the fatal injury, was not in immediate danger. While a partial defence of diminished responsibility could be taken, the key issue was that Humphreys' actions were triggered not by any mental disability, but by the words and taunts of Trevor Armitage. To plead diminished responsibility is for the defendant to be both catalyst and agent in the offence. Humphreys felt very strongly that, although she may have been the agent, she was not the catalyst for the events that led to the death of Trevor Armitage. On a partial defence of provocation, wherein the part played by Armitage could be reviewed, it had to be decided whether Humphreys could be said to have been provoked, as the law understands provocation, by the actions and/or words of Trevor Armitage when she stabbed him.

The definition of provocation in the 1957 Act is found in Section 3 of the Act:

> Where on a charge of murder there is evidence on which the jury can find that the person charged was provoked (whether by things done or by things said or by both together) to lose his [*sic*] self control, the question whether the provocation was enough to make a reasonable man [*sic*] do as he [*sic*] did shall be left to be determined by the jury; and in determining the question the jury shall take into account everything both done and said according to the effect which, in their opinion, it would have on a reasonable man [*sic*].

This Section is unambiguous in the matters of consideration of things said or done, and also in whether there was a loss of self-control. What is ambiguous is whether a reasonable [wo]man would have been so provoked by Armitage so as to lead to his death? What, in this context, is a reasonable [wo]man? How much should the defendant's own personality traits be taken into account? In the initial case in 1985, the judge seemed to take the view that the definition of a reasonable [wo]man should encompass any of the characteristics of the defendant except those which would be repugnant to the concept of a reasonable [wo]man. That is, self-inflicted character distortions should not be taken into account.[23] By viewing Humphreys' attempt to slash her wrists as self-inflicted and as 'attention-seeking', the judge removed from the jury's purview the whole range of experience that had led Humphreys to react in such a manner.

Legally this interpretation of the Act is sound. In *true* legal method the meaning of the term *reasonable man* cannot be moulded to fit a particular defendant's *own* personality. This is necessary in order to maintain the statute as a law applying to all men and women. In effect, the law removes any individual's personal history from being included when considering his or her actions.

The tools of legal method are designed to achieve consistency as a premium, but also to ensure the universality of application of the law. This must then be achieved by a form of rational, as opposed to intuitive, debate. The rules of legal precedent are, as with statutory interpretation, clearly acknowledged. Precedent follows the hierarchy of the courts, allows for persuasive precedents from other jurisdictions, and relies upon a clear and rational comparison of cases. The goal is, of course, a rational progression of analysis to ensure consistency in the treatment of *like* cases. In applying precedent, then, the object of counsel is to put forward the fundamental principle of law on which *like* cases were decided. In order to find the fundamental principle, the specifics of an individual case are removed, allowing for a generalized formulation of the law. The specifics of an individual's experience become secondary.

The use of precedent in Humphreys' initial case was based firmly on an idea of the universal application of the concept of the reasonable [wo]man.[24] The reasonable [wo]man was deemed to be someone of the same age and sex as the defendant, sharing some of Humphreys' characteristics such as would affect the impact of the provocation on her. But the reasonable [wo]man is never to be simply someone in the defendant's exact position with her same experiences. This effectively prevented the judge from directing the jury to consider the psychiatric report on Humphreys, or her experience of Trevor Armitage. The jury therefore returned a verdict of guilty to the charge of murder on the basis that Humphreys had not been provoked. Given that the jury were considering Humphreys' actions in the light of someone who was free of the trauma which she had suffered, their verdict is not surprising.

The Appeal

In the Humphreys appeal, the system of precedent was seen to be working at the boundaries of the existing law in past cases. In order to say that Humphreys' own character was not at odds with the concept of a reasonable [wo]man, and that therefore her 'immaturity' and 'attention-seeking' should have been left to the jury to decide whether a reasonable [wo]man with these characteristics would have been provoked, the court had to review the direction given by the judge in the initial case.

On appeal Humphreys' counsel relied upon different precedents and sought to present certain of her characteristics as being relevant to the concept of the reasonable [wo]man, so that these traits could be seen to be matters which the jury should consider in deciding on the issue of provocation. This turnabout in emphasis on past precedents was facilitated by a reconsideration of the report produced for the first trial by the consultant psychiatrist for the defence. His evidence was noted as 'critical for the appeal' by the appellate judges.[25] By extending the boundaries of the legal discourse being argued in court to cover not only the standard legal reference points of statutory and common law sources, but also the reference point of another rational, analytical science (namely medicine) as a valid contribution to the impartial, logical and even universal decision-making process, the court was able to redefine the concept of the reasonable [wo]man.

Using the psychiatrist's evidence, counsel for the appellant sought to show that Humphreys' immaturity and attention-seeking were permanent and intrinsic characteristics and were the direct subject of Armitage's taunts on the night he was killed. Therefore those characteristics would influence a reaction to the given provocation; because they were a permanent part of Humphreys' character, they should be allowed for consideration by the jury. The material facts of the case were effectively altered, allowing an alternative viewing of the events on the evening of 26 February, 1985.

Through legal method, the medical discourse of 'mad rather than bad' becomes another building-block in the law's construction of the female killer. However, if the psychiatric evidence was available at the first trial, why was the jury directed not to consider Humphreys' 'attention-seeking' as relevant to the reasonable [wo]man's reaction? It would seem that the psychiatric evidence *was* considered at the first trial, but the story of Humphreys' experience was told in a less compelling manner than it was in the appeal case. The feminist re-viewing of her behaviour enabled a more coherent story to be told.

In doing so, however, the law acknowledges the validity of medical evidence in cases where mental illness exists. Medicine, as with law, depends upon the assumption of objective and external criteria, of alleged proof in diagnosis. Therefore medical knowledge can be meshed with legal knowledge in terms of impartial and universal application. The problem for Humphreys, in the initial trial, was that she did not suffer from a specific mental illness that could be proven. Therefore Armitage's taunts levelled at her attempts to slash her wrists were not an attack on her mental illness, but an attack on what was deemed her attention-seeking nature.

When on appeal the psychiatric evidence was reconsidered it was told in a different manner. Instead of being likened to the behaviour of a spoilt child desperate for attention, Humphreys' wrist-slashing was compared to anorexia, which was, in the Court of Appeal's judgment, a recognized 'psychological illness or disorder'.[26] This is an especially interesting twist of logic, for as previously noted, self-injury is *not* a recognized psychological illness or disorder. Humphreys' transition from her place in the objective standard of 'reasonable [wo]man' had begun. She could now bring to the court a taste, although limited, of the specific quality of her experience under the umbrella of a medically-sanctioned disorder. Even now Humphreys could not, constrained by the rules of legal method, expect the court to decide her case on the basis of the singular nature of her own experience. What she *could* do, however, was bring to light as much of her own personality as would be commensurate with that of the reasonable [wo]man suffering from a similar disorder. The objective, universal standard, although expanded by the use of an alleged medical observation concerning Humphreys attention-seeking behaviour, is thus still maintained by legal method.

The second ground of appeal offered by counsel was that the judge had not given sufficient emphasis to, and analysis of, the cumulative provocation Humphreys had experienced. Again, traditionally the law will look to identifiable provocative actions, rather than a chain of experience, in deciding the existence of provocation. This, in terms of legal method, means that a certain objective criteria can be set rather than it being necessary to delve into each defendant's whole life experience. However, once Humphreys had been deemed to be a subject of psychiatric science, her character was effectively reconstructed, allowing for a more detailed consideration of her passage through life up to the point at which she stabbed Armitage. Had she not been so 'reconstructed', the specific details of her life would not have been deemed relevant to the case. In reality, a jury is less likely to deny a defence of provocation if they understand the whole passage of events.

From this case, and subsequent appeal, the significance of the function of legal method can be clearly understood. Whilst impartiality, universality and consistency are desirable in a legal system, there should be some means for reaching a just outcome other than by pathologizing the defendant. One of the reasons we suggest that some women's experiences of domestic killing will not be understood is the unholy – and usually sexist – alliance between psychiatry and law in their attempts to place all women's actions in one neat basket.

Intractable Stories?

To us the ultimate decision in this case is correct. Emma Humphreys did not deserve to spend ten years in prison for her act of 26 February, 1985. She also did not deserve to be considered a cold, calculating murderer.

But the law has not proved to be innovative, nor has it illuminated the material realities of many women's experiences of physical and sexual abuse. The method by which the law delivers its decision contributes to its inability to address the impact of cumulative abuse. When many women kill in intimate situations, the evidence continues to be overwhelming that women are choosing (whatever constitutes 'choice') self-preservation over abuse. When a man dies, the law must consider the culpability of an independent actor. The range of this consideration is limited by the very method through which law operates.

Rather than seeking to understand the specific circumstances of the death of a man, the law seeks to mould the female actor's motivations to its own logic. As such, the female killer will almost invariably be deemed a cold-blooded murderer, the only other option being 'madness'. But does madness explain why a woman chooses life over abuse?

We think not. Carol Smart, a leading commentator on feminist jurisprudence, suggests that law is a field that 'disqualifies women's accounts and experiences'.[27] By reaching to its companion, psychiatry, law merely magnifies the masculine imperative, thereby denying once again reasonable woman's motivation for choosing life over abuse. Criminology, too, joins in, through its continuous drive to label women offenders as 'deviant'. As it stands, women are still either mad or bad when they kill. The law continues to disqualify women's experiences by its failure to recognize that women are preserving life, even if in the process they take it.

Is there a way out of this? Not at this moment. The 'victory' of the Emma Humphreys case (as it was labeled in the media) for those searching for a fundamental principle by which to guide their own appeal, is hollow. The precedent embraces the primacy of law, whose logic, method and impact will continue to judge women by a masculine standard.

This is not to despair completely, however. The challenge to law is one brought by feminists who understand the devastation of physical and sexual abuse of women at the hands of men. It is the work of the activists that will keep this issue alive, and continue to agitate for change in the way we understand why some women kill. Although there is discussion of a new partial defence of self-preservation,[28] it remains in the hands of the law to determine whether this new defence could and should apply.

FIGHTING
FOR FREEDOM:

Suffragette Violence Against their State

Emily Hamer

Mass political female violence is usually seen as a recent and frightening phenomenon. Certainly the women-only camps at Greenham Common in Britain in the 1980s were presented in this way. However, the media representation of the violence of the Greenham women as new and as the product of the frightening 'masculinization' of women wrought by 1960s feminism is inaccurate. The most significant acts of organized female violence in Britain occurred during the women's suffrage campaigns in the period 1905 to 1914.

Women's struggle for the vote in Britain was a protracted one. Female enfranchisement was debated in meetings around the country, and eventually in Parliament, from the 1860s.[1] While at times it seemed that the women's cause was gaining ground, by 1900 there had been absolutely no progress on the basic issue of granting women the vote. However, the tactics of those working for women's suffrage were shaken up by the formation of the Women's Social and Political Union (WSPU) in 1905, and subsequently of the Women's Freedom League (WFL), a splinter group established in 1907. It was women from the WSPU, led by Mrs Emmeline Pankhurst and her daughters, along with the WFL who became 'suffragettes' and who began to campaign vociferously (and, eventually, violently) for the vote.

A much-reproduced image of the suffragettes shows women in large hats who have chained themselves to railings.[2] Film footage of the suffragettes inevitably includes Emily Wilding Davison's death at the 1913 Derby: she ran onto the race track and was trampled by the King's horse.[3] While we know that the suffragettes went on hungerstrikes while in prison, this too seems to be a peculiarly womanly and gentle gesture of defiance.

Current popular knowledge of suffragette violence is almost entirely limited to the violence that the suffragettes inflicted upon themselves. The accumulated effect of this kind of representation is to indicate that the main focus of suffragette violence was their own bodies. The violence of the suffragettes is presented as masochistic rather than aggressively directed at the men who refused to give them the vote. The activities of the suffragettes in the ten years before the First World War have been traduced to an image of gentle and impotent Edwardian ladies hurting only themselves. This version of the history of the suffragettes presents suffragette 'violence' as womanly and passive, a special kind of non-violent violence.

This touching and unthreatening picture is significantly different from the reality of the situation, however. Many suffragettes resorted to classic acts of terrorism, such as bombs, arson, hoaxes, and assassination attempts in response to the refusal of politicians and the Government to engage with their demand for the vote. Contemporary reports show that the suffragettes were perceived as a real and significant physical threat to the infrastructure of the nation.

Suffragette violence was initially focused solely on the political arena: disrupting political meetings, breaking windows on Government buildings and harassing politicians. However, many suffragettes had by 1912 broadened their range of targets. What came under attack was institution-alized male power; during this period in Britain, that was almost all power. Women had little access to education and were excluded from many professions, hence they wielded minimal economic power as a group. Thus the infrastructures that supported Britain's economic and political power and success were inalienably identified with male power and with men's ability to exclude women from a share of that power. By 1912, all the aspects of (male) control over British society were under physical threat from suffragette violence.

The first public appearance of the new militantly violent suffragettes occurred with the arrest and very brief imprisonment of Christabel

Pankhurst and Annie Kenney in 1905. Christabel Pankhurst wanted to be arrested while campaigning for the suffrage, believing that the resulting publicity would encourage debate and attract support from the public. In order to be arrested she assaulted a policeman by spitting at him. Spitting at someone can be construed as a technical assault, as it was in this case, a fact of which Christabel, who was studying law at Victoria University, Manchester, was surely well aware.[4]

It is significant that Christabel Pankhurst chose to link suffragette protests with physical assaults on men – and on those men who enforce the laws made by other men – rather than with more harmless and symbolic actions. Christabel Pankhurst showed that the focus of suffragette anger was to be men themselves. In the short term Christabel's assault was not immediately followed by further acts of blatant aggression, however, as there was hope that the election of a Liberal Government in 1906 would lead to a female suffrage bill being enacted.

In the next few years the suffrage cause entered the public arena as it had never done before: in 1907–8 there were more than 5,000 suffrage meetings.[5] The aim was 'to create an impression upon the public through-out the country, to set everyone talking about Votes for Women, to keep the subject in the Press, to leave the Government no peace from it'.[6] Large, public and well-publicized meetings and demonstrations led by women were in themselves seen as revolutionary acts of female militancy. There were clashes between suffragettes and the police at demonstrations, and arrests and imprisonment did result; in 1907–8, suffragette imprisonments totalled 350 weeks.[7]

The years between 1905 and 1912 were not entirely without explicit suffragette aggression, either. In 1909 Mary Leigh climbed upon the roof of a hall holding an anti-suffrage meeting in Liverpool brandishing a hatchet and hurling down tiles.[8] Marion Wallace-Dunlop was arrested for defacing St Stephen's Hall in Parliament with the slogan 'It is the right of the subject to petition the King, and all commitments and prosecutions for such petitioning are illegal.'[9] In the same week as Wallace-Dunlop's arrest, 13 women, all members of the WSPU, were also arrested for breaking windows in Government offices in a suffrage protest. Wallace-Dunlop and the WSPU 13 were all sentenced to imprisonment, and all went on hungerstrike while in gaol.

Window-breaking and the throwing of bricks and stones were basic and oft-repeated protest tactics for the suffragettes. These early actions were symbolic attacks upon the tyranny of male government. They were performed publicly, as the women involved wanted the publicity that arrests and trial would bring. Suffragette trials were used as propaganda vehicles for the cause: flags and banners were unfurled, eloquent women conducted their own defence, and sympathizers packed the court. In later years suffragette violence was to occur in the courts themselves, with defendants hurling missiles at the judges.

By the beginning of 1912 a significant number of suffragettes had come to believe that no amount of advocacy, lobbying, parliamentary negotia-tion or petitions would gain them the vote. Women were going to continue to be fobbed off with pleas for more time and calls for greater patience unless the suffragettes showed that angry women were a force too serious to be ignored and patronized. It was this group of suffragettes who began to undertake a wide variety of terrorist attacks on the infrastructure of British society. These suffragettes set out to damage private property, Crown property, the communications and transport system, and any other mechanism that supported and maintained the status quo.

An imaginative and widespread series of militant 'outrages' occurred during 1912–1914. It started in January relatively modestly with the breaking of the windows of the Reform Club in London and the burning down of the Tea Pavilion at Kew Gardens. In March, however, two railway stations, Saunderton and Crosley Green, were destroyed by suffragette arson. There was also extensive window-breaking in London's West End, interrupting the Winter sales, with hundreds of women intent on destroying the mercantile heart of ladies' fashion.

The violence had escalated by July, 1912. First two WSPU women, Helen Craggs and a Miss Smythe, were caught trying to set light to Nuneham House, home of the anti-suffragist minister Lewis Harcourt.[10] Then Mary Leigh and Gladys Evans tried to set light to the Theatre Royal, Dublin; one of them apparently also threw a hatchet into Prime Minister Asquith's carriage. Both Leigh and Evans were sentenced to five years' imprisonment.[11]

The autumn was marked by a campaign against post boxes; some were set alight, others had tar, kerosene or acid poured into them – all effective methods of emasculating the delivery of mail.

The new year (1913) was marked by an even more concerted effort to raise the profile of the suffrage cause:

[S]logans were burnt into golf courses, a jewel case was smashed at the Tower, refreshment pavilions were burnt down, telegraph and telephone wires were cut between London and Glasgow, and bogus telephone messages were sent calling up the Army Reserve and the Territorials. On 18th February a bomb was set off [and exploded] in the house that Lloyd George was having built in Surrey.[12]

February, 1913 also saw the wrecking of plants at Kew Gardens and the arson of the refreshment kiosk in Regents Park. Attacks like these on Royal Parks eventually led to a number of Royal Houses – such as those at Kensington, Kew, Hampton and Holyrood – being closed to the public due to fears of suffrage assaults. On the night of April 3, four houses were set on fire in Hampstead Garden Suburb, and a bomb exploded in an empty train carriage in Stockport. The next day a mansion near Chorley Wood was gutted by fire and a bomb went off at Oxted station. The day after that, Ayr racecourse stand was burnt down, causing £3,000 worth of damage.[13] Between the end of April and the middle of July there were a further 42 major cases of suffragette arson.[14]

By now suffragettes undertaking such violent crimes were doing so in well-planned secrecy. They no longer wanted to be caught in the act; they wanted buildings burnt down, not left slightly charred. Moreover, the prison sentences they now risked were too significant to be seen as useful publicity. Because of this necessary operational secrecy it is hard to tell how much control the Pankhursts and their controlling elite within the WSPU had over these women. The suffragette Micky (Naomi) Jacob reports trying to sign up with Sylvia Pankhurst for such active service; this indicates that the Pankhursts were directly involved in the operational planning of suffragette outrages.[15]

The official response of the WSPU to suffragette outrages was surprisingly prosaic and clearly supportive. The arson at Yarmouth pier, which destroyed the newly built concert pavilion and caused £20,000 of damage, occupied the entire front page of the *Daily Mirror*: 'Suffragettes fire Yarmouth pier: Bomb explosion heard a mile away.' The *Daily Mirror* included an interview with the WSPU in their coverage: '"Of course, wherever there is a fire we always get the blame," said Miss Hallon of the Women's Social and Political Union yesterday to the *Daily Mirror*. "We knew nothing of the Yarmouth fire, but I certainly fully approve if the fire was caused by [suffragette] militants."'[16]

The next year saw a further extension of suffrage activity:

> The destruction wrought in the seven months of 1914 excelled that
> of the previous year. Three Scotch castles were destroyed by fire on a
> single night. The Carnegie Library in Birmingham was burnt ... Many
> large empty houses in all parts of the country were set on fire,
> including Redlynch House, Somerset, where the damage was
> estimated at £40,000. Railway stations, piers, sports pavilions,
> haystacks were set on fire. Attempts were made to blow up reservoirs.
> A bomb exploded in Westminster Abbey, and in the fashionable
> church of St. George's, Hanover Square, where a famous stained-
> glass window from Malines was damaged. There were two explo-
> sions in St. John's, Westminster, and one in St. Martin's in the Fields,
> and in Spurgeon's Tabernacle ... One hundred and forty-one acts of
> destruction were chronicled in the Press during the first seven months
> of 1914.[17]

Men from Asquith on down were the subject of assaults by women. Ethel
Moorhead, a suffragette and artist living in Scotland, attacked with a dog-
whip a man who disagreed with her pro-suffrage views.[18]

While the suffragettes sought to avoid arrest, they did not leave their
crimes unmarked. At the site of the bomb in Spurgeon's Tabernacle the
militants left a calling card – 'Put your religion into practice and see that
women obtain their freedom.'[19] The Church was the object of much
suffragette anger, as this shows: the suffragettes were well aware of
the patriarchal nature of Christianity. This anger was inflamed by the refusal
of the Church to give shelter and sanctuary to suffragettes on
the run; the Archbishop of Canterbury turned Annie Kenney over to
the police and subsequently barred the gates of Lambeth Palace
against her.[20]

The failure of parliamentary democracy to respond to the petitions of the
suffragettes led a significant number of suffragettes to reject the authority of
Parliament. This resulted not only in criminal violence but also in a refusal
to pay taxes; suffragettes repeated the cry of the American colonies, 'No
taxation without representation.' Disgusted by the behaviour of Parliament
and the Government, suffragette agitation focused on the King. In May,
1914 suffragettes marched on Buckingham Palace to present a petition
directly to George V.

For the first time they carried not just banners but weapons. Mrs Pankhurst led a force of women armed with Indian clubs to the doors of the Royal family; a significant proportion of these women had served prison sentences for violent crimes. Violent revolution must have seemed no longer just a threat to weak foreign monarchs. No clubbing actually occurred, although eggs filled with coloured powder were thrown. More significantly, mass exposure of the truth of male power was threatened: one contingent of suffragettes 'made a systematic attempt to cut policemen's braces'.[21]

George V was harassed by suffragettes at the theatre, where they taunted him with shouts of 'You Russian Tsar', and while undertaking ceremonial duties; while being presented at Court, debutantes would cry 'Votes for Women.' The King was clearly unnerved; Royal garden parties were suspended in 1914 in an attempt to reduce his exposure to such unwelcome attentions. That summer Maude Edwardes slashed a portrait of George V at the Scottish Royal Academy – a clear indication that royal property, and perhaps even royal persons, were at risk from suffragette anger.[22]

Arson and attacks on museums continued. Wargrave Church, and the Bath Hotel, Felixstowe, were, for example, destroyed by fire, and many museums were closed as they could not be adequately protected against the suffragette threat.[23] National monuments, whether they were men or buildings, were not safe; Frances Parker was arrested for trying to burn down Robert Burns' birthplace.[24] In May 1914 a portrait of the Duke of Wellington, a British hero, was attacked.[25] In the same month Sargent's portrait of Henry James on exhibit at the Royal Academy was slashed by a suffragette. This was headlined in the *Daily Mirror* in true tabloid style as 'Hatchet Woman's Academy Smash'; the crowd who witnessed the outrage responded with cries of 'lynch her.'[26] This suffragette agitation and violence received widespread and regular coverage in the British press in the form of letters from interested parties and in reports, articles and leaders.

Much of the British press was explicitly against women's suffrage and was keen to stress how many women, as well as men, shared their views. The *Times*, in a leader in January, 1912, stated, 'we, as convinced and steady opponents of woman suffrage on principle, are glad to see the accumulating evidence that the great majority of women are themselves against the change.'[27] The *Times* seems to have been largely concerned with the views of 'ordinary' women, the non-political women in the street.

Militant violence was certainly explicitly rejected by a number of pro-suffragist women, such as Millicent Fawcett and Elizabeth Garrett Anderson, although whether this was on the grounds of pragmatic inefficacy or moral principle it is now hard to tell.

While suffragette arson was clearly dangerous and provoked under-standable anger, peaceful suffragette demonstrations were also seen as innately aggressive and dangerous. On 'Black Friday', 18 November 1910, the clash between 300 women presenting a deputation to Parliament and the police was described as an attack by women on the police in the *Times*, the *Standard*, the *Daily Mirror* and the *Daily Express*.[28] As Sylvia Pankhurst had already noted about an earlier incident, 'The Press described the scene with mendacious untruths, alleging that its participants were hysterical viragoes, biting, scratching and shrieking.'[29]

The march on Buckingham Palace in May, 1914 was described thus: '56 Arrests follow wild women's raid on Buckingham Palace … Blind charge on police at palace gates.' The suffragettes are described as 'furies' and as attacking the police with 'might and main'. They are charged with occasioning 'truncheon duels' and attempting to drag policemen from their horses.[30] The *Daily Mirror* claimed that one suffragette armed with a club knocked a policeman unconscious.[31] The alarm provoked by this demonstration is particularly surprising given that this was the action of 200 women facing a police presence of between 1,000 and 1,500 men.[32]

When suffragettes committed acts of violence against men and male institutions, men and their institutions were not slow to respond in kind. The prison sentences that the suffragettes received became increasingly punitive. When Ellen Pitfield, a dying midwife, started a small wastepaper basket fire, she was sentenced to six months' imprisonment although at the trial she had to be carried from the prison hospital and the prison doctor testified that she was so ill that she would never walk again.[33]

Force-feeding as a response to suffragette hungerstrikes was another example of harsh retribution. Suffragettes went on hungerstrike while in prison as a protest against the fact that they were classified as common criminals (Second and Third Division) instead of political prisoners (First Division).[34] For the suffragettes the fact that they were not treated as political prisoners meant that the very meaning of their acts of defiance was steadfastly ignored by the legal and prison system. Faced with women on hungerstrike the prison authorities, and ultimately the Home Office, responded with force-feeding.

This was carried out by holding the nose closed and pouring food (usually milk mixed with raw egg) through the mouth, or by forcing a tube through the mouth or nose and hence into the stomach. Medically, force-feeding was a dangerous practice which inevitably resulted in torn tissue in the throat and the mouth or nose, damage to the teeth and tongue, prolonged vomiting, breathing difficulties and stress to the heart. It was not uncommon for food to be forced in error into the lungs; this could lead to pneumonia. Force-feeding was also very unusual in British prisons; as Sylvia Pankhurst noted, 'In 1910 two ordinary criminals were forcibly fed: the man died during the first operation, the woman committed suicide.'[35]

Forcible feeding is in many ways akin to rape. This is perhaps particularly true in the case of women being force-fed by a male doctor. Bodily integrity is overcome by force, and the woman is penetrated by a foreign body ejecting milky fluid wielded by a man. The force-feeding of the suffragettes involves a complex web of cultural meanings; it cannot simply be seen as an unproblematic response to their refusal to eat. Commenting on Sylvia Pankhurst's description of being force-fed, Maud Ellman notes that 'what has been forced into her is not only the food but the ideology and even the identity of her oppressors. Under this torture starvation rather than ingestion has become the last remaining recipe for authenticity.'[36]

Force-feeding was seen as barbaric by many people, and public distaste reached huge proportions when it was revealed in the summer of 1914 that at least two women imprisoned in Perth had been force-fed via the rectum.[37] This was described in Scottish Office records, benignly, as the giving of a 'nutrient enema'.[38] The differences between 'rectal feeding' and 'anal rape' appear slight; at best rectal feeding is anal rape *for your own good*.

Women who 'resisted' force-feeding – and having tubes forced down their throat or up their rectum was resisted by most women – were perceived by the authorities to be committing further crimes of violence. At least two women, Theresa Garnet and Lilian Dove Wilcox, were charged in 1909 with assaulting wardresses because they resisted being force-fed.[39] Given that force-feeding only occurred when women were physically weak from lack of food, and that the prison team which conducted the feeding consisted of at least one prison official and one male doctor, it seems unlikely that a struggling suffragette posed a significant physical threat to anyone's safety. Yet even physically weak suffragettes were perceived by those dealing with them as dangerous.

The fact that suffragette prisoners called forth this violent and sexualized response is unsurprising, for the very aim of the women's suffrage movement was to question traditional beliefs about women's capacities and the female role in society. If women demonstrating in public and speaking at public meetings were seen by the press and many observers as frightening and unnatural spectacles, then how much more of an outrage must have been the sight of militant suffragettes physically attacking the most basic underpinnings of British society. Arson, bombs and physical assaults on men were seen as worryingly unfeminine acts by almost everybody.

Sylvia Pankhurst notes with considerable perception that 'officialdom everywhere treated this militancy as a pernicious form of hysteria.'[40] Women violently claiming such unwomanly rights were indeed seen as suffering from a form of sexualized madness. It is clear that the suffragettes were perceived as being sexually explosive. Their violence and their sex could not be viewed separately, and suffragettes were sexual anarchy made flesh. The response by individual men, and supported by the state, was to reassert women's proper role, as passive and physically weak objects sexually at the mercy of men, through violence. Aside from sexualized medical operations such as forcible feeding, there are indications that some suffragettes suffered sexual assaults while in prison.[41]

That the sexuality of the suffragettes was seen to be as wilful and ungovernable as their desire for the vote is supported by Sylvia Pankhurst's contention that while in prison they were often drugged with bromide.[42] Bromide was famously distributed to British troops in the trenches during the First World War in order to reduce their sexual appetite. For the suffragettes to have been dosed with bromide suggests that they were perceived as having uncontrollable sexual instincts on a par with soldiers, the epitome of virile and rapacious sexuality. On a more mundane level, it seems that the suffragettes' lingerie was also troublesome to the prison authorities. Sylvia Pankhurst's lack of stays was noted, and the women were told that they could not wear garters. The suffragettes were feared as 'unshackled' and sexually licentious, right down to their underclothes.[43]

On the streets of Britain, suffragettes were also the focus of sexualized violence as a result of their effrontery. The response of both male bystanders and the police to suffragette demonstrations often took the form of crudely sexual assaults. Describing the police response to a suffragette demonstration in 1906, Sylvia Pankhurst wrote that they 'sprang forward, thrusting with fists and knees'.[44] Of Black Friday in 1910 she says:

Again and again we saw the small deputations struggling through the crowd with their little purple bannerettes: 'Asquith has vetoed our Bill.' The police snatched the flags, tore them to shreds, and smashed the sticks, struck the women with fists and knees, knocked them down, some even kicked them, then dragged them up, carried them a few paces and flung them into the crowd of sightseers. For six hours this continued. From time to time we returned to Caxton Hall, where doctors and nurses were attending to women who had been hurt. We saw women go out and return exhausted, with black eyes, bleeding noses, bruises, sprains and dislocations. The cry went around: 'Be careful; they are dragging women down the side streets!' We knew this always meant greater ill-usage … violent and indecent treatment.[45]

The violence inflicted upon suffragettes and their allies by the police was the subject of Dr Jessie Murray and H. N. Brailsford's report (published in 1911), *Treatment of the Women's Deputations by the Police*, which was discussed in Parliament.[46] Section III was entitled 'Acts of Indecency' and gave detailed accounts of how women had their breasts and nipples grabbed and twisted and their skirts thrown over their heads by policemen on Black Friday. In fact it seems that the more extreme suffragette violence after 1912 was at least partly due to a desire to avoid police harassment; better to be a real criminal than to be sexually harassed and physically assaulted by the police when legally demonstrating.[47]

This argument was used to explain the new violent tactics of the militants by Emily Wilding Davison. She accepted that the suffragettes were now undertaking acts of criminal damage and violence which seemed 'most unwomanly, most unnatural and most illegal'. There had, she explained, been a change in suffragette reasoning:

The reason [for suffragette violence] was that when this militant agitation began woman cheerfully submitted to being punished in their bodies for whatever protest they made. The violence of their treatment increased in proportion as their determination increased, and the result was that women were very severely handled – so much so, that they became injured in their bodies.[48]

The response of the police to the suffragettes reflected the conflict felt generally by the anti-suffragist Establishment about the problem of suffragettes and violence. Theoretically the role of the police was to keep the peace and enable the suffragettes to express their rights as subjects of the King. Particularly among anti-suffragists, there was a widespread belief that women were different from men and their innocence and delicacy should be protected. From this perspective, the rough handling, including forcible feeding, that suffragettes suffered was unacceptable. Coverage in the anti-suffrage *Times*, while emphasizing the unpopularity of the suffragettes with headlines such as 'Militant Outrages – Headquarters Seized by Police – Rising Public Anger', also shows clear dismay at women being physically attacked for their beliefs.[49]

In one report, the *Times* details how a small group of suffragettes provoked public anger by handing out leaflets in Lyons in Piccadilly, London. The women were pelted with cutlery, sugar, bread and cake by hundreds of angry diners, and had to take refuge in a lift.[50] On the same day, suffragettes and their allies making speeches from a small wagon in Hyde Park were attacked by the public:

> Then a sudden rush was made for the vehicle, which was overturned just a second after its occupants had hastily left it, and smashed to pieces by the crowd. Meanwhile the speakers were receiving very rough treatment at the hands of the crowd, the women at first being particularly severely dealt with.[51]

Concurrent with this there was a strong feeling that suffragettes needed to be shown that their demands and their methods were profoundly wrong, and a bit of roughing up drove that point home. As suffragette violence and militancy increased, this dilemma – protection or attack – became more and more acute. On 15 April, 1913, the Home Secretary informed the WSPU that they could no longer be protected in public places, and banned them. In effect the Government withdrew the protection of the State from the suffragettes. This both symbolically and practically made attacks on suffragettes completely without reprisal; it legitimated assaults on suffragettes.

It was for these reasons that a number of women who had been actively involved in suffragette clashes with the police were very eager to establish either a women's police force or women police within the official police.

The motivating force behind the formation of women police was the sexist and sexual relationship that the suffragettes had suffered at the hands of the male police force. Mary Allen, arrested and imprisoned for window-breaking in 1909, went on to become a leading figure in the move to establish a recognized force of women police in the inter-war period. She was explicit about the connection between being manhandled by the police as a suffragette and her commitment to women police:

> Many of the women attracted by the idea of women police had been prominent workers for women's suffrage in the militant days before the war. Their efforts – whether rightly or wrongly exercised, is fortunately no longer in question – had not only shaken vast numbers of women out of their normal indifference to political questions, but had brought some into close, sometimes, painful touch with the police, teaching them how very unpleasant it is for an alleged woman culprit to be handled by men.[52]

Police women are one little-acknowledged and perhaps surprising legacy of the suffragettes' violence against their state.

ALL
TOO
FAMILIAR:

Gender, Violence, and National Politics
in the Fall of Winnie Mandela

Rachel Holmes

Winnie Mandela's Security Police file held in Pretoria, South Africa, contains
a copy of the contract in which she sold the rights to a movie about her life
to Camille and Bill Cosby for $110,000. If the film ever gets made, the
court-room scenes of the final dissolution of the marriage between Nelson
and Winnie Mandela will make for a suspenseful Hollywood-style
dramatic climax.

In March 1996, the world media focused its attentions on the courtroom
drama of the divorce proceedings of Nelson and Winnie Mandela. An
international press who once conferred a revered symbolic status upon the
Mandelas watched in fascination as Nelson Mandela – the man whose
political presence in the late twentieth century has become the watchword
for the power of reconciliation and negotiated political settlement – stated
the impossibility of reconciliation with his wife. After six years of public
statements stressing his support for Winnie Mandela and tempering the
increasingly evident rift between them, Nelson Mandela unambiguously
stated his position on the relationship: 'If the entire universe persuaded me
to reconcile with the defendant I would not. I am determined to get rid of
this marriage.'[1] In fact, the dissolution of this union provided no startling
new revelations for the media to get its teeth into. Rather, it simply
officially confirmed the long-standing alienation between the Mandelas,
finally ending what had in reality long been an empty shell of a marriage.

During the transitional times of the late 1980s and 1990s, as Nelson Mandela's name came to symbolize political endurance through an uncompromising will for negotiation and reconciliation, Winnie Mandela's name became linked with excess, violence and political unaccountability. Once a spirited champion of popular protest and a rocklike leader of opposition during the bleakest days of the stranglehold of the apartheid state, the Winnie Mandela of the 1990s has become a powerful symbol of the threat of populist nationalism to the processes of democratization through which multi-racial South Africa seeks to renew itself.

As her former husband expressed the absoluteness of the severance between them, Winnie Mandela's legal team spoke in farcical terms of the 'somewhat slight tensions' between their client and her husband. Winnie Mandela, for her part, claims that these tensions have their source in the allegations made against her concerning her involvement in kidnapping, assault and murder in Soweto in 1988, charges which culminated in her public trial in 1991. From the day this trial opened, Nelson Mandela appeared regularly in court to support her, publicly describing his belief in her innocence in any aspect of the murder of Stompie Moeketsi Sepei. In his best-selling autobiography, whose profits Winnie Mandela hoped for a share of in their divorce settlement, he again states that, as far as he was concerned, her innocence was not in doubt.[2]

Contrary to her claims that it was these public trials implicating her in the personal use of violence which exacerbated tensions between them, Nelson Mandela gives his reason for not previously dissolving the marriage as precisely because he did *not* 'want the world to think they were separating over the Stompie case'.[3] And despite these public protestations of his belief in her innocence, which increasingly lacked credibility in the face of the discrediting of all her alibis, the clarity of Winnie Mandela's own claim that these issues were and remain central to their irreparable estrangement is highly accurate.

Whilst the international media waited in anticipation of dirty laundry being washed by the Mandelas in the civil courts, Winnie Mandela's name was again featuring in the criminal courts in connection with gang violence. Simultaneous with the divorce hearings, two of Winnie Mandela's bodyguards were being charged with assault and attempted murder before a Soweto magistrate.

Even as Nelson Mandela expressed relief at the termination of their marriage, Winnie Madikizela-Mandela, as she is now calling herself, issued a statement in which she described the outcome of the divorce action as a 'travesty of justice' and a public defeat that 'undermines everything our marriage was about.'[4] Such words uncannily underwrite the sense of both fear and betrayal experienced by many in the struggle against apartheid since Winnie Mandela began to exploit her political status to mete out a personal brand of 'justice' in Soweto in the late 1980s. The activities of her personal bodyguards, styled the Mandela United Football Club (MUFC), brought Winnie Mandela and her household into increasingly bitter dispute with both local communities and the official ranks of the African National Congress (ANC). Of the many activities the MUFC was known for, skill on the football pitch was not amongst them. The reign of terror associated with this gang of about 30 personal male 'bodyguards' led to Winnie Mandela being effectively cast out of the anti-apartheid movement.

In January 1989, a community meeting gathered in Dobsonville, Soweto in the context of growing concern over the abduction of four youths from a local mission presided over by Methodist Minister Reverend Paul Verryn. About 150 activists from community, civic, women's and workers' organizations convened to listen to local grievances over the misconduct of the 'football club'. Of chief concern was the abduction and holding of the four youths at Winnie Mandela's home, compounded by the fact that Stompie Moeketsi Sepei, one of the kidnapped, was still missing. The community meeting, which decided that the matter should be taken up by the progressive movement, resolved to secure the return of Stompie from the 'football club'. After hearing the evidence against the conduct of the team, it was also decided that the community should cease to refer to it as the Mandela XI, as it was considered unfit to carry the name of the ANC leader.

Meanwhile, the Crisis Committee that had been convened at the direct request of Nelson Mandela in 1988 as a task force to control the activities of the 'football club' began to investigate the allegations regarding the abductions.[5] The Crisis Committee was composed of powerful leaders: Reverend Frank Chikane of the South African Council of Churches, Cyril Ramaphosa of the National Union of Mineworkers, Sister Bernard Ncube of the Federation of Transvaal Women, Sidney Mafumadi of the Congress of South African Trade Unions, and Aubrey Mokoena of the Release Mandela Committee. This team of prominent activists met frequently with Winnie Mandela and Mandela United, who finally allowed them to see three of the youths. The evidence of injuries from assault was apparent on two of them; the third appeared to be unhurt. The fourth, Stompie Moeketsi Sepei, was still missing. Pressure to release the youths was brought to bear on Winnie Mandela from a range of political and community representatives, including the leader of the ANC himself, who briefed his lawyer from Pollsmoor Prison to instruct her to release the hostages immediately. For a fortnight Winnie Mandela's household resisted these approaches, but on 16 January, 1988, the three were finally released. Stompie was, however, still missing.

On 27 January the 'Stompie story' broke in the local and foreign media. The *Weekly Mail* in Johannesburg and *The Guardian* in London were the first to run the story. Rumours about the conduct of both Winnie Mandela and her 'football club' of bodyguards had been circulating in newsrooms in South Africa for some time, but liberal leftist papers such as the *Weekly Mail* were reluctant to run what initially looked like another state-concocted campaign to discredit Winnie Mandela. However, following the Dobsonville community meeting there was proper scope for reporting events rather than rumours.

As the story broke, Dr Abu-Baker Asvat, a prominent Soweto physician and AZAPO (Azanian People's Organization) official closely connected with both Winnie Mandela and the resistance movement, was gunned down in his surgery, in a killing condemned by the ANC and the Black Consciousness Movement. When Winnie Mandela's case came to trial in 1991, it was revealed that Jerry Richardson, former 'coach' of the MUFC, had visited Asvat as a new patient on the day before his killing, 'sent by Winnie' as Asvat wrote on his medical card. It also emerged that Asvat had become involved in the gathering storm over the abduction of the four youths when Winnie Mandela had taken one of them to be examined by Asvat for evidence of the alleged homosexual abuse by the Reverend Paul Verryn. Whilst the storm over Stompie's disappearance continued to rage, Winnie Mandela herself claimed sinister links between Asvat's murder and the ongoing row over the 'football club'. She stated that she had hoped Asvat would be a key witness to substantiate the complaints she had made regarding the sexual abuse of the abducted boys, inferring he had been silenced in order to discredit her claims regarding the abuse. 'Dr Asvat was the only professional witness to back my story that the boys, alleged to be kept against their will in my house, were in fact victims of abuse.'[6]

At the trial, it was revealed that Asvat's medical records had been tampered with, but evidence of his examination of one of the abducted youths, Katiza Chebekhulu, was recovered. Winnie Mandela and her associate, Xoliswa Falati, who was also prosecuted in the 1991 trial, had visited Asvat's surgery with the request that he examine Chebekhulu for evidence of his having been raped. Asvat assured Chebekhulu that there was no evidence of anal penetration, and recommended that he seek psychiatric assistance. The medical card relating to this visit makes no mention of sexual abuse or the cause of Chebekhulu's distress, and records a prescription for mild tranquillizers to assist the patient's mental confusion. Although he never met with Verryn, Asvat recommended that he, too, might consider psychiatric guidance.

Stompie Seipei's body was finally found and identified on 14 February, 1989. Winnie Mandela initially denied that it was Stompie's body that had been discovered, and in a statement to the Dutch press claimed that in fact Stompie was still alive.[7] The discovery of the body finally led to the police opening a murder docket, and two days later the United Democratic Front (subsequently the Mass Democratic Movement, a broad umbrella group of resistance organizations) and Congress of South African Trade Unions (COSATU) publicly denounced the actions of Winnie Mandela and her 'football club', recommending to their affiliates – particularly Soweto residents – that they distance themselves from her, in a dignified manner. Winnie Mandela had fallen from grace within the resistance movement to which she was so committed.

In 1990 Jerry Richardson was brought to trial and convicted for the murder of Stompie Moeketsi. He received a death sentence, which was later commuted to life imprisonment. In their summing up, the court found that Winnie Mandela had in fact been present for some of the time during the kidnapping and physical assaults against the four held in her house.

The evidence of the three surviving complainants incriminated both Jerry Richardson and Winnie Mandela in kidnapping and assault. In the course of both the Richardson trial in 1990 and Winnie Mandela's trial in 1991, the three complainants gave testimony regarding the kinds of physical assault they had been subjected to whilst being held at Winnie Mandela's Diepkloof extension. Claiming that they had been instructed to call her 'Mummy', the three accused her in court of both being present and participating in assaults against them carried out by members of the 'football club'. The forms of abuse that they described included being punched, kicked, whipped with a cat-o-nine-tails, and hanged from the ceiling.

In effect, the Richardson trial became a rehearsal for Winnie Mandela's own trial which followed in 1991, during which her defence team elaborated on the line that she had acted to 'save' the youths from homosexual abuse. The story emerged as follows: The four youths had been kidnapped and taken to Winnie Mandela's Orlando West home, where they were beaten and held against their will. During attempts to secure their release, community representatives and the Crisis Committee had intervened, and were told that the youths were being protected from sexual abuse by the minister who presided over the refuge from which they had been taken.

Winnie Mandela's legal team adopted a homophobic defence strategy in order to justify the violence that had putatively taken place in her home. At the moment when the ANC formalized its commitment to lesbian, gay and bisexual human rights in the draft Bill of Rights, Winnie Mandela's defence team played upon popular prejudices against homosexuality by activating one of the most pernicious discourses in the canon of homophobic practice: the conflation of homosexuality with sexual child abuse. Winnie Mandela's lawyers defended the disastrous events of 1988 on the grounds that she was intervening to protect the four captives from further homosexual abuse by the Reverend Paul Verryn. Styling herself as a symbolic mother-figure protecting the lives of vulnerable young men, Winnie Mandela stated with regard to the unsubstantiated claims against Verryn:

> I could not believe that a minister of religion entrusted with children's lives would abuse them. Children who could not make any other choices but depend upon him. What kind of beast is this? Who wears a collar on Sunday, and goes to preach to parents of these children, and preaches the word of God even to some of these children? At night he becomes something else.[8]

Despite these claims, both community investigations and a church commission inquiry cleared Verryn of these imputations. In the apartheid state, where black children's social, civil and human rights had never been protected – indeed, where the state had historically acted with violence against black children – Winnie Mandela's claim to be taking responsibility for guarding children needed to be taken seriously. However, there were key factors which cast doubt on the Mother of the Nation's claim to be protecting 'children' from deviant paternalism.

First, the testimony of the complainants themselves underscored the difficult fact that what physical assault they had been subjected to had been experienced, not at Verryn's mission, but in the back rooms of Winnie Mandela's Diepkloof extension. Secondly, Winnie Mandela's repeated reference to the abducted youths as 'children' seemed somewhat tendentious when equated to the actual ages of the young people concerned: Kenny Kgase was 29, Thabiso Mono 18, Pelo Gabriel Mekgwe 19, and Stompie Moeketsi Seipei 14. In addition, as the radical uprisings of 1976 underscored, South Africa is a political culture in which children as young as eight or nine years of age are activists, growing up quickly in a culture of violence meted out by the heavy hand of the state. When Winnie Mandela's defence team attempted to connect homosexual practice with abuse in terms of exploiting the vulnerability of disadvantaged people, it rode roughshod over the political integrity and sexual independence of individuals whose subjecthood could not be reduced to the status of dependent children. Notably, this was most visibly the case in the instance of the youngest of those caught up in the 'football club' kidnappings, Stompie Seipei, a point that will be taken up later in this article.

The emerging lesbian, gay and bisexual movement in South Africa challenged the terms of the legal defence adopted by Winnie Mandela's lawyers to justify the violence that the kidnapped youths claimed had taken place in her house.[9] The defence team did not deny that violence had taken place at the Winnie Mandela household – rather it sought to establish that this violent action was 'justified' on the grounds that Winnie Mandela believed that she was acting to protect the youths concerned from further homosexual abuse. At the time, the defence line, playing as it did on the public's susceptibility to homophobia, damaged the confidence of the gay and lesbian activists who were lobbying for sexuality to be recognized as a human rights issue.

Winnie Mandela's political prominence as a leading pro-democracy activist in her own right had, to a significant extent, been built upon her central involvement in the founding of the Black Parents' Association during the Soweto uprisings in 1976. These famous uprisings, in which children and students mobilized against the military might of the apartheid state, revolutionized the face of resistance politics within South Africa in the 1970s. Emblematically an intergenerational sea-change which radicalized black youth throughout South Africa, these uprisings were in protest against the paternalism of the patriarchal white state. Informed through the political philosophies of Black Consciousness, these protests also confronted the strategies of existing political leaders, issuing a challenge to all forms of paternalism, black or white. The children and youth who organized and undertook these uprisings were also protesting against their parents and elders, by challenging the older generation's means of resistance against apartheid. The children and youth of 1976 also rejected their status as minors in a state where all black people were treated as social and political minors by the violently paternalistic white state.

The 1976 uprisings in Soweto soon spread to a national campaign of resistance, school boycotts and riots across South Africa. As is well known, the state responded with extreme military violence, gunning down children and students in the streets and arresting protesters in droves. The Black Parents' Association, established initially in Soweto, was formed to deal with this crisis, organizing assistance for the children and youths being held in police detention and prison, and making arrangements for the all-too-frequent funerals of the young South Africans murdered by the Afrikaner Nationalist state. The same state strongly targeted Winnie Mandela and other adult political leaders for their involvement in these events, paternalistically claiming that this mobilization of youth was in fact being orchestrated and incited by adult leaders of banned organizations. Winnie Mandela in particular was hounded by the Security Police for her part in these events.

As a key activist rallying to the support of what was at grass-roots level a youth- and student-led uprising, Winnie Mandela was justly accorded important political status for her involvement in the events of 1976, the repercussions of which continued throughout the late 1970s and 1980s. Indeed, it was Winnie Mandela herself who brought the importance of the political sea-change in the form of black resistance to the attention of the leader of the ANC, Nelson Mandela. In his autobiography, Nelson Mandela recalls the new intake of 'young men who had been arrested in the aftermath of the uprising' arriving on Robben Island, marking how he and his comrades saw the spirit of mass protest as renewed by this new generation of political activists:

In these young men we saw the angry revolutionary spirit of the times. I had had some warning. On a visit with Winnie a few months before, she had managed to tell me through our coded conversation that there was a rising class of discontented youths who were militant and Africanist in orientation. She said they were changing the nature of the struggle and that I should be aware of them.[10]

It is thus crucial to give proper scope to the political bond between the Mother of the Nation and activist youth that had developed in the context of the 1970s. This bond, founded on a recognition of the political rights and integrity of South Africa's black youth, helps to explain the consternation experienced when Winnie Mandela and her 'football club' were implicated in the use of unsanctioned political violence in the crisis-torn Soweto of the 1980s. Hitherto, the Mother of the Nation had been looked to as an ally and protector of the interests of South African youth; now it looked as if she were abusing this status. Nowhere was this more marked than in the allegations of her involvement in the murder of Stompie Moeketsi Seipei.

Following his abduction, 14-year-old youth activist and leader Stompie Moeketsi Seipei went missing, his whereabouts unknown until his mother identified his corpse, which had lain unidentified in a Soweto morgue.

At Stompie's funeral, his prominence as a youth activist was honoured and recalled by mourners. In 1985, aged ten, he had led a township protest of some 1,500 children known as the Under Fourteens, youth activists who battled against the black municipal police and allied conservative black vigilantes during the widescale civil unrest of the period. The Under Fourteens sometimes claimed that they were protecting adults from police harassment, and in an interview with the *Sunday Times* in 1987, Stompie stated, 'We are braver than the adults.' At the age of 11, the 'Little General' whose catchphrase was 'What is the direction, Comrade?' had been one of the youngest detainees in the country under the State of Emergency, and had spent his 12th birthday in a police cell. He was a well-known activist and speaker who addressed major anti-apartheid meetings. Stompie was a symbol of the determination of young people to resist the violent depredations and oppressions of apartheid.

As a political Mother venerated in the spirit of national resistance, it was devastating that Winnie Mandela's name should be linked to the death of so spirited and prominent a youth leader.

Winnie Mandela's defence team cast aspersions of sexualized deviance upon Verryn and the youths who sought refuge at his manse, yet within the symbolic rubric of the family of political resistance, it was Winnie Mandela who was increasingly looking like a 'deviant' national mother, caught up in a personal use of violence which refused political accountability to the local community and to the ANC which she so trenchantly represented.

Once lionized, Winnie Mandela had now become a liability. As the controversy over the activities of the 'football club' deepened and her credibility and standing tumbled, community leaders and the official ANC leadership distanced themselves from these activities, which apparently undermined everything that the democratizing forces of the resistance movement were about. Throughout the late 1980s, Winnie Mandela's actions and public statements increasingly contradicted the official policies of the ANC, most particularly concerning the use of violence. Once revered Mother of Revolution, strongly respected for her militant activism, Winnie Mandela's position on the ethics of violence fell increasingly out of step with the shifting political context of a South Africa moving towards political transition, wherein the ANC guided its international image away from that of 'terrorist' resistance movement to democratic government-in-waiting.

It is crucially important to remember, however, that even prior to these political changes Winnie Mandela had been an important spokeswoman for the integrity of the ANC's political strategy of the need to respond to the violence of the apartheid state with the legitimate violence of the oppressed. Confronted with the state repression and delegitimation of all other channels of resistance, the ANC had turned to armed struggle. Nelson Mandela was a central force in the formation of Umkhonto we Sizwe[11] in 1961, and a militant campaigner within existing resistance structures for the need to meet state violence with armed resistance. Since the Rivonia Trials (1963–4), in which Nelson Mandela was a key accused, the ethics of distinguishing between legitimate and illegitimate violence had been a key facet of the ANC's struggle with the apartheid state. Moreover, during the early 1990s the ANC and incumbent Nationalist Party had frequently clashed at CODESA (Congress for a Democratic South Africa) talks over the issue of the future role of MK, the ANC's official army. President F. W. De Klerk thumped lecterns demanding the dismemberment of MK, whilst Nelson Mandela pointed out that this could not be considered until national security services were sanctioned by a democratically elected non-racial state. Conflict over forms of the legitimate use of violence was, therefore, a high-profile political issue during the period when Winnie Mandela came to trial over her personal use of violence.

Prior to Winnie Mandela's political demise due to her increasingly problematic use of power through the MUFC and the direct linking of her name to a string of township murders and tactics of intimidation, she had been a prominent leader and speaker for the rationale of political violence in the struggle against apartheid.[12] A veteran of banning orders, house arrest, banishment and imprisonment without trial, Winnie Mandela was familiar with suffering. Hounded by the physical and mental depredations of the South African state for 25 years, she was well positioned to represent the voice of mass resistance. In 1985, at the peak of her power as Mama Wetu – Mother of the Nation – Winnie Mandela addressed loyal supporters in a strife-torn South Africa for whom her toughness and endurance were resonant political symbols:

> I will speak to you of violence ... I will tell you why we are violent. It is because those who oppress us are violent. The Afrikaner knows only one language: the language of violence. The white man will not hand over power in talks around a table. They will use every trick in the white man's book to keep us from power. Therefore, all that is left to us is this painful process of violence.[13]

At the time, Winnie Mandela's words matched the tenor of the political moment. The draconian imposition of successive States of Emergency throughout the crackdown of the 1980s had drastically narrowed the scope of politically strategic possibilities. Those committed to the ANC and the mass democratic movement remained loyal to the precepts of imprisoned and exiled leaders, whose banishment was a result of their political call to arms to resist the totalitarian violence of the apartheid state. Some 20 years older than Winnie Mandela, Nelson Mandela and his ANC comrades had cut their political teeth testing the limits of non-violent protest and passive resistance for fighting the newly-constituted might of the Afrikaner Nationalist state in the anti-removal campaigns of the 1950s. Commenting on what he learned politically from the Western Areas anti-removal campaign in the mid-1950s, however, Nelson Mandela states the following with regard to the political use of violence:

The lesson I took away from the campaign was that, in the end, we had no alternative to armed and resistant violence. Over and over again, we had used all the non-violent weapons in our arsenal – speeches, deputations, threats, marches, strikes, stay-aways, voluntary imprisonment – all to no avail, for whatever we did was met by an iron hand. A freedom fighter learns the hard way that it is the oppressor who defines the nature of the struggle, and the oppressed is often left no recourse but to use methods that mirror those of the oppressor. At a certain point, one can only fight fire with fire.[14]

In the context of a certain set of political conditions, there was concord between the positions of Nelson and Winnie Mandela on the use of violence for political ends. However, by the second half of the 1980s, conditions were radically changing, requiring adaptability on the part of political leaders. At the precise moment when the ANC was moderating its international image from 'terrorist organization' to government-in-waiting, Winnie Mandela made one of the most disastrous political speeches of her career, a speech which many commentators have argued heralded the beginning of her public embarrassments of the ANC. In April 1986 at Munsieville, she made her infamous 'necklacing' speech, 'We have no guns – we have only stones, boxes of matches and petrol ... Together, hand in hand, with our boxes of matches and our necklaces we shall liberate this country.'[15]

This statement was clearly in conflict with contemporary ANC policy, and signalled the beginning of Winnie Mandela's public alienation from ANC leadership, as well as the symbolic linking of her persona to images of violent excess. Such statements marked the beginning of Winnie Mandela's precipitous fall from Mother of the Nation to deviant 'Mugger of the Nation', in the headlines of the day.

These public embarrassments were compounded by revelations regarding Winnie's private life and handling of ANC affairs. Rumours escalated of her affair with 28-year-old Dali Mpofu, who worked with her at the ANC Department of Social Welfare, as a result of a letter (allegedly from Winnie to Dali) leaked to the *Sunday Times*. This scandal was further compounded by allegations of her misuse of power in the ANC Women's League and her misappropriation of Social Welfare funding, both of which charges were under investigation by the ANC during the early 1990s.

Increasingly, the 'good mother' of the nation was being demoted to the status of sexually voracious and politically irresponsible 'bad mother', disloyal to the name of her husband.

The ramifications of Winnie Mandela's fall from political grace raise trenchant questions about the ways in which women's political roles in national liberation struggles are both represented and understood. As the prominent South African journalist Mark Gevisser has pointed out, Winnie Mandela was created in the popular imagination as being 'bigger-than-life, a fantasy vessel for so many gender stereotypes'. In the iconography that built up around her, Winnie Mandela was portrayed as:

> ... the pushy girl from the provinces; the adventuress who hitched her wagon to a rising star; the loyal and devoted wife; the essential Mama Afrika; the power-queen who couldn't deal with power; Imelda, Evita and Maggie rolled into one, and set against a backdrop of one of this century's most compelling liberation struggles.[16]

Gevisser's analysis is important because it astutely identifies the symbolic overload that weighed (and continues to weigh) upon Winnie Mandela as both political leader and wife to Nelson Mandela. It is obvious, he states, that 'Winnie Mandela is the victim of one system that tried to crush her and another that tried to crown her.'[17] Revered and reviled, Winnie Mandela herself is the victim of the depredations meted out to her by a violent and abusive state. At the same time she is a politicized woman whose life has been permanently strained by the public's expectation that she perform the role of perfect wife and mother for over 30 difficult years.

An understanding of the gendering of women's relationships to power and authority is central to the Winnie Mandela story. As icons of national liberation, women are symbolically associated with the spirit and principle of freedom, and with nurturing roles such as motherhood and the life-giving properties of the land itself. Where freedom, of necessity, militantly arms herself for struggle, her association with the firebrand of political violence repositions her relationship to both sexual and maternal metaphors, sometimes consolidating them, sometimes contradicting them. Whilst the use of forms of violence is naturalized within the dynamics of masculine political activism, the language and symbolism of sexual difference make women's relationship to violence more visible and culturally problematic. As Gevisser wryly asks concerning the unanswered questions in the Winnie Mandela mythology, 'Why must the world have both a nurturing mother and a castrating bitch in its cultural genealogy?'[18]

Stripped of the media-glitzed veneer, there was and remains a deep political dispute at the heart of the Mandela marriage, a dispute over the personal and political uses of violence. But in the international media's oversimplification of the complexities of local and national South African politics, Winnie Mandela was either demonized as the imperfect mother and wife, or complacently exonerated by commentators who felt that to question her use of power was to align themselves with the oppressive apartheid system. Rather than tackling the need to represent and report on the difficulties of collective political struggle, and the specific ways in which the vital roles of women are represented in that struggle, the world media which once hailed Winnie Mandela as mythologized mother and 'African Queen', came to demonize her as 'disreputable', 'wicked', 'wayward' and 'betraying'. She was 'a shrieking shrew of a wife', a murderess and overreacher who reduced her husband to a 'doting' and 'lovesick fool'.[19] As one foreign correspondent put it, '*Private Eye* ... was not entirely exaggerating when it drew a line of descent for Mrs Mandela through Lucrezia Borgia, Myra Hindley and Lady Macbeth.'[20]

These stereotypes of Winnie Mandela were inveterately sexist, and drew on cultural references of little relevance to South Africa. Moreover, the media's alacrity to construct Winnie Mandela in the image of monstrous female power obscured the possibility for a fair and rational analysis of her position. As Elleke Boehmer points out in her discussion on the gendering of nationalism, the idea of nationhood bears a masculine identity, though national ideals may wear a feminine face.[21] In gendered discourses of national identity, woman appears in a metaphoric or symbolic role, a role which highlights the relationship between patriarchy and nationalism. Such projections are central to the pitfalls of nationalism which, as a political concept, represents relationships to both political power and to the technologies of violence.[22] Popular responses to women's relationships to the technologies of violence are crucially indicative of the central role of gender within the ideas of nationhood.

When Nelson Mandela and Nomzamo Winifred Madikizela got married in 1958, the father of the bride told his daughter that 'she was marrying a man already married to the struggle.'[23] Politically, Winnie Mandela's public persona has always been inextricably linked to that of her husband, whether in amity or, as more recently, in dispute. The roles of political wife and mother compromise the integrity of women's independent political activism. As Anne McClintock succinctly puts it, 'the heterosexual family within the sanction of matrimony acquires the inevitability of destiny, and women are seen not as independent members of the national community, but as wives responsible to the nation through their service to individual men.'[24]

It is in fact discourses surrounding the family and heterosexuality which have led to the popular framing of Winnie Mandela as deviant mother. Whether framed in progressive or reactionary ways, myths investing heterosexual maternity and marriage with special status and power reduplicate the unchallenged role of the family as the central component of legitimate national identity. The gendering of nationalism is revealed when women who are symbolically venerated remain, in practice, disempowered. Caught in the crossfire of competing patriarchal discourses of male-dominated political conflict, where both oppression and resistance have been seen as the proper domain of masculinity, Winnie Mandela's life tells the success story of a woman determined to challenge this disempowerment. She has often done so by deliberately exploiting and working within such discourses as the family and idealized 'hetero-normality', in communities where 'motherhood' is a symbol of communal sharing and responsibility. Speaking of her marriage to Nelson, Winnie Mandela once expressed the hope that 'someday we will also have the luxury of having the nucleus of a family: some day we'll also know what it would have been like to lead a normal family.'[25]

Winnie Mandela's political star seemed to reascend in 1994, with her cabinet appointment as Minister of Arts, Culture, Science and Technology. This portfolio was, however, taken away from her in 1995 as a result of a political dispute; though no longer a member of the cabinet, she is still a Member of Parliament. Winnie Mandela remains a highly controversial figure, in whom the contradictory images of maternity, political militancy and personal violence are inextricably linked. One of the radical successes of women in the ANC has been their effectiveness in showing motherhood to be a social category that undergoes constant transformation. Most important in terms of the role of black women in the social and political transformation of South Africa, the trials of Winnie Mandela have thrown into relief the collective challenge women face in transforming the patriarchal character of national consciousness – the challenge to demonstrate that women's roles can extend beyond those of 'political handmaiden' or 'good mother'. Her struggles have also uncovered, for all to see, the gendering of personal and political violence at the heart of the national family.

PHALLOCENTRIC SLICING:

20/20's Reporting of Lorena and John Bobbitt

Patricia J. Priest, Cindy Jenefsky, and Jill D. Swenson

> On that June night, a domestic quarrel reached the point of
> unthinkable violence. That barrier was crossed when Mrs. Bobbitt
> picked up this knife...
> *20/20*, 24 SEPTEMBER, 1993

American press coverage of John and Lorena Bobbitt emphasized her
act of slicing off her husband's penis as 'unthinkable' and 'abhorrent'.
Superlatives were common; *Vanity Fair* magazine described Lorena's
retaliation as 'a heinous act like no other'; *Newsweek* labeled her action
'primordial'; and the television program *American Journal* noted the 'cruel
and unusual nature of the crime'.[1] The expressed horror of the Bobbitt tale
has thus focused on the severance of John Bobbitt's penis, not on his
protracted sexual torture and abuse of his wife. The typical media outcry
directed toward Lorena's actions drew attention away from the terror of
living with the enemy and, in an abrupt but invisible turn, shifted full blame
to the woman as nemesis lying in wait. The focus on the exceptional and
cruel nature solely of Lorena's behavior framed her response to spousal
abuse as an act 'beyond belief' – the title for an ABC *20/20* report on the
Bobbitts – in the process implying that marital rape is 'thinkable,' a mild
transgression. In short, the media's judgmental superlatives were reserved
exclusively for what *20/20* labeled *her* 'degenerate act'.

In this essay we closely examine ABC's *20/20* report of 24 September, 1993, because it is riddled with examples of bias seen throughout wider media coverage of the Bobbitts and because of its prominence: more than 17 million viewers in the US watched *20/20* that night.[2] The half-hour piece, produced three months after the news story originally broke, offered the first in-depth mass media treatment in the US of the Bobbitts.

We begin with a brief overview of recent critical analyses of the newspaper coverage of sexual/domestic violence cases. Significant insights within this body of research – namely, the recycling of rape myths, the individual pathologizing of stories of rape and spousal abuse, and news routines that give preference to 'the unusual' – are combined with feminist scholarship on sexual and domestic violence to analyze *20/20*'s reporting on the Bobbitts. Overall, we maintain that *20/20*'s minimization of John's cruel behavior naturalizes male violence, while forcefully condemning retaliation against wife abuse and rape.

Print Reporting on Sexual/Domestic Violence

Recent works on press coverage of rape and wife battery provide detailed evidence of systematic bias. For example, in *Virgin or Vamp: How the Press Covers Sex Crimes*, Helen Benedict illustrates how societal myths about sexual assault are not only rarely dispelled by reporters but are, in fact, compounded by the media's unexamined usage of them. These myths include the well-worn beliefs that rape is not much different than having sex, that women bring rape upon themselves through provocative behavior, and that women vengefully bring forward false rape charges.[3] In addition to the overt use of rape myths, other more subtle and structural press practices function to minimize rape and domestic violence: the decontextualization and individualization of sexual/domestic violence stories, and the reliance upon press routines that privilege 'the unusual' as news topics. Benedict describes the propensity of the press to focus exclusively on the individual traits of the perpetrator and the victim: 'Rape as a societal problem has lost interest for the public and the press, and the press is reverting to its pre-1970 focus on sex crimes as individual, bizarre, or sensational case histories.'[4]

Marian Meyers identifies this same pattern in her analysis of the *Atlanta Journal and Constitution*'s coverage of a man who murdered his wife. She claims that the 'interpretive framework' employed for narrating stories of wife battery situates stories about batterers who kill their wives as aberrant events, depicting the men as temporarily out of control because of a pathological state. Meyers, like Benedict, points to a recurring pattern in the press reporting of sex crimes and domestic violence that is 'socially distorted, rooted in assumptions, myths, and stereotypes that link it to individual and family pathology rather than to social structures and gendered patterns of domination and control'.[5] Similarly, Barbara Johnson notes in her study of San Francisco newspaper coverage of domestic violence incidents that the press rarely turns to experts on spousal abuse to provide a larger context for a story. Isolating events from larger societal dynamics obscures the systemic and widespread character of sexual violence by presenting rape stories as unusual, deviant acts by deviant people.[6]

One of the most imposing constraints on the coverage of sex crimes is that newsworthiness is often defined by 'unusualness'. One radio reporter, when queried about the kinds of sexual assault or wife abuse cases that warrant press attention, replied that a rape is likely to be covered 'if the person is beaten up badly, gang raped, if it's something like she's been stalked or it happened in a public place'. Researchers comparing police and newspaper reports have found that newspapers are far more likely to carry a report of sexual assault when the attacker is a stranger rather than an acquaintance. Furthermore, Marlyss Schwengels and James Lemert note that information about women's attempts to resist their attackers is rarely mentioned in newspapers.[7]

The Bobbitt case differs from the incidents analyzed in the studies above because of Lorena Bobbitt's explicit act of resistance. The media's focus on 'the unusual' and their obfuscation of the larger issue of male supremacy take a slightly different form in a case where that which is aberrant, and therefore newsworthy, is a woman's violent retaliation against her abuser. Here, the elision of the larger social context amplifies her behavior as 'abhorrent' and renders it inexplicable – in short, 'beyond belief'. This structurally situates John's injuries at the center of the narrative and, in turn, effectively minimizes marital rape, normalizes male violence, positions him as the most aggrieved party, and constructs Lorena's actions alone as extreme and inhumane.

Phallocentrism in the Narrative Structure:
Minimizing Male Sexual Violence

There is a contradictory tension that persists throughout 'Beyond Belief', between the framing narrative provided by the journalists' script, and the embedded narrative spun from story components provided by sources.[8] The framing narrative is a multi-layered story iterated by 20/20's newscasters: Hugh Downs and Barbara Walters, who host the show, and Tom Jarriel, who reports the feature story on the Bobbitts. The news team's words frame the narrative on all sides – prior to the segment with opening teasers, before and after the commercial break within the piece, in Jarriel's transitions facilitating thematic shifts within the story, and at the end, when all three converse about the story. The embedded narrative in 'Beyond Belief' is constructed mostly of an assortment of testimonies, as well as reenactments of dramatic events, all strung together by Jarriel's voice-overs.

The framing narrative narrowly focuses the segment on 'that June night' which 'reached the point of unthinkable violence' – the singular night when Lorena severed John's penis. In contrast, the embedded narrative contextualizes Lorena's action within a more longitudinal view of John Bobbitt's history of violence in their marriage, even though it, too, focuses mainly on that single evening. The tension between the framing and embedded dimensions of the narrative is sustained throughout the report, even though, as we will demonstrate, the journalists' narrower approach is accorded greater presence and credibility overall.

The constricted framing begins in the teaser before the commercial break preceding 'Beyond Belief'.[9] Barbara Walters states dramatically: 'Well, next, perhaps, the most provocative story that we have ever presented – the story of Lorena Bobbitt, the woman who sexually mutilated her husband with a knife and threw his sex organ out of the window.' Following the commercials, Hugh Downs' opening lines reinforce the narrow focus on the pathological character of Lorena's actions. After a line about the serious and far-reaching nature of the story, he omits any mention of John's history of sexual/domestic violence and immediately isolates Lorena's deviance: 'A Virginia woman, with no warning, sexually mutilated her husband and then claimed he had raped her. What kind of a woman could strike out in such a shocking way?' Such phallocentric slicing of the couple's history removes a key component of the story – John's documented history of wife abuse and rape.

Feminist writer Andrea Dworkin states that 'The favorite conceit of male culture is that experience can be fractured, literally its bones split, and that one can examine the splinters as if they were not part of the bone.'[10] Such fracturing is noticeable in *20/20*'s narrow emphasis on 'that awful night' and 'the night of mayhem', also inaccurately described by Hugh Downs as 'that single night of violence'. This parsing of the stream of events in the Bobbitts' married life excises the years of abuse preceding Lorena's retaliatory act.[11] It is important to note that this same evening is never described as the night John committed his last rape and/or attack against Lorena. An ahistorical bent is common to news writing;[12] but, in this case, the circumscribed version is not merely undercontextualized, but false: it positions John as the victim of mere craziness and vengeance, and Lorena alone as the irrational perpetrator who lashes out 'without warning'. Only Lorena, in Hugh Downs' words, 'did the unthinkable'.

The viciousness, severity and duration of John Bobbitt's violence is ignored by the newscasters throughout the segment – it is literally never the subject of discussion between the journalists. Even though *20/20* devotes significant time within the embedded narrative of 'Beyond Belief' to construct John's violent history, only Lorena's act of violence is positioned, within any of the narrative layers, as egregious and as a violation of normal behavior. A woman's retaliation to rape and battery is characterized as outrageous, while a man's violence is rendered routine.[13]

This imbalance in gender portrayals is further evidenced by the journalists' choice of words throughout this news program. Jarriel labels Lorena's act as 'the point of unthinkable violence' and 'extraordinary violence'. Downs calls her behavior 'vengeance of a high-voltage nature', and Walters refers to Lorena's 'vicious act' on 'that awful night in June'. No such condemnatory or intense words are used when referring to John's violent behavior. This difference normalizes, and even erases, male violence while it demonizes female retaliation as, in the words of John Bobbitt's lawyer during the program, 'a real danger which I don't think in a civilized society anybody should accept'.

While the framing narrative narrows its view exclusively to one night of violence and amplifies the deviance of Lorena's behavior, the embedded narrative contextualizes Lorena's violent act (albeit only within the history of the Bobbitt's marriage, and not within the social context of pervasive male sexual violence against women) and is sympathetic to Lorena's victimization. This more compassionate portrait is created, in part, by

Lorena's physical presence recounting her side of the story, in contrast to John's absence.[14] This sympathy is also created by the weight of witness testimony corroborating Lorena's tales of abuse: three neighbors, Lorena's employer/best friend, and a police officer all confirm John's violence against Lorena.

The embedded narrative does not, however, construct Lorena as an innocent; John's lawyer describes her as sexually greedy, and several minutes are devoted to details of her arrest for theft and embezzlement. But she is also depicted as an unlikely perpetrator: mention of her petite frame contrasts with descriptions of John as a 175–200-pound [12.5–14 stone] Marine 'trained to fight without a weapon using hand-to-hand combat'. Her family is presented as 'devout', 'close-knit' and economically 'comfortable' (cultural signifiers implying an absence of pathological or dysfunctional family origins) in contrast to John's less romanticized upbringing 'by relatives after his parents split up'. Lorena is portrayed as faithful in comparison to his womanizing; she is presented as steadily employed, while he is shown to have an erratic work history. Her move to the US from Venezuela is characterized as a starry-eyed pursuit of the 'American dream' thwarted, it is implied, by John's abusive or irresponsible behavior.

The dialectical tension between the framing and embedded narratives creates an impression of objectivity and balance: one story narrowly focuses on the night of the penis severance, while the other provides a more macroscopic view of the couple's marital history; one story casts Lorena as a vengeful castrator and John as the victim of heinous violence, while the other casts her as an unfortunate victim and him a likely perpetrator. This is not a tension that hangs in equitable balance, however. First, as already noted, the journalists' expressions of shock and horror are reserved exclusively for Lorena's violence, thereby denoting only her behavior as an 'act that defies understanding'.

Second, even though numerous witnesses confirm Lorena's tales of battery, John's abuse of her is marginalized within the segment as a whole. As the title and framing narrative make clear, the focal point of 'Beyond Belief' is the 'unthinkable' severance of John's penis. Jarriel's interviews with Lorena and others are presented as an attempt to understand, in Downs' words, 'What kind of woman would strike out in such a shocking way?' and 'What would drive her to such abhorrent behavior?' After Lorena's friend and an apartment manager testify to the bruises they had seen, and Lorena describes the beatings and rapes, Walters remarks: 'You've heard Lorena Bobbitt's version of what was going on behind closed doors. Violence was not new to their marriage. In fact, it appears to have been an integral part of the relationship. But what happened that night that prompted this vicious act?' Similarly, Jarriel queries, 'What led to the extraordinary violence that has focused such attention on Lorena Bobbitt and her kitchen knife?' Thus, the embedded narrative is circumscribed within the pursuit to uncover the mysterious motives behind *her* 'abhorrent' crime. The larger picture of wife abuse is cropped by framing John's severed penis as the focal point.

Third, the framing narrative lingers on her violence against him. In simplest terms, more minutes are devoted to 'that awful night in June' (Walters' introduction to the second half of the segment) than to John's years of violence against Lorena. This fact alone accords greater significance to Lorena's violent retaliation. Furthermore, her violence against him is amplified within the story through minutely detailed (and poorly executed) recreations of events on that singular June night.[15] No such detailed coverage is devoted to any of his acts of violence against her.[16] This imbalanced visual amplification of 'the [single] night of mayhem' functions to reinforce the visual presence and significance of Lorena's act.

Fourth, the surface appearance of balanced coverage conveyed by the dialectical tension between the framing and embedded narratives is undermined by the absence of a social context for this story. Like news coverage of rape and battering generally,[17] 'Beyond Belief' obscures the relationship of the Bobbitts' story with male supremacy generally and with gendered patterns of violence specifically. *20/20* personalizes the Bobbitt story as a case of one man and one woman in a 'marriage gone wrong'.[18] Lorena's actions become inexplicable and pathological only in the absence of knowledge about systematic sexual violence against women. FBI statistics for 1993 indicate that four women are killed *every day* in the US by current or former husbands or lovers or by prospective suitors. Tragically, too, one in every four women is raped in her lifetime.[19] In light of such systematic abuse and terrorization of women, is it not more surprising that so few women have lopped off penises than that Lorena Bobbitt did so?

Explicit Trivialization of Male Sexual Violence

The minimization of male violence in this program also results from explicit trivialization of John's abusive behavior. Recall Walters' remark, stated earlier in this essay, that violence 'appears to have been an integral part of the relationship'. Such a phrasing equalizes the violence between them, as if it were inflicted mutually. Jarriel similarly euphemizes John's abusive behavior by using the term 'domestic quarrel' to refer to the rape that preceded the maiming. This phrase carries little emotional weight when used opposite such terms as 'mutilation' and 'degenerate act' – terms characterizing Lorena's actions. Throughout the program, Jarriel glosses over John's violence by referring to his repeated acts of torture and rape as: 'a turbulent marriage', a 'stormy marriage' and 'conflicts at home'.[20] These phrases suggest that both partners played equally culpable roles in the marital violence, when the evidence about the case – including that presented throughout 20/20's report – proves otherwise.

In the latter half of the segment, after Lorena describes fighting John as he raped her, Jarriel responds with questions that repeatedly trivialize the violence she recounts. 'How emphatic were you when you said, "No sex"?' he asks. She replies, 'When I said "no" I wanted him to respect that. Well, he didn't.' Jarriel's response constitutes the rape incident *as* sex: 'He never agreed to stop, and he knew – he knew very clearly – that you were fighting him and you were resisting him?' Lorena states, 'Like always, he would not listen.' Despite her explicit descriptions of being held down, her underwear ripped, and being forced into sex, Jarriel manages to reconstrue the situation as mere miscommunication about sex. This interchange reflects prevailing social attitudes toward marital rape as a variation on sexual activity – pushy and mean-spirited rather than the terror-filled and painful humiliation survivors report. Finally, during the concluding roundtable discussion among Jarriel, Downs, and Walters, Jarriel summarizes the Bobbitt's story as a reflection of 'a huge gulf between men and women and communicating about sex that we almost hate to admit.'

An unspoken sense of entitlement for husbands underlies the press and public outrage about Lorena's actions.[21] Timothy Beneke's extensive study of men's attitudes about rape indicates that this sense of sexual entitlement is commonplace among men. A quote from one young man in Beneke's study typifies this belief: 'If a guy has to rape his wife, she ought to consider something that she's doing wrong ... She's gotta be puttin' it off for a good while before a husband will rape his wife.'[22] Similarly, an audience member commented on the television program *Jenny Jones* about Lorena's actions: 'I think it was cold-blooded. I don't think anybody would deserve that, after – He was married to the woman, right?'[23]

In contrast, when a woman in Mississippi fought back against her attacker that same year in an incident of stranger rape by twisting his scrotum until he begged her to call the police, columnist Mike Royko and others in the press cheered her. It is important to note that the woman involved was in her home at the time and was described as a 'middle-aged nurse who lives with an elderly aunt in the rural hamlet of Edwards, Mississippi' – a rather peerless profile of a survivor that is hard for the press to disparage.[24] Yet an immigrant wife who strikes back at her husband after years of abuse and repeated rape is scorned for her actions.

A deputy district attorney quoted in Beneke's study talks about marital rape laws as unworkable and impossible to treat as seriously as stranger rape: 'I mean, God, you marry the guy, you've slept with him before. Where's the horror?[25] Where's the shame of being raped?'[26] By not educating the public about the terror of wife rape – the long-lasting loss of trust, the degradation, and the brutality – *20/20* positions Lorena's actions as unjustified and hysterical.

Severed Parts: The Social Context Cut from Reports of Violence Against Women

Benedict points to the dearth of discussion in the press about the violent nature of wife abuse, despite the fact that the first well-publicized case of marital rape in the US occurred more than 15 years ago.[27] A persistent point of public misunderstanding – common to caseworkers, attorneys and the police alike – is the simplistic notion that women can easily leave battering situations if they really want to.[28] The *20/20* narrative immediately suggests that Lorena refused to take this option by noting early in the report's audio introduction that a neighbor offered to let her stay overnight. Lorena later explained to Jarriel that she had returned to her apartment that night because she felt that John would not try to rape her because his friend was visiting. Jarriel then summarizes her behavior this way:

> Lorena had more than one option. Remember, a neighbor offered to take her in that night. She could have obtained that legal order against John, and she might have sought help from John's friend sleeping nearby in the living room. She chose the knife.

These comments suggest, first, that Lorena is to blame for placing herself in a dangerous situation. Second, this analysis of her choices implies that restraining orders are infallible, that *his* friend would have come to her rescue, and that staying with neighbors or friends is a safe harbor from domestic violence. Furthermore, Jarriel's comments frame the violence, once again, as a single night of danger she could have avoided.

In the 1990s, when so much more is known about wife abuse, the press again neglected to provide necessary information about why battered women often strike out when their abusers are sleeping or drunk, or about the very real dangers faced by women who leave batterers. Research about the dangerous role of macho attitudes in the propensity to rape, and the higher incidence of domestic violence in military homes, could have been especially useful contexts in this case. For example, according to a 1994 military report, spousal abuse occurs in approximately one in three army households – twice the level found in civilian families.[29]

While the obvious context should have been the tragedy of domestic violence, the story could have also have been couched as one about America being fed up and fighting back against crime. Instead, it became a story solely about the battle of the sexes, with women portrayed as irrational and dangerous. For this reason, the not guilty verdict Lorena won is not an advance for women's rights advocacy, because it hinged on depicting her as temporarily insane rather than justified in fighting back.

Kathleen Lawrence notes that much of the press reporting of the Bobbitts treated the story as high farce. Cartoons prevalent after the incident depict women as ready to strike back at the slightest provocation. A representative example shows a man in bed with a pillow stuffed between his legs. The caption reads, 'He couldn't sleep ... had he pushed his wife "over the edge" when he made that remark about her casserole?'[30] These treatments trivialize the terror faced by women in battering situations. In Melanie Kaye/Kantrowitz's analysis of this historical trivialization, she explains that 'the jovial image of "the war between the sexes," suggesting as it does sexual bantering, cloaks an authentic war waged by men against women.'[31] *20/20* never allows for the fact that dire retaliation may be justified when husbands or boyfriends batter and rape women.

Phallocentrism in Wider Press Coverage

20/20's biased pattern of coverage of the Bobbitts is not an isolated occurrence but embodies trends in wider media coverage.[32] Euphemistic descriptions of John's actions are evident elsewhere; newspaper and magazine accounts refer to his actions variously as 'marital travails' (*The Atlanta Journal and Constitution*) or, as in *People* magazine, merely the problem of an inexpert lover who did not know how to satisfy his demanding wife. During the second trial, a headline in *The New York Times* read 'Witnesses say mutilated man often hit wife,' yet the bulk of evidence presented about John's behavior that day would have been better summarized with verbs such as 'terrorized' or 'brutalized.'[33] US journalistic legal stipulations work in John's favor, as claims against him had to be labeled 'allegations', a practice which suggested that Lorena's accusations were questionable. Furthermore, under Virginia state law the charges against him were not technically defined as rape because the couple was living together and he used no weapon as he pinned her down, twisted her arms and forced sex on her. Instead, the term 'marital assault' was used at trial. However, Lorena's behavior was rarely referred to solely as a 'malicious wounding', the legal term for her offense, but was instead described frequently as mutilation; the Canadian magazine *MacLean's* used the term 'amputate'.[34] *20/20*'s caption for Lorena contained the inflammatory phrase, 'castrated her husband'.

This myopic focus on Lorena's actions lasted throughout the half-year of media coverage. After her acquittal, for example, a flurry of questions centered on whether the jury's finding signalled an open season on men. Concerns about John's acquittal were never mentioned, despite the fact that many who had heard all the evidence felt John had abused Lorena brutally and often,[35] and despite the alarmingly low conviction rate for crimes of sexual assault which puts dangerous men back on the street. John was arrested, in fact, within the year for battering another woman, but his stint in prison for this assault generated very little press attention.

The media's bias is also reflected in the concern frequently expressed for John's recovery, as if he were the only party suffering injuries. Press accounts of the public debate contain many mentions of Lorena hurting him, as John's brother Brett said on *Jenny Jones*, 'in the worst way possible, for any man'.[36] Such language is never used to address the crippling effect of rape on both male and female survivors. Talk inevitably turns to questions of John's healing and sexual functioning. There were many missed opportunities to address the long-term emotional scarring experienced by survivors of sexual violence.

Reporters' framing of events is partly the consequence of deadlines and competitive pressures.[37] The systematic nature of the bias described here – whether due to reporter insensitivity or ignorance or misogynistic attitudes – further calcifies persistent stereotypes and reinforces public denial about the magnitude of violence against women. Sociologist Herbert Gans claims in his book, *Deciding What's News*, that news stories about 'the unusual' are often about threats to the reigning 'white male social order'.[38] The myths invoked and the strong terminology used to describe Lorena in *20/20*'s news story reveal that her actions were seen as a threat to the status quo, an order based on age-old beliefs about male entitlement to sexual access to women. The press seems to pull out all the stops in its efforts to describe retaliation against an acquaintance rapist as out-of-bounds, unthinkable. News reports that demonize women who fight back keep victims of spousal abuse trapped in a Catch-22: they are either blamed for not leaving or are blamed for retaliating, while the legal system they are supposed to rely on does not adequately safeguard their lives.

The biased depictions throughout the *20/20* piece reflect society's tolerance of rape and wife abuse. Portraying violence against women as unremarkable, but fighting back as 'unthinkable', further reinforces the patriarchal order that limits and endangers women's lives. The phallocentric nature of much of the coverage creates a serious obstacle for activists trying to reform rape laws, when reports of rape position viewers' sympathies with John, a batterer and rapist.

A key problem, as noted earlier, is that news is about oddities, not the mundane. The grim statistics that millions of women are raped and battered each year rarely cause a stir unless they are illuminated during a sensational case. The public can learn from other high-profile cases, such as O. J. Simpson's or William Kennedy Smith's, only if the facts are put in context and myths about victims are dispelled. Coverage of sex crimes which is not placed within the context of gendered patterns of such violence greatly diminishes the possibility for meaningful social change.

WOMEN WHO KILL AND THE MADE-FOR-TV MOVIE:

The Betty Broderick Story[1]

Stephanie Savage

Homicides by women are exceedingly rare and more frequently are the result of one woman's desperate attempt to rid herself of an abusive man. Unlike men, who are apt to kill a total stranger in a bar during a drunken brawl, women tend to kill their cheating lovers, violent husbands, and unwanted newborn babes. In short, women kill those they have *loved*.[2]

LISA PRIEST, *WOMEN WHO KILLED*

The whole title of that movie makes you want to gag … I was *never* a woman scorned. They're using my name, pretending it's *my* voice, leading people to believe it was *my* story. Hah!! I don't think so.[3]

BETTY BRODERICK, QUOTED IN *TV GUIDE*

Introduction

In the past several years, stories about women who kill have inundated the popular press and television programming – and have been extremely popular with the public. One of the main forms to have taken up this topic is the made-for-TV movie. In the 1991–92 US television season, for example, no fewer than eight of these movies earned over 20 million viewers each and reached the top 25 in the weekly ratings.[4] Many of these movies were based on the headline-grabbing stories of actual women. The 1992–3 season continued this trend, with telefeatures on Wanda Holloway, Bambi Bembenek, and Aileen Wuornos – not to mention the now infamous all-Amy Fisher weekend, when each of the three major networks aired a docudrama of the Fisher-Buttafuoco story (25–8 December, 1992).[5] These TV movies can be seen in the context of recent 'psycho-femme' feature films in the *Fatal Attraction* (1987) tradition (for example, *Basic Instinct, Hand that Rocks the Cradle, Single White Female* and *Poison Ivy*, all 1992) as well as docu- and tabloid-TV shows that often feature the 'real life' exploits of criminals, such as *Hard Copy* and *A Current Affair*. It was within this context that I first came across the Betty Broderick story.

I watched the made-for-TV movie *A Woman Scorned: The Betty Broderick Story*, on the night it was first aired (1 March, 1992), rather distractedly out of my peripheral vision, while doing something else. I had no knowledge at the time of Broderick's real-life headlines, and didn't view the program with a critical eye or a mind to write about it. In the weeks that followed, however, I became more and more preoccupied with it. Its pacing and tone had struck me as inexplicably strange, and its construction of the Betty Broderick character made me feel profoundly ambivalent toward her actions. *This* was the Betty Broderick story? Despite Meredith Baxter's congenial voice-over as Broderick, it seemed unlikely that anyone would characterize her own experiences in the manner that this movie did. The tension that built between an increasingly wacko Betty and the assertion that this was *her* narration of *her* story was extraordinary, and seemed to point to broader concerns about fact-based telefeatures as a whole. In particular, I wondered, did this tension result from the difficulty of integrating the story of a woman who is found guilty of second-degree murder with the current model of representing real women's experience in television narrative?

In her recent book on the made-for-TV movie, *The Movie of the Week: Private Stories, Public Events*, Elaine Rapping points out the limits of television as 'a perfect model of democratic representation', but remains somewhat optimistic about the made-for-TV movie as 'a discursive site upon which conflicts and contradictions inherent in the existence of the family as an institution within bourgeois society are worked out' and where there may be 'encoded the oppositional voices of feminists and other women'.[6] Rapping's study, however, focuses on the popular woman-in-jeopardy narratives which flourished in the eighties, typified by *The Burning Bed* (1984), based on the story of a real woman, Francine Hughes, who was acquitted of killing the husband who had physically abused her for years.

The Betty Broderick story is also a story of a woman who fights back, but the circumstances of Broderick's crime are more disputed than those of Hughes'; her status as a victim, less clear-cut. Broderick is also something of a spectacle. Her widely publicized transgressions in the landscape of suburbia across the specific borders of wife- and motherhood are often reported with an element of awe and fascination. There is something surreal in the scenes of rebellion that are conjured in one's mind: custom-tailored suits go up in smoke on the fresh green lawn; home-made pie gets smeared around the adulterer's bedroom; the front of the new tudor-style home gets smashed by the Chevy van with 'LODEMUP' vanity plates; children listen as their mother uses explicit language on the family answering machine to describe their father's sexual activities with another woman. Most importantly, however, unlike Hughes, Broderick was found guilty. Since her real-life actions were not ultimately sanctioned by the state, she is an unlikely candidate for woman-in-jeopardy. If the Broderick case illustrates anything, it is that the inherent 'contradictions' that structure the lives of women cannot be 'worked out' peaceably within the system as it stands. It is for this reason that her story cannot easily be told within the prevailing made-for-TV movie format.

In the press, the twists and turns of Broderick's case were taken up as raising 'a really rich series of questions' and becoming 'a morality play for the community'.[7] But this notion seems lost to the television program that bears Broderick's name. A comparison of a sampling of Betty Broderick stories (found in newspapers, the popular press, tabloids, a supermarket 'mini-mag' and a 'true crime' novel) with the CBS made-for-TV movie reveals that the TV version is the most pathologizing, most politically conservative and most anti-feminist of all the 'stories'. In comparing these stories we can discover more about how fact-based narratives of female violence are produced, as well as the strange tale that is *A Woman Scorned*.[8]

The Betty Broderick Stories

Daniel and Betty Broderick divorced after 16 years of marriage in 1986. Almost four years later, after intensive ongoing legal battling over property settlements, child custody and alimony payments, Betty Broderick entered the home of her ex-husband and his second wife on the morning of 5 November, 1989, and shot them in bed. Both died, Linda Kolkena-Broderick instantly, and Daniel T. Broderick III a few moments later. Hours after Betty Broderick shot Dan and Linda, she surrendered herself to the police. She was held without bail until her trial in October, 1990. After a month-long trial, the jury deliberated for four days and returned hung: two jurors wanted to find Broderick guilty of manslaughter, while the other ten wanted to find her guilty of murder in the second degree. Almost exactly one year later, Broderick was re-tried, found guilty of second-degree murder, and sentenced to 32 years-to-life in prison.

The circumstances that led up to these events are complex and, ultimately, unknowable. And yet, in order to make sense of them, stories must be told. Of course, which narrative materializes depends on whom you talk to, and where the story appears.

Broderick contended that her husband, a prominent San Diego medical malpractice attorney and president of the San Diego Bar Association, used his legal influence to beleaguer her and to deprive her of a fair divorce settlement: her share of his more than $1 million a year income, and custody of their two youngest children. Betty was devoted to Dan, working to put him through medical and then law school, caring for their four children and running a well-ordered household. Dan became cold and withholding as he approached middle-age; he drank, intimidated the family with violent outbursts, had an affair. Once the couple separated he asked Betty for a divorce over lunch, and planned to serve her papers at one of their children's school functions.

Dan and Linda Broderick's families portray Betty in a different light, as a selfish psychopath who abandoned her children and relentlessly harassed the happy couple. This polarization of viewpoints is integral to the news reports of the trial. The issue of whether Dan's treatment of Betty was the cause of her actions, or the result of them, became key early on. The notion that Broderick's actions might somehow be 'defensive', or even 'justified', became the crux of community interest in the case, as well as the main tension throughout the various Betty Broderick stories I examine below.

Amy Wallace's 'scoop' story of Broderick's confession in the *Los Angeles Times* was instrumental in shaping interpretations of the Broderick case. Betty Broderick told Wallace in a phone interview at the end of March, 1990, that she had killed her husband and his second wife, but described the murder as a 'desperate act of self-defense' against a man who wanted 'to control [her] totally'.[9] Reporter Wallace was a creative consultant for the made-for-TV movie, and the script went into production before the second trial was over and a verdict reached.[10] As a consequence, *A Woman Scorned* is based more on Wallace's pre-trial interviews with Broderick than on evidence that came out during the two trials (and in fact, as will be shown, details of the TV show contradict the trial evidence in significant ways). Wallace wrote a lengthy (ten-page) article for the *LA Times Magazine* that appeared on 3 June, 1990, while Broderick was still in custody awaiting her first trial.[11] Attempting to compensate for the fact that 'Dan, by all accounts an eloquent litigator, could no longer speak for himself,' Wallace interviewed numerous friends and family of Dan and Linda, and Betty's estranged eldest daughter, Kim, as support for Dan's 'side of the story'.[12] The result of this strategy is not a balanced piece that explores the various complexities of the case and its implications; rather, Betty Broderick's version of events remains unsupported in the face of the multiple, corroborated version told by the friends and relatives of Dan and Linda.

Given this framework, it follows that Dan's and Linda's characterizations would be extremely positive. Most importantly, their affair during Dan's marriage to Betty is referred to only once, and only as Betty's groundless suspicion. Meredith Baxter (the actress who portrayed Broderick) is quoted in a *Times* article about *A Woman Scorned*, 'I felt convinced [Dan and Linda] were having an affair, but because it was never substantiated in the trial we couldn't just editorialize.'[13] The affair was, however, substantiated in court, to the point of having a clinical therapist who specializes in the effects of extramarital affairs testify. Even prosecuting attorney Kerry Wells has gone on record as stating, 'I think he [Dan] felt tremendously guilty about having an affair with Linda and not exactly knowing what to do about the situation.'[14]

In addition, Steve Kelley, who was dating Linda while she was seeing the still-married Dan and whose story significantly shapes an article on Broderick written for *Ladies Home Journal*, was not consulted for Wallace's piece.[15]

Dan Broderick employed Linda, a former airline attendant with no legal training, as his assistant. Kelley reports being astounded by the size and luxury of Linda's office, 'and on her wall, she had this photograph of Dan Broderick on horseback, with the horse rearing up. It was like a knight in shining armor.'[16] Eventually, Kelley recalls, he confronted Linda about her feelings for her boss. She admitted to having an affair with Dan and broke off relations with Kelley.

In Wallace's account, Betty Broderick's 'story' is not only undermined by the fact that she does not attempt to substantiate Betty's claims, but that she frames these claims with her own antagonistic assertions. Although the statements of others are reprinted with minimal characterization, Betty's comments are accompanied by descriptions implying shrillness and hysteria. Wallace uses a series of negative editorializing comments to undermine Broderick's credibility and attack her reasoning and logic, interrupting the flow of her narrative account to declare that there is a 'flaw' in Betty's 'argument', or that 'the more pieces Betty Broderick added to her puzzle, the fewer seemed to fit.'[17] This idea that Betty's puzzle is a few pieces short of a picture is a motif that runs throughout the article. For example, Betty contends that Dan's 'cruel side' was linked to alcohol abuse, but according to Wallace, Dan's liver 'seemed to tell a different story' – despite the coroner's assertion that 'not all chronic drinkers have visibly damaged livers'.[18] Further, this type of comment often takes on the legalistic tone of a cross-examination, and is often supported by the 'testimony' of lawyers. Thus the article puts Betty Broderick 'on the stand' and encourages the reader to participate in the interrogation.

While ostensibly dealing with the same issues and events, this article stands in striking contrast to the story found in *Ladies Home Journal*. The *Journal* article takes up Broderick's story in terms of the 'failed marriage' genre, framing the piece with a juxtaposition of young Betty's expectations about marriage with her actual experience. 'No longer does she have the perfect life of her girlhood fantasies ... Betty says all that really ended six years ago, when her husband left her for Linda Kolkena, a younger woman he eventually married.'[19] The different tacks taken by each article are exemplified by their contextualization of one of Betty's commonly reprinted claims. Wallace reports in the *Times*:

Suddenly, Betty says, 'I wasn't Mrs. Anything.' She had a house, a car, a closet full of $8,000 ball gowns and $2,000 outfits. A long-legged, slender 38-year-old, she was receiving $9,036 a month, tax free from Dan. She had a teaching credential, a real estate license and plenty of friends.[20]

The same quote appears in the *Journal*:

As the battle wore on, Betty felt adrift. Suddenly, she said, 'I wasn't Mrs. Anything.' Some of her friends advised her to let go, to get on with her life. But Betty felt she had no life to get on with. She had lost her husband, her children, her house, many of her friends and her position in the community. And the legal wars weren't over.[21]

The Wallace article uses Betty's self-reflection as an opportunity to enumerate her assets (particularly material possessions) and undermine her point of view. The *Journal* article, in contrast, takes the occasion to identify with Betty and detail her losses. In a later *Journal* article on killers in the news, 'The Devil Inside', Broderick ('out of control, at the end of [her] rope') gets taken up as the killer with whom readers are most likely to identify, reinforcing the characterization established in the earlier profile of Broderick as 'driven' to kill by circumstance.[22]

Another women's magazine, *Mirabella*, takes perhaps the most progressive, but also the most glib approach of the magazines I examined. It sets up Broderick's story with the tag, 'If you kind of liked Jean Harris, you'll love Betty Broderick'; first trial jury member Walter Polk's widely quoted question, 'What took her so long?' appears on the magazine's cover. This somewhat flippant attitude continues in the article, but its author also takes Betty at her word, focuses on Dan's legal abuses, and places Betty in the paradigm of 'women who fight back'. She even quotes a legal expert who is optimistic about the possibility that Broderick's second trial might lead to an acquittal. While Wallace focuses on the opulence of the Brodericks' lifestyle and implies that Dan left Betty with plenty of money of her own, *Mirabella* does not find Betty's standard of living after the divorce particularly lavish.

This might not be surprising, given upscale *Mirabella*'s target audience; however, a booklet entitled *Crimes of Passion* put out by 'Globe Mini-Mag' takes a similar stance.[23] The 99-cent 'Mini-Mag' is found at the checkout counter of the supermarket, tucked in with astrological guides and *Thin Thighs in Thirty Days*. Neither article presents Betty's alimony as an extremely generous portion of Dan Broderick's monthly income of over $100,000. Susan Lehman writes in *Mirabella* that Betty's lawyers figured that, after taking care of her debts, 'she'd have just $843.00 of the $16,000.00 left each month;' the 'Mini-Mag' states that Broderick's property settlement provided her with 'only a small fraction of Dan's earnings'.[24] Moreover, the Globe publication is taken aback at Linda's salary: 'The bubbling cauldron of love gone sour spilled over after Dan hired Linda as his legal assistant at an eye-popping $30,000 a year.'[25]

At this point, it cannot go unnoticed that Wallace's *Times* article is the only text we have been examining that is not marketed explicitly to women.[26] How exactly this might figure into each construction of the Betty Broderick story is difficult to say, but it does seem to be the case that the women's magazines – regardless of market – attempt to be more sympathetic to Broderick's position and to engage some of the larger issues raised by her story.[27] We can thus read the women's magazine construction of Betty Broderick as a particular configuration that collectively presents a picture of Broderick which is by no means unified, but which *does* stand in opposition to non-gender specific accounts such as Wallace's. Susan Ohmer contends that 'women's magazines can be viewed as a mediating force in American culture, a relay system that transmits ideas and images between the public and private spheres.'[28] It is this space between the public and private sphere that seems to be the very place in which the creation of a non-pathologizing reading of Betty Broderick is allowed. That is to say, if a certain account does not portray Broderick as a manipulative psychopath and menace to society, it is only because her experience in the private sphere (as a mother, as a wife who put her husband's career ahead of her own, as a woman over 30 who was left for a younger woman) is considered in relation to her actions in the public sphere (as a citizen accused of murder). This sensitivity is imbued with a more radical critique of culture, one which suggests that a fair and equitable society would place a political value on what happens in private.

When a 12-person jury could not be convinced of a unified, coherent story that established what happened and who was responsible for it after listening to an entire month of testimony, the difficulty of creating a two-hour linear narrative for television that will air to almost 30 million people is understandable. However, if as Bryna Taubman asserts in her 'True

Crime' novel *Hell Hath No Fury*, 'the problem with the prosecution's argument for the first degree murder was its lack of inner logic. The cold-blooded, materialistic, greedy woman described by the state's witnesses would not have deliberately killed the man providing her with nearly $200,000 a year,' we must ask ourselves: why is it that *this* Betty Broderick is brought to life on TV?[29]

A Woman Scorned: The Betty Broderick Story

Having examined the sources outlined above, we can begin to get a sense of the Betty Broderick stories – not one, monolithic 'true' story, but a nexus of polyvalent texts, sometimes overlapping, sometimes contradictory, which nevertheless support each other.[30] We have noted that the women's magazines significantly differ from Wallace's *Times* article, yet there is no reason to think that these sources reached only their target markets and did not interact with each other (that is, that men did not read or hear talk of the articles in women's magazines, or that women did not read the newspapers; that only well-off women read *Mirabella*, or that only low-income women read *Crimes of Passion*). We can assume that sources were variously consumed, sometimes in conjunction with each other, in diverse contexts.[31] Thus we are able to posit a relationship of 'family resemblance' between the various Betty Broderick stories. It is not that each of the stories shares a particular (essential) fact or characterization, but that together they constitute a body of texts that are 'similar'. In constructing a Betty Broderick 'mega-text' that includes the entire 'family' of stories, we create a standard against which we can compare the made-for-TV movie. By isolating the events that occur only in the made-for-TV movie and noting where the portrayals of key incidents seem to vary significantly from other accounts in tone or emphasis, we can begin to see the ways in which it is distinct.

The following details or characterizations are a sampling of those which are unique to the television version of *A Woman Scorned*:

> *Dan is a Cub Scout Leader for his son Grant's[32] Scout troop*
> *Dan buys Betty an expensive ring for Christmas. She throws it in his face because it is not the one she wanted: 'It's not what I asked for and that makes it a piece of crap.'*
> *Dan comes home one night to find his youngest son Grant (about age six or seven in the movie) waiting alone on his front steps.*

Betty is seen talking to the media in her home.

Betty enters Dan's home and sits under the Christmas tree. She rips apart a present and slaps Katie, who tries to intercept her.

Betty's bedroom is covered with clippings of society reports of Dan and Linda's relationship.

Dan and Linda help coach a child's soccer team. Betty looms on a nearby hill.

How might we characterize these idiosyncrasies?

Dan is played up as a family man, while these scenes of Betty reinforce her character as ungrateful, histrionic and violent. These characterizations are not simply more sensational than others; the TV version does not dig up the worst 'dirt'. For example, a drunken Dan ducking DWI (driving while intoxicated) tickets, flopping around on the floor like an alligator, kicking the dog, and Betty's birthday suicide attempt, would certainly have added to the sordid character of the story.[33] Instead, the majority of potentially sensational details that have been omitted are those which might lend sympathy to Betty, while those that have been added serve to buttress Dan's identity as a solid citizen and caring family man.

In addition to this, a few 'facts' have also been altered. The Broderick children, for example, are all closer in age and younger than they were in real life, and the entire show takes on the shape of a single calendar year (St Patrick's Day, summer, Thanksgiving, Christmas, high school graduation) rather than the more than six years that stretched between the beginning of Dan's affair and the murders. Several figures are totally absent, such as the various governesses Dan Broderick hired to help care for the children while they lived with him. A citizens' group which provided much support for Betty, HALT (Help Abolish Legal Tyranny), is also not figured in the movie.

A Woman Scorned implicitly plays on its audience's knowledge of specific details from media reports on the real Brodericks by including particulars that do not work to advance the plot or add narrative meaning in any way. Betty's 'LODEMUP' licence plate, Dan and Linda's Notre Dame sweatshirts, and the attempted reproduction of the Broderick's actual (and widely published) wedding photo all play on extra-textual knowledge about media reporting of the real story. For this reason, details that can be read as *reversals* of reports in other sources are of particular interest. For example, Bryna Taubman writes:

'When I was brought into the Broderick family,' Betty testified, 'Larry Broderick said to me, "Now you're a yuck!" And I said, "What's a yuck?" He said, "It's too low to kick and too wet to step on." That's what they called their sisters, the yucks.'[34]

In contrast, *A Woman Scorned* shows Betty, pacing back and forth, proclaiming into a cellular phone, 'You're just a slug in a fancy suit, Dan. Too low to kick and too wet to step on.'

Multiple articles describe Linda as looking very much like Betty at the same age, a fact well supported by photographs. The casting of the two actresses in *A Woman Scorned* does not reflect this similarity, and the narrative actually distorts it. One incident is particularly telling: in real-life, Linda sent Betty ads for weight loss products and wrinkle cream, as well as a photo of Dan and Linda at the Blackstone Ball with the caption 'Eat your heart out, Bitch;' in *A Woman Scorned*, Linda finds a card with two photos – one of Dan and Linda, and one of Dan and Betty – 'Don't we look alike?' is written across the bottom in Betty's handwriting. This reverses the identity of the mean-spirited and obsessive woman guilty of assembling and sending vindictive mail. Thus Betty's card, 'Don't we look alike?' capitalizes on the fact that the real Linda did in fact bear a remarkable resemblance to the young Betty, but in the context of the movie this only serves to make the Betty character seem narcissistic (Linda looks like *her*) and obsessed (her bedroom is covered with Dan and Linda memorabilia). It also erases any evidence of Dan's penchant for young, slim blondes. Further, Betty's experience of aging is minimized by the fact that her 'self-improvement' efforts to grow her hair long and fix a cracked tooth are absent from the TV narrative. The movie does not display any awareness of the discourse around women's self-esteem, or body image as it relates to weight or aging (something that the women's magazines all acknowledge to some extent).

Perhaps most disturbing is the way in which the events of the night of the murder are figured so as to work against a verdict of second-degree murder or manslaughter. Betty goes directly to the house, enters through the main bedroom door, comes completely into the room and shoots without anyone yelling. All of these factors contribute to the notion that Betty had formed intent, the key element in the crime of first-degree murder. During the trial there was much debate over whether or not Betty wrapped the cord around the phone after she pulled it out of the wall. Wrapping the cord while Dan choked on his own blood suggests premeditated cruelty, while pulling and fleeing suggests a frantic rush, and allows for the possibility that Broderick's contention that she did not know her victims had actually been hit was true. In court, it was established that the cord was not wrapped around the phone. In *A Woman Scorned*, however, not only does Betty wrap the cord, she *takes the phone with her* when she flees the house. Finally, Betty is seen at a pay phone, stating 'I finally shot the son-of-a-bitch,' although the first person Betty called testified that '"I need help" were the first words [she] heard.'[35] The made-for-TV movie essentially indicts Broderick of a crime of which two juries found her not guilty.

Also contributing to this verdict is the cause-and-effect narrative of the movie. Dan's restraining order follows on the heels of Betty's vandalism, and the lunch when Dan announces he wants a divorce follows Betty's hysterical refusal of his Christmas present. The placement of commercial breaks during the program also reinforces the idea that Dan is always reacting to Betty's active (negative) behavior: blocks of action are created where Betty does something extreme, the family gets upset, and Dan reacts calmly and punishes her. Despite Baxter's occasional voice-over, any enunciative power the Betty character might have is undermined by the fact that we are not encouraged to identify with her. We are thus positioned more voyeuristically (looking at Betty and the spectacles she creates) than subjectively (seeing 'with' her, from her point of view).

It is not that all murder is unsanctionable in popular culture. This is clearly not the case, as many examples attest – Francine Hughes included. But the cultural status of Broderick's crime, 'fighting back' against an *emotionally* abusive husband, is tentative and contested. If Francine Hughes' murder of her husband is sanctioned because 'her motives were familial … [s]he acted as a mother,' Broderick is not let off the hook so easily.[36] *A Woman Scorned* goes to considerable lengths to discredit her abilities as a mother, presenting a relationship with her children based primarily on domination and manipulation, and showing us children who both dislike and fear their mother. Unlike mother Francine Hughes, Broderick is, above all else it would seem, a murderer.

Although during the trial it was established that Betty's two youngest sons wanted to live with her rather than their father, *A Woman Scorned* suggests that her children were essentially happy with the custody arrangement. This disparity is perhaps most poignantly revealed in the scene when Betty speaks with Grant (the youngest son) on the phone. He is extremely upset and crying over the fact that Betty keeps leaving obscene messages on the answering machine. This conversation is based on a lengthy, dramatic tape of a telephone call between Danny (the eldest son) and Betty that was heard in court. *A Woman Scorned* includes dialogue about the son's discomfort with his mother's language, and concern that she is upsetting everyone, but it omits the dialogue (from the trial tape) that suggests his desire to live with his mother. For example:

> [sobbing] Well … we don't even know what you sound like or look like if you keep saying those stupid bad words.
> … he's not going to let us come over there – ever, so you'd better stop doing it or you're just going to make your whole family mad at you – everybody who wants to come over there.
> … We want to live with you, but you're just making it harder for all of us that want to live over there.[37]

By omitting this aspect of the conversation, *A Woman Scorned* is able to assert that Betty's children would actually be better off without her, and that she has failed at the only real goal she professes for herself.[38]

On *The Oprah Winfrey Show*, Maggie Kolkena-Seats, Linda Kolkena's sister, described Betty Broderick in the following way: 'It's such a myth that she was a loving wife and mother … these poor kids were torn in half and she continues to proclaim what a wonderful mother she was. And that offends me because I consider myself a very good mother.'[39] Not surprisingly, Kolkena-Seats' definition of 'a very good mother' does not include a mother who kills the father of her children, but it is curious that she is 'offended' by this claim. Later in Kolkena-Seats' discussion, the idea that Betty Broderick is offensive in other ways becomes more clear: 'She had such a foul, trash mouth. She never referred to Linda – Linda was always a four-letter word beginning with the letter C.'[40]

Betty's habit of referring to Linda almost exclusively as 'the cunt' and Dan as 'the fuckhead' is often alluded to in narratives of the case. She left obscene messages on Dan's answering machine in response to the terse legalese in which all of his communications to her were written, and his decision to call the police any time she attempted to speak to him in person. She slashed out his name in the divorce papers and wrote in 'God'; she slyly re-defined words, referring to Dan's bifurcation order, a legal divorce without a property settlement, as 'a bifornication order: it's a way to legally fuck your wife and your girlfriend at the same time.'[41] Her response to the official, public, channels of communication (legal documents, law enforcement) was a vulgar, bodily – sexualized, even pornographic – language. But whereas in other accounts this language is construed as reasonable and intelligent – even funny – in *A Woman Scorned*, it is merely offensive.

In the construction of Betty Broderick on TV we find a mother who is contemptible, a mother whose vulgar language and selfish actions affront her children, her community, and the pastel landscape against which she is placed. These processes of inclusion, omission, refiguration and characterization overwhelmingly contribute to what can only be described as a gleefully misogynist construction of the Betty Broderick character. Her more famous deeds – driving her Suburban into the front of Dan's house, trashing his bedroom, leaving obscene messages on his answering machine – are presented, but without the context of a husband who leaves his family for another woman, commits his wife to a mental institution (and sends her the bill), to name but a few omissions, she comes off as not only extreme, but unprovoked. It is Betty Broderick who disrupts orderly suburbia, and who becomes increasingly isolated, violent – and ultimately punished.

Women Who Kill and the Made-for-TV Movie

The history of made-for-TV movies suggests the possibility of treating women sympathetically, of not punishing them for 'fighting back' against their oppressors – be they husbands, fathers, or the 'system' itself. Yet it is clear that the real woman who kills presents a problem for television dramatization. In the case of Betty Broderick, as with Amy Fisher or Aileen Wuornos, a TV movie that would resolve 'the conflicts and contradictions within families and between family values and those of capitalism in ways that the real world does not in fact allow' would mean divorcing the TV narrative from the facts of the real case.[42] And the real 'resolution of the contradictions' – in Betty Broderick's story, the double murder – cannot be represented as an appropriate response to this conflict. In an article written in 1985, Elaine Rapping claims: 'TV raises and resolves issues. It offers guidance, models and hope. Life makes sense, follows a neat path from crisis to resolution, even if the world it creates is emotionally flattened and intellectually and politically simplistic.'[43] This is the point where the most progressive and most conservative elements of the telefeature narrative come together. On the one hand, TV may represent women's difficulties in negotiating the private and public spheres. The representation of women's struggles within society is a relatively progressive thing in the face of the possibility (and the long history) of not dealing with women's experiences at all. On the other hand, since the TV movie asserts that all the structures necessary to effect a happy ending are already in place, it reinforces the sense that larger social action is unnecessary. 'Its real concerns … are not so much our problems themselves as the need to convince us of where to seek help, and how much we can reasonably expect to get.'[44] This leads us to the most problematic aspect of A Woman Scorned as a telefeature.

If made-for-TV movies are meant to deal with social issues and problems, albeit it in a facile, politically inert way, where is the problem in The Betty Broderick Story? What social ill has its significant action displaced onto the private realm? The obvious potential choices are not made. One could tell the story of a woman abused by the legal system, for example, denied a fair divorce hearing and a fair murder trial, supported by HALT, and continuing her fight from behind bars. The issues of 'white collar domestic violence' or even gun control could also be explored. Given these possible social problems, the Betty Broderick story could take on the traditional shape of the woman-in-jeopardy genre. This possibility is blocked, however, by the story's origin in reality. The real story points precisely to the impossibility of negotiating the conflicts experienced by women within the system as it stands. To validate Broderick's murdering, or to suggest that larger social change is necessary in order to avoid similar 'conflicts' in the future, is a radical message unsupportable by the genre. The extremely divided or profoundly ambivalent reaction in the media to the real Broderick trial is at odds with the narrative requirements of the made-for-TV movie. The facts of the real case block the reliable liberal happy ending for TV women-in-jeopardy – that a smart lawyer and a level-headed, sympathetic jury validate her experiences and enable her to go unpunished (as happened to fictional husband-killers on L.A. Law and The Young and the Restless around the same time as the Broderick made-for-TV movie). On television, triumph is simply a matter of finding a right-minded pro-bono lawyer to argue your case in court, or the appropriate support group to bring media attention to your cause. Faced with having to decide between backing the liberal legal framework, the great hero of women-in-jeopardy genre, or a woman who feels victimized by the law, A Woman Scorned chooses to support the law.

Conclusion

The Betty Broderick character in *A Woman Scorned* exists in a complex media space surrounded by TV news, women's magazines, prime-time melodramas and true-crime shows. For this reason it is extremely difficult to suggest how *A Woman Scorned* is taken up by audiences. It taps into talk show chat, the latest episode of *Knots Landing*, *L.A. Law*, or the evening news in some very complicated ways. And while it is highly over-simplistic to suggest that people's notions of right and wrong are *construct-ed* by television programming, the notion that TV might play an intercessor role in mainstreaming new ways of thinking about cultural phenomena such as women who kill is not outrageous. TV certainly constructs *itself* in this way: many television shows are suggested as family viewing, intended to promote discussion about difficult issues such as incest, eating disorders, child abduction, drug abuse and domestic violence. *Soap Opera Digest* now gives an award for 'Best Social Issue Storyline', and some programs include helpline numbers and the names of helpful organizations. A CBS sequel to *A Woman Scorned*, *Her Final Fury: Betty Broderick the Last Chapter*, commenced with a voice-over asking viewers to 'see it all and decide for yourself,' and was followed on ABC by two days of Broderick coverage on *The Oprah Winfrey Show* (including a visit to Betty in prison and interviews with her children). TV is also often championed by feminist critics as a potential forum for progressive discourse around a variety of women's issues. But the Betty Broderick story exists beyond the line where television's hospitality ends. Television's manifestation of a 'Betty-backlash' seems to point to televisual culture's inability to respect the complexity of real life, and to endorse real social change.

I have been following the Broderick case for years, and yet, in my final analysis, I feel my mother first said it best. 'Oh ... *that*,' she responded wearily when I asked her if she had watched *A Woman Scorned*. 'That was ...' she searched for the appropriately descriptive words, '*not* a good show.' After investigating how the Betty Broderick story was taken up by the news, women's magazines and television, and considering its relation to the made-for-TV movie, I think this sums up my conclusions quite well: *A Woman Scorned* is emblematic of the most cynical and misogynist aspects of television programming today.

I do not wish to locate a true Betty Broderick story, or to suggest improvements for those that are extant. I do not wish to end on a prescrip-tive note at all. Rather, I would like to suggest a cautionary one. Instead of trying to focus our energy and resources on discovering how-to-build-a-better-Betty-Broderick-story, I would suggest that we need to be wary of television's seemingly insatiable appetite for real-life which eats up the experiences of real women and spits them out in its own co-opted, pathologized form. Any sites of negotiation these narratives might open up can be easily closed, critiquing not the system, but the women that it fails. A *Woman Scorned* stands in opposition to other texts found in women's magazines, supermarket pamphlets and pulp fiction: it is less complicated, more distanced, and decidedly more anti-feminist. Even studying texts critically, it is easy to get caught up in the giddy, freakish nature of television characters. And in a world where literary studies debates the ethics of representing other people's unique experiences, it might seem surprising that we allow television to speak for anyone, and that we are satisfied with the timbre of that voice. Such is its allure, or our supposition that it doesn't matter anyway – 'it's only TV'. But sometimes reality intrudes.

My mother's calm concern and dead-pan generosity temper the heady exuberance with which I report that Betty Broderick has phoned me: 'Is she okay in there? Does she have enough to do? Should I send her some knitting patterns?' My mother reminds me that there is a real woman spending at least 19 years in a Northern California prison, and that her story has yet to be told.

VICTIMLESS CRIMES AND CRIMELESS VICTIMS:

Lindy Chamberlain and Fairlie Arrow

Helen Yeates

Visibility and credibility have always been problematic for the voiceless in our society. Women have suffered taken-for-granted invisibility and incredibility before a male-dominated and defined legal system, as well as in the mass media. Traditionally, the media silence, distort or trivialize women's voices, in ways similar to women's experience with the law. Where women are visible before the law they are often seen in relation to violent crime, either as hapless victims needing men to rescue them, or as deadly perpetrators, guilty of unspeakable crimes, usually against men.[1] At both extremes, innocent or guilty, victim or perpetrator, women are often inscribed in our cultural texts as unreliable, this essentializing attribute tending to inform and colour our general views of women in popular culture. It will be argued here that there exists an inverse relationship between exposure and reliability: the more exposure to the law and the media a woman has, the less reliable she appears to become in the eyes of the community.

Two supposedly unreliable Australian women, Lindy Chamberlain and Fairlie Arrow, have reached a considerable level of media saturation because of their involvement in 'criminal' activities. After the death of her baby daughter Azaria in August, 1980, Chamberlain was charged with murder, found guilty and jailed in 1982; she was subsequently released after some evidence came to light in 1986, but has been fighting to clear her name in the face of public scepticism ever since. This case could be said to revolve around the issue of whether Chamberlain, called in some quarters an 'evil angel' and a 'witch', is, in actuality, a crimeless victim. For nearly two decades Chamberlain has received a veritable glut of media exposure, and her credibility has often been called into question.[2]

On the other hand, Fairlie Arrow's self-abduction hoax gained media attention on and off for barely 12 months in the Australian media in the early 1990s. Her crime, which took the form of an escapade staged for media attention, could be termed a 'victimless crime'. Despite the comparative brevity of her media exposure, this woman has also entered Australian mythology about women and their unreliability.

Television and other popular media (magazines, newspapers) play a significant role in constructing such pervasive myths about gender and crime, and where such women stand on the cultural credibility spectrum. Both of them mothers, Chamberlain and Arrow are painted as anything but credible and angelic by a media and legal system out for virtual revenge against such transgressive women.

Fairlie Arrow: A Flight from Reality

In December, 1991, when the media spotlight focused on Fairlie Arrow, an unknown Australian nightclub singer, the crucial issue of the vexed relationship between women, crime, the legal system and the media was glaringly raised. Arrow was convicted of making a false complaint to police in relation to an elaborately faked abduction. Her dramatic 'disappearance', bondage and supposed attempted murder by an obsessed male stalker had caused widespread concern in the community. When exposed as a fraud, she claimed in the local press that she only wanted to alert the police to her plight as a potential victim, having been hounded by a 'demented and infatuated fan' for some time.[3] Arrow was fined $23,000 for her actions. She was also fined an extra $600 as a result of striking a lawyer after her trial, allegedly because he called her a 'femme fatale' and 'a slut'.[4] For a considerable period of time between December 1991 and September 1992, she gained much media attention including front-page coverage and stories occasionally leading the nightly television news. The saga proceeded in a rather bizarre fashion; for instance, the balance of her repayment of police expenses (about $18,500) was overdue because, crying poor, she claimed she had to outfit herself expensively for a series of *Penthouse* photographs in various stages of undress.[5] While she technically committed a 'victimless crime', with herself as the mythic victim, the duped public did in a sense become the victim, as well as, it was argued in the media, genuine crime victims who may have suffered while her hoax wasted the time and resources of the police.

At first glance, it would seem that Fairlie Arrow profited both personally and professionally through her self-abduction and attempted murder hoax, namely by posing for the *Penthouse* photographs (August, 1992) and by signing a recording contract in the US: 'The notoriety will certainly help sell albums in Australia, and if she gets big in America ... the stuff from Australia will obviously leak out.'[6] On the other hand, a subsequent print media report claimed sardonically that she had 'had her singing career in this country destroyed by the media' and that a Fairlie Arrow tour of Queensland was scheduled, called 'Tak'n for Ransom', presumably to compensate for this.[7] She had admitted her guilt regarding the hoax, but, despite her admission, the flighty Arrow suffered an acute credibility crisis. In the eye of her self-created crime/media storm, she was excessively visible for a time. This ambivalent relationship between credibility and visibility may be understood more clearly through a closer analysis of some of the television coverage she was given.

Hard Copy was a tabloid-style weekly programme on Australian commercial television in the early nineties, a carbon-copy of the US version. Armed with a craggy-faced anchorperson who looked like he had just stepped out of a boxing ring, the programme had a typically strong masculine style, hard-hitting and pulling no punches. One *Hard Copy* television report (25 June, 1992) gave an unsympathetic, damning summary of the Fairlie Arrow case. Appearing to revel in the exposure of Arrow as a total fraud, the disdainful female interviewer asked, with very arched eyebrows, how Fairlie felt about her stunt, and how she could now be believed by anyone. Fairlie's persona was constructed in the segment as the embodiment of unreliability and greed, and her inane and often contradictory answers to similar questions underlined this impression.

The report showed her singing sexy adult songs with her toddler son present. To highlight her apparent inappropriateness as a mother, the producers of the show intercut revealing stills from the (then) forthcoming *Penthouse*, in which she posed in a most unmotherly fashion. Thus Arrow's maternity and sexuality sat in unresolved and uneasy conflict with each other within the television frame. The programme's construction of Arrow was of a mother resistant to traditional ideals of selfless, reliable motherhood. While this may be read as an ironic, liberatory discourse for women, the programme undercut Arrow's unruly spirit by reinforcing sexist notions of female sexuality and the woman's body on available display. Significantly, the contradictory facets – resistant, liberated mother, scheming, reactionary hoaxer, and willing toygirl – combined to exaggerate her flagrant inauthenticity.[8] In sum, the *Hard Copy* television report was a sensationalist production with a tough masculine ideology, reinforced by the female interviewer who morally and physically distanced herself from Fairlie Arrow. This case underlines the intensely gendered nature of television regarding ways that women may represent themselves or be represented.[9]

Arrow's *Penthouse* magazine spread, coyly shown in the television report, was entitled 'Fairlie Nude! The naked truth about Fairlie Arrow.' The photographs depicted her as a cavorting bondage slave, displaying her body in various stages of undress, along with pasted-up media references to her self-abduction. This soft porn revelled in such stereotypes as woman as temptress and trickster, as well as mere body. The conflation of sex and violence was also a significant element in the *Penthouse* spread.

Arrow's very few minutes of celebrity may therefore be read as an anti-feminist event, as such media exposure of Arrow merely heightened dominant masculine values about feminine shallowness and pretence, as well as the titillating promotion of bondage itself as sexually exciting. Such a feminist reading of Arrow's media representations would deem that her self-abduction hoax involved serious regressive behaviour. For the ostensibly frivolous, selfish reasons of promoting her singing career, she set herself up as a victim of an abhorrent crime, one which has multiple resonances for women everywhere.[10] Like the 'boy who cried wolf', Arrow's mediated voice rebounds on itself, losing authentic resonance. More seriously, the implication is that women kidnapped from now on will have to 'pump up the volume', so to speak, and somehow reclaim both the right to be heard and the credibility gap caused by this case.

Women have always had to substantiate their claims regarding violent crime such as rape, which has often been seen by police and the wider society as either the woman's fault – she 'asked for it', or as a 'figment of her imagination'.[11] Therefore, the media's construction of Arrow's own irresponsible 'flight' of imagination may rebound against herself and against other women. Although Arrow has not spent time in prison, her hoax and its subsequent media coverage did, in a sense, help condemn future vulnerable women to another heinous form of cultural prison: that of further doubt, suspicion and questionable authenticity. Predictably, the Australian media gave no space to feminist voices concerned about the ramifications of Arrow's case for women. In the *Hard Copy* television report, the event was packaged as a snide, incredulous 'blonde-bimbo-strikes-again' story.

A subsequent case in Britain showed that the 'Fairlie Arrow effect' had negative and unexpected consequences there. Exactly a year to the day after the Arrow debacle in Australia, a copycat hoax was committed in Britain by a woman called Joanna Grenside.[12] At first vehemently denying any link, Grenside eventually confessed to copying Arrow, although her own motive was unclear. According to one media report, Arrow herself helpfully told the British media: 'The coincidences between what I did and this affair in England are too great to miss.'[13]

Curiously, these antics could be seen to turn such powerful abduction fictions as *The Collector* and *The Silence of the Lambs* virtually on their heads. Females are actually plotting and enacting their own pseudo-savage kidnappings, victimizing themselves within nightmare self-abduction scenarios. These women construct themselves as a very special kind of victim for a few exaltant moments of empowerment over the law and the media, risking their freedom and laying their credibility decidedly on the line.

Feminism and Fairlie – Another Way of Seeing
An alternative, more sympathetic feminist reading of the way the Arrow case has been articulated by the media raises interesting questions about this victim-within-a-victim conjuring trick, as well as the nature of victimless crime. From all reports, the extensive media exposure appeared to increase Arrow's earning capacity, and the old adage that 'any publicity is good publicity' certainly seemed to be true for Fairlie Arrow. However, at the same time her body image was appropriated and exploited by the media because of its commodity value.

The creator of a media event soon turned into the creature formed by it, and Arrow became the sado-masochistic fantasy victim of countless voyeurs. Thus, another way of arguing the Fairlie case is this: the entertainment industry may well have been a sexist jungle for her; in order to increase her career value, she thought she had to go through this media charade. At this juncture, however, a certain kind of cynical cross-appropriation occurred: who, after all, was running the charade? The *Hard Copy* pictures merely affirmed the silliness of a female trickster, and the *Penthouse* photographs remain male trophies rather than any kind of real triumph (apart from, perhaps, an economic one) for Arrow.

From this perspective the media have exploited her, treating her merely as a bizarre self-promotist, and, in the *Hard Copy* report, as a 'problem' (because sexy) mother. She exploited the media in the first instance to gain attention and a career opportunity. But perhaps the earlier press reports were actually true; perhaps she had been hounded by a demented fan and her hoax was an actual, if unorthodox, cry for help. This original claim was glossed over subsequently and given no credence by the media.

Once she was exposed and punished, the media counter-exploited her; the *Hard Copy* report stands accused on this point. For instance, the grating tone of the female voice-over asserts, 'She's sure got a well-developed [pause] sense of humour.' This sexist comment was made immediately after footage of Fairlie baring her breasts for Penthouse. Indeed, this case is quite a potent example of the self-reflexivity of mainstream, male-centred television, with in this instance the obvious complicity of a female presenter. The media do not take kindly to someone (let alone a woman) who has duped them and/or made them look foolish. It seems they want to construct their own realities, not someone else's. Once Arrow's scam was exposed, an excessive media punishment ensued, particularly on television. Any fragile authenticity she may have had initially (the 'demented fan' story) was blown away by her intense visibility in the media as a figure of ridicule.

For instance, on one local television magazine programme, *Brisbane Extra*, a piece featured the staging of the kidnap and bondage of a Fairlie 'garden gnome', further trivializing the case. A national television comedy show, *Fast Forward*, also featured a satirical sketch about her escapade, while the national radio station Triple J mocked Arrow's assault of the lawyer by announcing 'National Slap-a-Lawyer Day'. Fairlie's self-sought publicity multiplied in media forms which she certainly did not plan.

In effect, the cheated media could only reinstate their own credibility by destroying Arrow's public image. She did instigate further publicity through a rather extraordinary Fairlie Arrow self-abduction phone-in tape called *Fairlie Urgent*, where people could hear her justification of what happened. On the tape she claimed the tape was made to rebuild her flagging media credibility: 'Over the past six months my life has been made a public issue. It's about time the public had a chance to hear the facts without the fiction.' For legal reasons, apparently, this bid for authenticity was discontinued almost immediately it began.

Relating to the *Hard Copy* programme again, it could be argued that Arrow's particularly incorrigible form of self-parody (including the phone-in tape) did not fit comfortably into the narrow *Hard Copy* paradigm. Continually surprising the audience and the presenter by breaking out of that paradigm, Fairlie emerged as a self-styled character playing with what could be seen as an essentially fictional television genre – that is, current affairs.[14] She became a teasing chameleon within a televised fiction, in a sense out-manoeuvring the media by hijacking their agenda for a time and resisting closure. She shifted from the scheming hoaxer to the loving mother, to the naughty girl, the slick career singer, then to the bold woman trying to authenticate herself, and finally to the pert body on display. Perhaps she was all, or none, of these competing subjectivities. However, the result was that her very unorthodoxy meant she had to pay the vengeful media's price.

Despite the fact that the media and the legal system at the time asserted that Arrow acted beyond the limits of both the law and popular notions of decorum by committing her victimless crime, the hidden question is really about the quality of choices facing many women, and furthermore the definition of those choices. Even though her media-constructed images represent a blatant affirmation of hegemonic masculine values, they may actually be less harmful for women than more subtle, less obvious affirmations. The very showiness of the media's articulation of Arrow revealed and underlined the inherent power relationships when men look at women and place them in the frame. More clearly than other more conventional representations, therefore, the Arrow case articulates the spurious kinds of ladders of opportunity society permits women to climb, and the way the media render powerless an earthy, decidedly non-angelic woman whose main 'crime' is to play the media at their own often duplicitous game. Arrow's unruly kind of masquerade does not, however, give the female viewer the easy and obvious pleasure of identification and recognition.[15]

Lindy Chamberlain: A Fight for Authenticity

Lindy Chamberlain represents a different kind of challenge for any media analyst of the slippery category of transgressive-woman-as-criminal. Like Arrow, her cultural narrative resists closure, but in a different way. For years Lindy Chamberlain has endured, and more recently courted, the media spotlight. She has achieved far-reaching if ambiguous visibility and voice in all Western cultures, and in Australia, a country seemingly starved of icons, she has become a kind of celebrity.

In the early 1980s, Chamberlain was accused of the crime of infanticide, found guilty, sent to prison, and later acquitted because of the discovery of a baby's jacket and the discrediting of forensic evidence.[16] Nevertheless, she has never been fully pardoned, and a recent appeal (late 1995) failed to establish her and her 'accessory' husband Michael's complete innocence. She has always maintained that a dingo took and killed her nine-week-old baby, Azaria, whose body has never been found. A convincing reading of her case today is that she was the victim of a virulent campaign by legal instrumentalities to find her guilty at all costs, despite very dubious 'evidence', and that the notion of her guilt was mercilessly fanned by the media.[17] Thus, as argued earlier, in contrast to Arrow with her 'victimless crime' concoction, Chamberlain could be defined as a 'crimeless victim'. In the absence of a real crime, Chamberlain suffered the consequences of the bizarre, unspeakable imaginary crime that was committed and re-committed in the hostile, horrified minds of many people both in Australia and throughout the world.

A plethora of material has been published about Lindy Chamberlain, and the Lindy saga continues. She has been written about in academic articles across more than a decade;[18] represented in a multiplicity of newspapers and women's magazines; and her story was told again in the 1988 film based on the book of the same name, *Evil Angels* (released under the title *A Cry in the Dark* outside Australia), directed by Fred Schepisi.[19] Lindy Chamberlain has written her autobiography, and she has created art works for an exhibition. Apparently there is even an opera being penned. In a 'world exclusive', *Woman's Day* reported that Lindy, 'Australia's most notorious woman', was to marry again[20] and, in a subsequent issue, the same popular magazine gave us 'Lindy's lavish wedding spectacle'.[21] She appears (for hefty appearance fees these days) on national television at regular intervals. Thus she is still 'hot media property'.

With the tenth anniversary of the Chamberlain case (1990), the unrepentant media had a field day of reminiscences and self-justification. More recently, the media have been churning out gossipy stories of her glamorous, newly-reconstructed self, divorcing her husband, involvement in custody wrangles, and finding a new love. Dredging up an old myth about her toughness, at the time of her million-dollar compensation pay-out the Australian television reporter in the *Sixty Minutes* segment 'The Pay-Off' coolly asked her 'how hard she was' (the imputation being that she is 'cast iron', a phrase suggested in the interview). Further, she was quizzed on how she felt about the supposed statistical truth that one third of the Australian public still thinks that she committed the murder.[22] The subtext here is that her image (as presented by the media) was generally interpreted by the Australian public as hard and unfeeling, 'unnatural' for a mother at the time of the disappearance of her baby. At her subsequent trial, her cool self-presentation was interpreted as guilt. In the 1992 *Sixty Minutes* report, her on-camera discomfort was obvious, especially when asked very personal questions about the breakdown of her marriage and about the disappearance of baby Azaria. Although at this stage she had been acquitted and paid a generous compensation, the shadow of doubt continued to linger over this possibly evil mother who was now expressing her sexuality once more by falling in love with a younger man. Sex and motherhood do not sit well in the frame.

The film *Evil Angels* throws some light onto this televisual spectacle of the ensnared, doubted woman, plagued by questions about her sexuality and maternity. In the film the deliberate construction of Lindy as the 'misunderstood innocent' is, despite every effort seemingly to the contrary, beset by some equivocation and complexity. On the one hand we find the endorsement of a different, more conventional private 'motherliness' through the filmic construction of her intimate world, where she is shown as grieving and caring. Such an image works actively against the harsh media stereotypes Chamberlain has always endured. On the other hand, this sanctioned credibility is undercut by the apparent contradiction between her sexuality and maternity, both in the passionate bedroom scenes with her husband and, more significantly, when she is seen as the heavily pregnant woman-on-trial. Her sexual activity in the obvious form of her pregnancy is affirmed, this being especially offensive to those who thought of her as a killer mother. 'Good' mothers are not supposed to be killers, nor are they supposed to reveal their breasts in light, immodest summer dresses, as Lindy did daily at her trial. Lindy Chamberlain does emerge from the film as a believable, 'crimeless victim', yet the dark ambivalence is still there. She remains an 'incredible' woman in society's eyes partly because of the unresolved, visible dissonance between her sexuality and maternity.[23]

This dissonance is emphasized, for instance, in the *Sixty Minutes* report discussed here, and in the magazine report of her marriage to her 'American sweetheart'. Her three children (one of them born while she was in prison) are shown 'giving their mother away', but the sinister clouds of the 'dingo case' and further legal battles over child custody are still present in this portrait of (yet again) 'Australia's most notorious woman'.[24] With a surprising change of perspective, *Woman's Day* ran a story the following year that helps vindicate Lindy.[25] In this article, her son Reagan, now in his late teens, finally tells of his experiences on the fateful night. He claims to remember that the dingo 'walked on him' as he lay in the tent. The article points out that this could not be used in the court at the trial, as a four-year-old's evidence could not be corroborated. The article also discusses the fact that Lindy (now aged 46) wants another baby. Thus her problematic motherhood and sexuality are still under contentious scrutiny, even in an article claiming to give a new insight into her innocence.

It is important to note, however, that there has been a considerable shift recently in mainstream media representations of Lindy Chamberlain. For instance, after the loss of her appeal for a full pardon, a sympathetic front-page newspaper article attacks what is termed the 'Macho conspiracy against Lindy'. The male writer, McGregor, states that the vehement 'vendetta' against Chamberlain occurred largely because she was viewed as a feminist:

> The Territory [where the baby disappeared] is a macho, frontier society where the ambiance of menace and violence towards black women conditions attitudes to all women. They [the Northern Territory Government and legal system] couldn't cope with Mrs Chamberlain's intransigence and reacted with a smouldering resentment – as males have to feminists everywhere.[26]

Such a liberal view of her dilemma is a welcome shift, showing a more discerning reflection on the key issues involved in this complex case and representing a definite change in the tide of public opinion since, for instance, the 1992 *Sixty Minutes* programme. Chamberlain has had many prominent champions over the past bitter years, for instance film-maker Fred Schepisi, and it would seem that a more rational view of the case is finally prevailing, as the evidence for her innocence is reiterated time and again.

Increased Visibility and Decreased Credibility

To some observers, the Fairlie Arrow case discussed here may seem trivial and unworthy of critical analysis, a kind of low-life, low-culture embarrassment, best forgotten. There are no films, books or operas on the Fairlie Arrow saga. It was merely a minor hysterical ripple in the Australian media, encroaching rather extraordinarily on Britain as well with the engraving there of a copycat crime. The case does, however, raise questions about the nature and status of popular culture texts, and points to the paradox of the new kind of 'high' status within popular culture that Chamberlain has attained by being enshrined in film and books, as against Arrow's status as the ultimate post-modern media text – ephemeral, contradictory, unpredictable, superficial and flashy, a playful fabrication without explanation or closure, revelling in its 'authentic inauthenticity'.[27]

From another viewpoint, both the Arrow and the Chamberlain case reveal the ongoing problems of women's positioning within mainstream Western media. Both women have tried to gain a voice and redefine themselves by using the media: Arrow through an ultimately destructive escapade, and Chamberlain through a (relatively speaking) carefully orchestrated media exposure. Despite her efforts at control through staging press conferences and giving certain media outlets exclusive rights, Chamberlain's life has been turned into yet another sordid soap opera. The reality of Lindy as a strong woman wronged is being upheld now in some sympathetic media coverage, but the quashing of her appeal for total exoneration shows that she is still suffering a credibility problem in the legal realm.

Female reliability is therefore a passionately disputed terrain in relation to fundamental discourses in our culture, specifically motherhood, sexuality, and crime. As mothers and as sexual beings, Lindy Chamberlain and Fairlie Arrow were caricatured by the media, given the challenges posed by these women's unconventional maternity and their alleged links with crime. Lindy Chamberlain dared to become pregnant again when she was on trial for the murder of her newborn infant, and she had the baby in jail. Later, at the age of 46, she was still longing for another child. Fairlie Arrow was also constructed by the media as a deviant mother, whose sexuality is contentious in the sense that it also appears contradictory – untamable in its defiance of societal norms (mothers 'don't' pose for *Penthouse*) yet contained by the media (the framing of Arrow in *Hard Copy* and the soft-porn bondage poses in *Penthouse*).

Such women are placed in a state of siege with regard to the cumulative power of the media, whether they attempt personally to orchestrate their public image or not. While the Chamberlain case is obviously more weighty and resonant in the Australian 'collective imaginary' than the Arrow 'fly by night' case, both illustrate the cultural dilemma posed for women in gaining a credible voice in relation to crime and the media. Fairlie Arrow's fabricated crime and Lindy Chamberlain's imagined crime both had strong elements of horror and revulsion, an important issue confounding the credibility stakes of these two women.

Significantly, this study of gendered crime and the Australian media demonstrates that an inverse, profoundly gendered relationship exists between media exposure and authenticity. In other words, the more media coverage given to a woman under legalistic scrutiny, the less credibility she has. The media circus surrounding the Anita Hill case in the US, while different in its emphasis and concerns, also demonstrates this dilemma of a woman's word being doubted and contested on a grand public scale.[28] The thorny old question still needing to be addressed is how women in general may create their own identities and cultures, at the same time controlling the redefinition of themselves by media institutions, through the language of the media to heterogeneous audiences. In particular, women with both media and legal profiles urgently need that control in order to negotiate the pleasurable power of articulation for themselves. Visibility, credibility and even unruly notoriety will then be forged together in a new and positively mediated relationship.

RE-MEMBERING
JOHN BOBBITT:

Castration Anxiety, Male Hysteria, and the Phallus[1]

Laura Grindstaff and Martha McCaughey

Introduction: A Slice of Life
We begin by invoking two stories, one ancient, the other (post)modern. The first is the Egyptian myth of Isis and Osiris, summarized by Jean-Joseph Goux in a recent essay on the phallus and masculine identity:

> The god Osiris is killed by Typhon who dismembers his corpse into pieces which he then scatters in all directions. Osiris' faithful companion, Isis, patiently retrieves the fourteen pieces to reassemble and reanimate them. However, there is one part of Osiris' body which she cannot find: his virile member. To replace this missing piece which is irrevocably lost, Isis erects a simulacrum which she orders everyone to honor.[2]

As Goux observes, 'the myth thus presents itself as the justification of a rite: the exhibition of the phallus, which has become the object of a cult in temples and which is carried in procession during festivals.'[3] The phallus stands in for the missing penis, but is also something more. As a fabrication, an artifact, the phallus both simulates what's missing and renders it larger than life, a kind of cult object. More importantly for Goux, the myth demonstrates that the initial trial of dismemberment must first be endured in order for the male organ to transcend its material base – that is, the 'death' of the penis is essential to its subsequent resurrection as phallic signifier, sign of rationality, power, and cultural authority.

The second story takes place closer to home: Manassas, Virginia, 1993. In the early morning hours of June 23, John Bobbitt returned home to his wife Lorena after a night out drinking with a friend. Desiring sex, he woke her, allegedly raped her, and promptly fell asleep. Lorena Bobbitt then made American history by cutting off her husband's penis with a kitchen knife and throwing the severed organ away in a nearby vacant lot. Police recovered the organ (after Lorena herself notified them of its location) and surgeons spent nine hours re-attaching it to John. In subsequent months, the media reassembled and reanimated the incident in a frenzy of national and international coverage.

At first glance, there appear only superficial similarities between the myth of Isis and Osiris and the Bobbitt case. After all, John was no god, killed and chopped into pieces by a male rival, nor was Lorena the faithful companion who pays homage to her lover's missing member. By all accounts, the couple had a volatile and abusive union strained by financial and other hardships – hardly the stuff of which myths are made. But what link the two tales are the clarity and precision with which they dramatize the inextricable relationship between the organic penis and symbolic phallus, despite our culture's refusal to acknowledge this relationship, as well as the necessity of the penis' initial dis-membering to its subsequent re-membering as phallic substitute.

In the Bobbitt scenario, however, unlike the Egyptian myth, re-membering the phallus was not accomplished without a certain amount of struggle and contestation over the very concept of masculinity itself. Indeed, cultural tensions and anxieties over the definition of masculinity were central to media discourse in the year following the penis-severing incident.

More specifically, we are interested in the ways in which certain narratives in the media are symptomatic of social and psychic conflict around sexual difference, masculine identity, and heterosexual male privilege, and we use the concepts of castration anxiety, hysteria and the phallus as a framework for this discussion. The phallus supposedly soars 'free', its corporeal origins rigorously denied in modern social and religious doctrine. But the phallus is none the less haunted by the penis, a haunting in which psychoanalysis has played a most useful ghost-busting role.[4]

While American men may experience their concern over John Bobbitt's missing manhood as 'natural' and therefore 'innocent' (that is, divorced from issues of male sexual privilege), the great contribution of psycho-analysis is, as Jacqueline Rose suggests, to challenge the self-evidence and obviousness of everyday life and language.[5] A psychoanalytic approach sees certain external behaviors as symptomatic of underlying, unconscious psycho-sexual activity, activity which reveals not only the inscription of patriarchal relations and ideology but the *failures* of that inscription. According to Rose, this is what differentiates psychoanalysis from sociological accounts of gender: whereas the latter assumes that gender norms are successfully internalized, the basic premise and indeed starting-point of psychoanalysis is that they are not. Nor does psychoanalysis see such 'failure' as an aberration – rather, failure is constitutive of identity formation, something endlessly repeated and relived as part of the struggle to secure and maintain a stable sense of self.[6] More importantly for Rose, the recognition that resistance to 'normal' gender identity exists at the very heart of psychic life is what links psychoanalytic projects in crucial ways to feminist ones. Psychoanalysis becomes one of the few places in our culture where it is recognized as more than a fact of individual pathology that many women (and men) do not painlessly slip into their roles, if indeed they do at all.[7]

Because the sexes are positioned unequally in the cultural order, men and women exhibit psycho-sexual neuroses differently, and with different consequences. One of the lessons of feminist theorizing is that women are often constrained to act in the realm traditionally given them, that of the body (nature), while men, having greater authority, get to express themselves through speech and language (culture). At one level, the Bobbitt conflict and its media coverage illustrate this point well: Lorena's so-called 'hysterical' behavior, like that of Freud's Dora, was a bodily response to the sexual abuse of which she could not speak; male 'experts' and commentators then gave voice and meaning to her actions through societal institutions they still dominate, the popular media. At the same time, however, the intense media coverage of the Bobbitt case challenges any neat assumptions linking hysteria to women (while Freud did not deny that men could also qualify as hysterics, it was a label typically associated with women and, to a lesser degree, homosexuals). Indeed, we want to read the coverage itself as a form of straight male hysteria, one we call 'privileged hysteria', which, because of straight men's greater cultural authority, was primarily discursive and textual rather than bodily or somatic, and therefore never seen as neurotic or a form of 'acting out'.

This is not to say that in the wake of the Bobbitt case men did not somatize their anxieties about castration, both phallic (symbolic) and penile (actual). As we shall see, there were endless displays of such anxiety, and it was John Bobbitt himself who most clearly exposed what is at stake for feminists in this whole debate: the intimate connection of heterosexual masculine identity with the penis as the privileged signifier of sexual difference and naturalized male power. It was precisely because of this connection that Lorena's (literal) emasculation of her husband was conflated in media accounts with feminism's (metaphorical) emasculation of men. But since male privilege works in part by denying the relationship between penis and phallus, any aggressive behavior on the part of women which exposes and critiques this relationship tends to generate hostility toward women rather than toward the larger system of gender inequality.

Touted in the media as the ultimate example of 'male bashing', male hysteria over the Bobbitt case was not unlike that over the film *Thelma and Louise*; both illustrate a tired double standard where isolated cases of female aggression ('real' and Hollywood) are read as evidence of the routine victimization of white men rather than as rational responses to male oppression. This double standard highlights white men's greater power to voice their complaints in the media (while silencing women's), as well as their sense of entitlement to sexual invulnerability.

Coverage of the Bobbitt case also opened up a discussion among feminists over the subject of female victimhood, specifically whether the continued emphasis on women as victims of rape and abuse perpetuates a negative stereotype of women as passive, weak, helpless and masochistic. Lorena's 'sadistic' knife-wielding behavior seemed to contradict this stereotype; at this same time, her tearful courtroom testimony during the subsequent trial seemed to reinforce it. Either way, her acquittal on charges of malicious wounding was highly unusual, for aggressive women are typically punished more severely than aggressive men because their behavior violates normative standards of femininity. Thus, in order for a feminist critique of victimhood to make sense, cultural notions of proper feminine conduct must also be challenged.

We now turn to the media coverage of the event, which served as a synecdoche for already existing cultural tensions surrounding gender relations, and in particular the so-called battle of the sexes. Mass media accounts are of course interpretive and constitutive, not 'above' or 'outside' the events they describe, thus our aim is not to 'set the record straight' but to investigate with a critical eye the particular kinds of narratives that emerged.

Framing the Bobbitt Conflict

The Bobbitt case spawned numerous jokes, t-shirts, fodder for radio and TV talk shows, and over 1,600 news articles and opinion pieces throughout the US.[8] Of course, news is never just what's 'out there', but rather what someone deems important, the more unusual the better – especially when it comes to sex and violence. When Lorena Bobbitt severed her husband's penis, the bulk of media coverage centered on what men are most interested in: the status of John Bobbitt's John Thomas, including the length of the knife used to sever it, the length of time his manhood lay in a vacant field, the length of time needed to surgically re-attach it to him, and how long before he'd be able to do 'it' again. Even the several trenchant feminist analyses that appeared in the popular press mainly responded to a discourse initiated by men and reflecting men's concerns.

Most media accounts suggested that men and women nationwide seized upon the Bobbitt case as a symbol of the ongoing power struggle between the sexes, in part because Lorena Bobbitt did what many men supposedly fear and many women supposedly fantasize about. 'Fantasize' is the key word here, since actual incidents of penis-severing are extremely rare. Given Lorena's claim that *her* violence was in retaliation to *his*, some accounts even positioned the young woman as a feminist heroine. The following passage from the *Los Angeles Times* is illustrative: 'Overnight, the 24-year old manicurist became a heroine to a handful of feminists who took the dismemberment and unceremonious disposal as an exquisite revolutionary act on behalf of the abused women of the world.'[9] Similarly, Rush Limbaugh complained in a *Newsweek* editorial that 'those [feminists] who view all men as "potential rapists" have made Lorena into a symbol for the plight of battered women,'[10] while Peter Jennings of ABC's *World News Tonight* accused American feminists of using the Bobbitt case to 'advance their own agenda'[11] (as if educating the public about wife abuse is neither a legitimate response to the Bobbitt conflict nor an agenda worth advancing). Of course, it is possible to suggest that media professionals were the ones advancing their own agenda, for if Lorena's actions sparked a trend, it was not a rash of penis-cutting but a rash of talk shows and news articles which consistently used the Bobbitt affair as a convenient way to discredit feminism and reassert male sexual privilege.

Ironically, the few feminist intellectuals who expressed support for Lorena are precisely those feminists most likely to agree with Rush Limbaugh that women need to stop viewing all men as 'potential rapists' and to stop whining about how victimized they are. Katie Roiphe, for example, who believes that date rape is merely a charge feminists have invented so women can punish men for any regrettable sexual encounter,[12] approvingly called Lorena 'a symbol of female rage' in an Op-Ed piece for the *New York Times*.[13] The *New York Times* also printed an essay by an Australian feminist who described Mrs. Bobbitt as 'a symbol of innovative resistance against gender oppression everywhere', while the American Camille Paglia said that Lorena's cutting of her husband's penis sounded a 'wake-up call' to every man in the world, comparable in impact to the Boston Tea Party.[14]

However, most other feminist critics refused to frame the Bobbitt conflict in these terms. 'The universal feminist response I see reflected in the press', wrote Mim Udovich in the *Village Voice*, 'is one of guarded sympathy for Lorena Bobbitt as a rape victim, coupled with an unconditional disapproval of marital rape law and a conditional disapproval of penis-severing as a reasonable response to domestic violence'.[15] Robin Abcarian further insisted that 'to make Lorena Bobbitt into a symbol for anything other than a sick marriage between two, immature, angry people is to compromise the legitimacy that has finally been conferred on battered women who strike back in self-defense.'[16]

Feminists writing in the press also emphasized that Lorena's attempt to 'take back the night' is not the sort of politics feminists espouse; that Lorena Bobbitt is not another Anita Hill doing for marital rape what Hill did for sexual harassment; and, most importantly, that men's sexual violence against women (including genital mutilation) is unfortunately too commonplace to be newsworthy. As Cynthia Heimel wrote in *Newsweek*, quoting a friend: 'rapists are chopping off women's arms and getting out on parole two years later, and maybe it's covered once in the news. But let one woman touch one single penis and the whole country goes ballistic.'[17] Perhaps this friend was referring to Robert Keith Smith, who wrote a letter to *People* magazine complaining that 'being a male in America today is like being a Jew in Nazi Germany.'[18] Or maybe she read the *Los Angeles Times* article in which the director of a Virginia-based women's center said 'there is no justification for what she did. Her abuse of him was so barbaric that the fact she was allegedly abused is hardly an issue.'[19]

Thus, while many media accounts tended to sympathize with John Wayne Bobbitt and worry about women on the rampage, some feminists tried to refocus the debate around sexual violence in general, which is overwhelmingly male against female. Interestingly, feminist critiques of such violence were seen as either hostile and partisan or unnecessarily plaintive, while the national obsession with the sexual victimization of one man was framed as a nonpartisan, apolitical and entirely justified concern. Consider, for example, the confrontation between panelists on the *Maury Povich* show devoted to the Bobbitt conflict. The two 'resident feminists' on the panel, while not condoning Lorena's actions, nevertheless repeatedly tried to situate discussion of the Bobbitts within a larger social context in which male violence contributes significantly to women's oppression. When one of the feminists (Ann Siminton) pointed out that men commonly masturbate to pornographic images of female genital mutilation and nobody in the media objects, the 'resident psychologist' said, 'Here we go again! You are still on the political thing! Get off the politics! Be real!' A few moments later Siminton noted that women who kill their husbands tend to receive prison terms twice as long as men who kill their wives, and the psychologist gave a similar response, to considerable laughter and applause from the audience: 'Wind her up and you get the party line!' This man also got the last word when he said, 'this [case] is not about politics or vengeance; this is about sensitivity, sensitivity between men and women.' Thus the feminist insistence that we see the entire Bobbitt affair – John's alleged abuse of his wife, her violent retaliation, and the public response – within a larger context characterized by systemic gender inequality, was belittled as partisan and political, while the psychologist's insistence that we view John Bobbitt as an individual victim was framed as an apolitical matter of 'sensitivity' between the sexes.[20]

Isolated cases of female aggression tend to generate a climate of concerned debate about proper 'role models' for girls, the possibility of 'copycat crimes' and the ever-popular subject of 'male-bashing', which men's routine victimization of women does not. While feminists have consistently challenged male sexual violence, charges of 'male-bashing' imply that women's complaints about male aggression are just as victimizing as the systemic violence which produces the complaints in the first place. Of course, what discussions of male-bashing in newspapers, magazines and on television and radio talk shows reveal is that men still have privileged access to the media, and further, that female aggression is intolerable – especially when directed at a white man.

Violent Women: Villains and Victims

Q: What did Jeffrey Dahmer say to Lorena Bobbitt?
A: You gonna eat that?

This joke is remarkable for suggesting a likeness between Lorena Bobbitt and serial killer Jeffrey Dahmer (and their actions), while at the same time exposing *her* violence as relatively wimpy – what Lorena threw away in a vacant field, Dahmer would have considered a 'pièce de résistance'. On a talk radio program, host Joy Beher indirectly made this same point when she said, 'hey, she just threw it out, it's not like she put it in a Cuisinart.'[21]

Wimpy or not, some may argue that Lorena Bobbitt's acquittal on charges of malicious wounding in fact indicates a new social tolerance for female violence. But a closer look reveals that her courtroom behavior as a proper feminine subject helped ensure her acquittal. Lorena Bobbitt played the consummate victim, crying profusely and acting confused. Both the defense and the prosecution agreed that temporary insanity, perhaps caused by spousal abuse, caused the violence – not surprisingly, since women's violence is rarely lawful and is typically authorized only once proper femininity has been established. Neither Mr nor Mrs Bobbitt was known for maturity or intelligence, but the lack of such qualities in Lorena's case may have worked to her advantage, because female savvy, like female violence, challenges the gender status quo. Thus, while female violence is generally intolerable, exceptions are made for extra-feminine, extra-helpless, extra-naïve women. In any event, the pervasive media attention to the case has ensured that Lorena's acquittal will not establish a precedent but will be a one-of-a-kind event, because no woman anywhere who hereafter cuts off a penis can insist the act was not premeditated. That is, given the intense, high-profile coverage, it would be extremely difficult for any penis-severing woman to claim ignorance of Lorena Bobbitt, and hence to claim that her own actions were spontaneous rather than premeditated and modeled after Lorena's.

Many men, on the other hand, feel entitled to violent retaliation when their boundaries are violated. The 1985 Bernhard Goetz case illustrates this gendered (and, in this case, racist) double standard. Goetz, a white man, was acquitted for shooting several Black youths on the New York subway during an altercation in which Goetz claimed he was being assaulted. His violence was defended as a refusal to be victimized, whereas Lorena had to be a victim in order to be acquitted. Goetz's racial violence was considered rational, whereas Lorena's gender violence cast her rationality into doubt. Goetz re-established his entitlement to social authority and personal boundaries through violence in a racist society; Lorena didn't dare claim that kind of respect – if she had, she might now be in prison.

The fact that social tolerance for aggression is gendered reflects the cultural equation of violence and masculinity in a way which naturalizes their coincidence. Both men's self-defensive violence and their sexual violence against women fit neatly into what we understand as natural masculinity, while women's aggression is seen as unnatural and therefore pathological.[22] Conventional gender identity does not emerge naturally or unproblematically, however, but rather involves parameters set by a culture invested in gender inequality. Freud suggested that all children have narcissistic and aggressive impulses, and that in girls these impulses are eventually channeled into passivity and masochism.[23] If we understand such channeling to be the result of unequal positioning in the cultural order, then notions of proper womanhood, and a social commitment to rigid gender polarity more generally, underlie the double standard around violence. Put differently, aggression is a primary marker of masculine/feminine difference, and construing women's aggression as unnatural helps mask the political character of gender inequality (indeed, of gender itself).

We see the construction of 'the battered women's syndrome' defense in this context. Women have to be beaten for years before they can legally act in their own defense against violent partners, and even then they use violence only because the other person's has driven them insane. Models of sanity are gendered, and female sanity, or proper femininity, revolves specifically around a lack of anger, aggression, and inviolable bodily boundaries. In other words, violent women are seen as either not-sane or not-women, because sane women are never violent. Media discourse, then, fails to challenge our cultural insistence on women's natural passivity, which permits women's violence only under conditions of extreme victimization.

The debate also throws into sharp relief the great standoff around the subject of victimhood. As Barbara Ehrenreich describes it, on one side are the domestic abuse specialists who focus on women's long weepy history of rape and abuse; on the other side are feminist scholars who claim women are turning away from feminism because they are tired of hearing about battering, foot binding, and clitoridectomies.[24] These anti-victim-hood feminists say that it's time to stop whining and go for the power.[25] Sabine Reichel epitomized this position in a *Los Angeles Times* article entitled 'Some Women Nurture Misery.' Lorena Bobbitt has no one to blame for her plight but herself, Reichel contends. Indeed, women have run out of excuses for their own inept, irresponsible behavior, which includes tolerating outrageous and abusive acts by men: 'The times when parents sold their daughters for a couple of cows are over. Most women can pick whom they want, be what they want, do what they want when and how they want it. If they wind up with a jerk, a woman-hater, a philandering Mama's boy or a sadistic two-timer, it's because that's what they chose; it's their own fault.'[26]

Katha Pollitt suggests that the current attack on 'victim feminism' is also partly a class phenomenon, in that it reflects the desire of educated female professionals to distance themselves from stereotypes of women as passive, dependent, helpless and irrational – stereotypes which simultane-ously contribute to women's victimization and ensure the punishment of aggressive women who violate these stereotypes.[27] Lorena Bobbitt can stand as a 'mascot' for either side, since she was framed as both a victim (of domestic abuse) and an aggressor (against her abuser). What this debate fails to highlight, however, is the extent to which women are disproportion-ately punished for aggressive behavior, including violent acts of self-defense.[28] Thus the entreaty of anti-victimhood feminists to 'stop whining and go for the power' is itself victimizing if gendered stereotypes about 'proper' (that is, nonviolent) feminine conduct don't also change.

No matter which way feminists slice it, there was undeniable grass-roots support for Lorena Bobbitt among many ordinary women outside of official academic and activist circles. Indeed, what was most interesting for Ehrenreich about the whole Bobbitt affair was the huge divergence it revealed between high-powered feminist intellectuals and your average housewife, waitress, or female retail clerk. While the former were tripping over one another to distance themselves from Lorena Bobbitt and from charges of male-bashing, she says, the latter were 'discussing fascinating new possibilities for cutlery commercials' and 'making V signs by raising two fingers and bringing them together with snipping motions'.[29] Ehrenreich admits feminism has a lot to do with this new 'beyond-bitch' attitude, but she also suggests that for most women the feminist revolution hasn't come along fast enough. 'All too many women still go home to Bobbitt-like fellows who regard the penis as a portable battering ram,' she insists, and women are sick and tired of it. Consequently, feminist intellectuals have it wrong: your average woman doesn't shrink from feminism because feminists are perceived to be militant ball-busters, but in fact because they aren't militant enough.[30]

But it is not only the limited social tolerance for female aggression which accounted for Bobbitt-mania. The specific focus of Lorena's aggression cut right to the heart of gender inequality. Lorena did not shoot John, or chop off his arm or leg. No, she did something so uncommon the act has been named after her: she 'bobbittized' him. Men express their social power to dominate women in specifically sexual ways (which is why rapists don't just hit women), and Lorena's actions simultaneously acknowledged and protested this domination. But men's eroticization and naturalization of their social power means that they tend not to experience their fixation with the penis as political. Neither do they recognize or experience as political their assumption of sexual invulnerability, an assumption Lorena explicitly challenged.

Taking Freud Literally

Most contemporary psychoanalytic theorizing about masculinity and the phallus at some point deals with the specific relation between phallus and penis. Lacan himself points to the myth of Isis and Osiris as evidence of an ancient phallic discourse that our own culture has repressed but that psychoanalysis can excavate or unveil.[31] At the same time, however, he insists that neither women nor men can ever actually 'have' the phallus, insofar as the phallus is a cultural fiction, a transcendental signifier of the wholeness, plenitude and mastery which human subjects by very definition lack (and therefore desire). The desire for completeness is thus an act of phallic identification for both sexes, which is always in some sense 'failed.'[32]

But, as a number of feminist theorists have pointed out, this failure is not identical for men and women because the phallus – with its emphasis on verticality, ascension, elevation and erection – undeniably derives part of its signifying power from the male organ itself. Kaja Silverman puts it this way: 'as long as the phallus is designated the "image of the penis," and the penis as the "real phallus," there can never be less than an analogical relation between those two terms, a relation that often gives way to complete identification.'[33] Consequently, the penis functions as the 'natural' signifier both of maleness and cultural dominance. This is why, to most guys, manhood is simply the natural result of having a penis, while to feminists it's a political category central to gender inequality. The penis is, to borrow a phrase from Frank Krutnik, the male 'membership card' permitting access into the club of the cultural elite, which, because of the general valorization of the penis in patriarchal culture, offers security in its very possession.[34] Thus, when Freud proposed his Oedipal theory of castration anxiety, he meant it quite literally, although scholars since Freud have often emphasized the fear of losing the social power and privilege associated with masculinity rather than of losing the male member itself.

The public concern over John Bobbitt's John Thomas illustrates the extent to which penis and phallus remain closely aligned. The notion that the penis is a man's manhood, a literal and figurative substitute for the man himself, was a trope heard over and over in the media discourse on the Bobbitt conflict. In *Elle* magazine, Vince Passaro confessed that 'men are admittedly odd about this body part,' listing 15 synonyms for penis including 'dick cock prick tool member boner hose joint woody wiener'. He writes, 'we have lots of words for it, but none of them express how, day to day, hour to hour, we feel about those squiggly little fellows we carry in our pants.'[35]

While it's possible that Lorena, in an uncontrollable fit of penis envy, cut off John's bobbitt (predictably, the latest synonym for penis) in an attempt to make him just as miserable as she was – after all, hadn't she endured a state of penislessness for 24 years? – more than likely she aimed below the belt because she knew perfectly well where his seminal sense of self lay. This is not to suggest penis envy is necessarily a woman's lament of an anatomical defect, as Freud first proposed;[36] rather, it's a resentment of being deprived of the political, cultural, social – including sexual – advantages many men routinely enjoy.[37] Lorena claimed that John repeatedly gained sexual gratification without treating her as someone with her own sexual needs; if this is true, then perhaps Lorena can appropriately be said to have had 'penis envy'. Her attempt to acquire phallic power took such a literal form precisely because our culture itself is so literal about it.

For example, John's brother Todd, who appeared on the *Jenny Jones* show with John and the entire Bobbitt clan, got an enthusiastic round of applause when he said: 'She did worse than kill him, she took away that thing that means most to a man' – a pronouncement that popped up repeatedly on television talk shows. Of all John's many such appearances, the two-part interview with Jenny Jones was perhaps most remarkable for its explicit discourse about the severed organ.[38] Claiming she was only asking what everyone else was dying to know, Jones posed pointed and detailed questions about John and Lorena's sex life, the experience of dismemberment, the surgery to re-attach the penis, and its current status as a functioning sexual organ. She seemed especially interested in the condition of John's penis now, whether it was 'working' (that is, whether he could get an erection), and whether, after frequent sex with Lorena (they were reported to have had sex over 900 times in four years) he was anxious to 'test it out soon'.

John admitted that he'd tried intercourse with an old girlfriend, but so far only the lower third of his penis could maintain an erection. But he insisted it was healing rapidly and would be 'fully functional' in just a couple of years. Jones then noted that a full recovery would be quite unusual, medically speaking, and the following exchange took place:

> *Bobbitt:* I feel I will fully recover … actually, I don't know, it's healing real well now, I think it's going to be a lot better than it was.
> *Jones:* Better how?
> *Bobbitt:* It'll be stronger and bigger!
> *Jones:* You think it's getting bigger now?
> *Bobbitt:* Not now, but it will be, because the nerves will grow back, you know, rejuvenate.

Jones was rather astounded by this, and after a break she returned to the subject (note how John's penis seems to grow as they talk about it):

> *Jones:* You're healing well, in fact, you expect when you're healed for your penis to be bigger?
> *Bobbitt:* Yeah, I feel I'm getting stronger, and through the new nerve rejuvenation it'll be a lot better.
> *Jones:* Is it getting wider or longer?
> *Bobbitt:* I wouldn't say wider … it's a little longer than it was.

Jones then asked, 'where would you be now, emotionally, physically, if they hadn't found your penis and re-attached it?' John shook his head and said, 'I'd be real depressed, I'd probably be bottled up in some corner somewhere, not talking about it at all, probably even contemplating suicide.' Things apparently wouldn't have been so great for Lorena Bobbitt, either, had the police not found her husband's penis in a nearby vacant lot and had doctors not been able to surgically re-attach it. A *Vanity Fair* article featuring Lorena's side of the story suggested that, if the penis hadn't been recovered, Lorena might have faced a possible prison sentence of 40 years instead of 20.[39]

In Freudian terms, the horror of John Bobbitt's close call with 'lack' is in part a horror of the feminine itself – and the subordinate position of women. With characteristic aplomb, John told Jenny Jones that having his penis cut off was particularly terrible because he might not be able to stand while urinating:

> *Bobbitt:* They said I'd have to sit down to urinate for the rest of my life. I said 'What?!' You know, I started to get real depressed, I thought, how am I going to handle this, what kind of life am I going to have?
> *Jones:* What did the thought of having to urinate sitting down do to you?
> *Bobbitt:* It's terrible! It's not normal!
> *Jones:* Did it make you suicidal?
> *Bobbitt:* Well, I thought about that, because, you know, it's so depressing.

According to Freud, the threat of castration is not fully real to a little boy until the devastating moment when he witnesses for the first time the 'inadequate' female genitalia (usually that of a younger sister or playmate). No wonder men were reported to cringe when they heard the details of John Bobbitt's ordeal; he certainly underwent an experience more disturbing than catching a glimpse of a little girl at her bath. Psychiatrists and anthropologists cited in *Vanity Fair* agreed that the cutting of the penis 'is an act that would be freighted with symbolism in any culture', a kind of universal no-no. One author quoted put it this way: 'the response [to the threat of castration] is so rooted in the neural substratum and reptilian back brain that men cannot find words to express their shock.'[40] Given this, either men are on an evolutionary par with birds and snakes, or Freud was right – in a patriarchal society, the male genital organ has a socially constructed meaning that plays a leading role in both psychosexual and social relations.

This leads to something else Freud clearly had a hand on. Compulsive repetition, such as the media coverage of the severed penis, is really nothing more than a fruitless attempt to fix or pin down what can never be fixed or pinned down: an essential masculinity (and an essential femininity). As Krutnik puts it, 'the phallic regime of masculine identity is by no means a secure option that can be taken for granted once it is set in place for the male subject.'[41] Rather, it has to be endlessly narrativized, idealized, and defended against threats, both internal and external, revealing that men have castration anxiety precisely because their masculinity isn't as unproblematic or invulnerable as they'd like to believe. And in the Bobbitt case as in much of our popular culture, a woman figures as the castrating *femme fatale*, the feminine projection of a man's deepest fears and figure of his ultimate demise.

The constant valorization of the phallus in popular discourse – despite the conspicuous absence of visual representations of the penis itself – exposes the perpetual effort necessary to secure male privilege as natural and inevitable. Ironically, this absence of visual representation is one of the principal mechanisms by which the penis is idealized. Just as Osiris' missing member engendered the erection of the phallus as cult object, the literal invisibility of the penis in most forms of popular culture serves to maintain its sacred status, while its display threatens to render it profane. In the one place where men's naked bodies are almost as visible as women's – hard-core film and video pornography – the penis is invariably represented in a way which maintains the myth of perpetual potency: it is longer than average, usually erect, and constantly in motion. Rarely is the penis depicted in its more common but decidedly unphallic state.

The substitution of 'erect penis' for 'penis' in popular culture is itself a deliberate mechanism for securing and sustaining phallic power, one that, according to Charles Bernheimer, has been neglected in feminist psychoanalytic theorizing. Merely exposing the phallus' anatomical dependence leaves woefully unanalyzed the actual male organ itself, as if the penis represents the limits of theoretical discourse, its meaning clear, transparent and unambiguous. For Bernheimer, just as our culture tends to conflate phallus and penis while simultaneously mystifying the conflation, much feminist theorizing does the same thing at the level of the penis when it conflates the idealized, erect penis – the phallic penis – with 'penis' in general. Acknowledging the difference – that is, acknowledging the diversity of the penis in terms of size, state, color, functioning, ontological status (organic versus strap-on), etc., would serve not only to emphasize the fact that physical bodies are as shifting and provisional as any other semiotic construction, but to destabilize the notion of the phallus itself by revealing the phallus to be a kind of theoretical dream or projection – a dream of perpetual erection and potency that clearly doesn't exist.[42]

Conclusion: Dis-membering Male Sexual Privilege

Lorena Bobbitt's violence is particularly frightening for many men because of something that the media has failed to deconstruct: under a system of compulsory heterosexuality, the use of the penis to have sex with women is central to securing a 'natural' heterosexual male identity. This is why men don't experience the Bobbitt incident as threatening to their *privilege* but simply, 'innocently', to their sense of who they are. A man's sense of entitlement to use his penis whenever he wants, with or without a woman's consent, a 'natural right' that defines rape culture, is what women are describing when they say that a man uses his penis as a weapon. And, as Barbara Ehrenreich notes, 'if a fellow insists on using his penis as a weapon, I say that, one way or another, he ought to be swiftly disarmed.'[43] This statement so outraged talk show host Montel Williams that he read it repeatedly on the air as evidence that feminists have declared 'open season' on men's genitals. Heterosexual men are 'real men' because they have sex with women, and 'sex' itself is practically synonymous with vaginal penetration. Thus we tend to think of women who have had clitoridectomies – but not men without penises – as still capable of having 'sex'. Hence, one man's lost penis generates a national fixation which a woman's lost clitoris never has. At the same time, masculinity is racially tiered; hence, a white guy's castration generates a national fixation which black man's never has.

The centrality of the penis in forming masculine identity not only leads to genuinely horrified reactions to John Wayne's missing manhood, but is partly responsible for the high incidence of rape in the first place. Because intercourse, whether forced *or* consensual, is a crucial way for men to establish themselves as manly, a woman's refusal to have sex is easily construed as emasculating and therefore intolerable. Likewise, feminism's insistence that men honor women's sexual boundaries must feel, well, castrating. From this vantage point, the conflation of Lorena Bobbitt's (literal) emasculation of her husband with feminism's (metaphorical) emasculation of men is entirely apropos, because it reveals the extent to which the sexual functioning of the penis figures in the construction of masculinity, across class and across race. Were it not for this particular construction of masculinity, Lorena's retaliation would not have been emasculating in the same sense. But in that kind of world, rape itself, the violence which prompted Lorena's, would be less compelling, as it would no longer be 'masculating' in the first place.[44]

As John told Jenny Jones, it would be 'just a matter of time' before he could put his penis back to work, and he even insisted that it would be better, stronger and bigger. Unfortunately, media coverage of the Bobbitt extravaganza failed to make this a growth experience in any other way. That John himself remained remarkably unchanged by his ordeal (save for the size of his penis) was made clear by his appearance on *Rolanda*, another daytime talk show. On this show we learned not only that John had been arrested for battering his new fiancée in the months following his trial, but that another woman had named John in a paternity suit. He admitted to being the father of the child in question, and insisted he would take partial responsibility for it. John said he was especially interested in teaching his son to choose a mate wisely, and would do everything in his power to prevent the boy from getting *his* penis cut off, since, after all, 'women are dangerous.'[45]

Thus the media coverage of Lorena's actions ultimately served to perpetuate gender inequality rather than dismantle it, because the media never challenged the presumed naturalness of male sexual identity. Instead of spawning discussions of male sexual violence, and how men often use sex to establish themselves as naturally different from and superior to women, popular attention remained fixated on John's penis, without which he presumably could not have sex, or a sexed identity. Further, John's ordeal will long afterwards be associated with the protection of male sexual privilege. For example, a legislative bill under consideration requiring the chemical regulation of convicted rapists' sex hormones was referred to in the media as 'the Bobbitt bill', as if any move to control men's sexuality (even violent sexuality) is castrating, emasculating, bobbittizing. Indeed, an Italian sculptor invented a male chastity belt made of stainless steel and leather for men to wear at night so their wives can't 'do a Mrs. Bobbitt'. If only the phallus could be similarly secured!

We have argued that men's defensive posturing with regard to their genitals constitutes what we call 'privileged hysteria', privileged in the sense that men have in the mass media a readily available cultural forum in which to voice their outrage over the violation of both John's penis and their own sense of sexual invulnerability. Whereas Lorena, like Freud's Dora, employed the language of the body, journalists, reporters, critics and talk show hosts employed the language of words and images.[46] We have also tried to show that the fixation with the penis is really a fixation with political and cultural authority (the naturalization of which helps justify and maintain it), and that the conflation between 'penis' and 'phallus' is not surprising precisely because the penis remains the signifier of a falsely naturalized cultural dominance.

At the same time, the phallic regime of masculine identity is by no means stable or secure; it must constantly be reinforced, reasserted, and re-articulated. Thus men's anxiety about 'those squiggly little fellows' in their pants – their desire to talk about the penis, valorize it, put it into 'action' – is in fact a somatization of psychic stress over heterosexual male identity, an anxious 'speech of the body' – hysteria in the classic sense. From this perspective, Dora's nervous cough, which belied her unconscious psychic turmoil, finds its contemporary parallel not in the castrating action of Lorena Bobbitt, but in the male-dominated media brouhaha that accompanied it.

Not surprisingly, the recent porn video dramatizing John Bobbitt's version of the story is the one document that most explicitly exposes John's concern with his penis as a somatization of his insecurity about his masculinity. In *John Wayne Bobbitt: Uncut*, when we finally get to see 'it', we see him 'doing it', reasserting his manhood through endless scenes of heterosexual intercourse, including the infamous cum shots as the undeniable proof of his virility.[47] When John and the other porn actors appeared on the daytime talk show *Geraldo* in order to promote the video's release, audience members wanted to know why he'd chosen to star in 'that kind' of film. John said that making a XXX-rated video was the best way to tell his story. 'Lots of people have a curiosity about my penis,' he explained, 'so an adult film was the best way to show everybody it works.' A man in the audience then asked him if he felt 'more of a man' for having made the film. 'Definitely,' John replied without hesitation.[48]

But while the video may try to persuade us that his manhood is intact, it does little to establish John as the 'sensitive' individual he claims to be, nor does it seriously discredit Lorena's charges that he raped her. The video's primal scene shows John coming home drunk from a local strip club, waking Lorena for sex and, despite her repeated refusals, climbing on top of her. At this moment Lorena miraculously changes her mind and is in fact excited by his failure to respect her wishes – a sudden reversal of attitude consistent with much heterosexual porn fantasy, and a bit of revisionist history that breathes life into the tired old myth that 'no' means 'yes'. John orgasms and falls back unconscious, while Lorena pouts, obviously dissatisfied with the encounter. In this manner the scenario is brought to a head: Lorena, provoked by frustrated desire rather than vengeance for rape and years of abuse, grabs a knife from the kitchen and smites the offending member.

John Bobbitt apparently hopes the video will exonerate him and restore his sense of manhood. Maybe it will. But it may also expose 'manhood' – both the 'natural' category and the penis which serves as its privileged signifier – as a particularly impoverished cultural fiction. Unlike most discussions in the media, *John Wayne Bobbitt: Uncut* makes no bones about what was at stake for men on that fateful June night. Thus the video's release may actually serve, however unintentionally, to parody our cultural obsession with manhood and offer on its own the very critique we have developed in these pages.

We began by invoking the ancient myth of Isis and Osiris, juxtaposing it to the contemporary narrative of John and Lorena Bobbitt. The former is an originary tale offering an account of the connection between penis and phallus; the latter is a modern-day reminder of both the strength of this connection and, more importantly, the strength of growing challenges to the male privilege that requires and sustains it. It is because of the slippage between phallus and penis that Lorena cut John's off, that the media went ballistic, and that John Wayne Bobbitt himself decided a porn video would be the best way to reconstitute his damaged sense of manhood. But at the same time, because the phallus is not reducible to the penis, there is space to maneuver an alternative kind of discourse around masculine power, privilege, and responsibility.

NOTES

Introduction – Wight and Myers

1. *Independent*, 18 March, 1996.
2. See Ann Lloyd, *Doubly Deviant, Doubly Damned: Society's Treatment of Violent Women* (Harmondsworth: Penguin, 1995): 55.
3. For further discussion, Helen Birch (ed.), *Moving Targets: Women, Murder and Representation* (London: Virago, 1993); Lloyd, *Doubly Deviant, Doubly Damned*, op cit.; Helena Kennedy, *Eve Was Framed: Women and British Justice* (London: Vintage, 1992); Lynda Hart, *Fatal Women: Lesbian Sexuality and the Mark of Aggression* (London: Routledge, 1994).
4. Kennedy, *Eve Was Framed*: 23.
5. Sara Thornton, in a letter to the Registrar of Criminal Appeals (Master McKenzie), 23 May 1991, as quoted in J. Nadel, *Sara Thornton: The Story of a Woman Who Killed* (London: Gollancz, 1993): 193–4. See Anette Ballinger's chapter in this collection for a fuller discussion.
6. Betty Broderick, as quoted in Deborah Starr Seibel, 'Caged Fury', *TV Guide*, 31 October, 1992: 18. See Stephanie Savage's chapter in this book for a full discussion.

The Guilt of the Innocent – Ballinger

Thank you to Kristi Ballinger, Tia Ballinger, Penny Gill, Tony Jefferson and Marion Price for inspiring comments. Thanks especially to Joe Sim for his unerring support and encouragement throughout the preparation of this chapter.

1. Extract from trial transcript of the Marie Fahmy case, reproduced in the *Times*, 14 September, 1923: 7.
2. Extract from trial transcript of the Ruth Ellis case, reproduced in the *Sun*, 21 September, 1972.
3. A. Morris and A. Wilczynski, (1993) 'Rocking the Cradle: Mothers who Kill their Children', in H. Birch (ed.), *Moving Targets* (London: Virago, 1993): 199.
4. H. Allen, *Justice Unbalanced* (Milton Keynes: Open University Press, 1987): 73; 101. Emphasis in the original. See also Lloyd, *Doubly Deviant, Doubly Damned: Society's Treatment of Violent Women* (Harmondsworth: Penguin, 1995): 49 for a discussion on 'woman as victim'.
5. P. Carlen (ed.), *Criminal Women* (Cambridge: Polity Press, 1985): 10.
6. Carlen, *Criminal Women*: 11; Barrister Helena Kennedy, as quoted in *The Guardian*, 12 March, 1991.
7. See, for example, M. Benn, 'Body Talk: The Sexual Politics of PMT' in Birch, *Moving Targets*: 152–71. Moreover, of the 130 women who were sentenced to death during the first half of this century, 100 had been found guilty of murdering their children. Yet, although murder during this period carried a mandatory death sentence, and the plea of Diminished Responsibility had not yet come into being, not one of them was executed. This figure does not include the 512 women who were convicted of infanticide (the murder of a child less than 12 months old) between 1923 and 1948 (1922 being the year when the Infanticide Act was introduced) – see *Royal Commission on Capital Punishment 1949–1953 Report*: 58.
8. See, for example, the case of Suzanne Oatley, who was put on probation for two years after killing her baby; reported in *The Guardian*, 1 September, 1995: 8.
9. See, for example, A. Kirsta, *Deadlier than the Male* (London: HarperCollins, 1994): 5–8.
10. Morris and Wilczynski: 199–200.
11. Stuart Hall has defined 'discourse' as 'a group of statements which

provide a language for talking about – i.e. a way of representing – a particular kind of knowledge about a topic. When statements about a topic are made within a particular discourse, the discourse makes it possible to construct the topic in a certain way. It also limits the other ways in which the topic can be constructed.' (S. Hall, 'The West and the Rest: Discourse and Power' in S. Hall and B. Gieben [eds], *Formations of Modernity* [Cambridge: Polity Press, 1992]: 291). My use of the term 'discourse' is taken from Hall's definition throughout this chapter.

12. L. Stanley and S. Wise, 'Method, Methodology and Epistemology in Feminist Research Processes', in L. Stanley (ed.), *Feminist Praxis* (London: Routledge, 1990): 25.

13. A. Worrall, *Offending Women* (London: Routledge, 1990): 11.

14. For example, in a medical report dated 3 June, 1955, Principal Medical Officer at Holloway prison Penry Williams describes Ruth as 'pleasant and co-operative in manner' (Ruth Ellis file CRIM 1/2582 Royal Courts of Justice, Strand, London). There were many examples of Ruth's politeness – for example: 'when charged she said "Thanks"' (*The Times*, 29 April, 1955).

15. As quoted in J. Goodman and P. Pringle (eds), *The Trial of Ruth Ellis* (Newton Abbott: David and Charles, 1974): 40.

16. Worrall, *Offending Women*: 5.

17. J. Ritchie, *Myra Hindley: Inside the Mind of a Murderess* (London: Grafton, 1991): 281.

18. Medical Report of Marie Fahmy by J. Morton MD in CRIM 1/247 21629 PRO, Chancery Lane, London; F. Jones, *Murderous Women* (London: Headline, 1991): 82–3.

19. One trial witness testified that 'they used to insult and "smack" each other openly' (*The Times*, 13 July, 1923: 9). See also Deposition File CRIM 1/247 21629 PRO, Chancery Lane, London, which lists numerous examples of the insults which took place between the couple, for example, when Marie called Ali 'a pimp', he retaliated by calling her 'a prostitute'. Moreover, on the night of the murder, Marie was heard to say to Ali in the Savoy restaurant: 'You shut up or I'll smash this [a champagne bottle] over your head'(as quoted in *The Times*, 11 September, 1923: 7; also in H. Kingsley and G. Tibballs, *No Way Out* [London: Headline, 1994]: 88; see also Jones, *Murderous Women*: 85). During the trial Marie denied having

threatened Ali, but did admit to having 'boxed his ears' in response to a beating (*The Times*, 13 September, 1923: 7).

20. Ali apparently failed to pay the full amount to Marie, and instead handed over £450 and an IOU note for the rest of the amount (*The Times*, 12 September, 1923: 7).

21. Jones, *Murderous Women*: 93.

22. At one point during dinner at the Savoy Grill, the music conductor offered to play a piece of music of Madame's choosing; she replied (in the presence of her husband), 'Thank you very much. My husband is going to kill me in 24 hours and I am not very anxious for music.' (*The Times*, 13 September, 1923: 7; see also testimony of Said Enani, 18 July, 1923 in CRIM 1/247 21629, PRO, Chancery Lane, London).

23. Jones, *Murderous Women*:76–7; *The Times*, 11 September, 1923: 7.

24. Testimony of Arthur Marini, 21 July, 1923, CRIM 1/247 21629 Public Record Office, Chancery Lane, London.

25. Deposition File CRIM 1/247 21629, Public Record Office, Chancery Lane, London.

26. *The Times*, 13 July, 1923: 9.

27. *The Times*, 11 July, 1923: 9.

28. *The Times*, 11 September, 1923: 7.

29. Extract from trial transcript, reproduced in *The Times*, 13 September, 1923: 7.

30. B. Eastlea, *Science and Sexual Oppression* (London: Weidenfeld and Nicolson, 1981): 68–72.

31. Extract from trial transcript reproduced in *The Times*, 14 September, 1923: 7.

32. F. Heidensohn, *Women & Crime* (Basingstoke: Macmillan, 1986): 112.

33. A. Oakley, 'Normal Motherhood: An Exercise in Self-Control?', in B. Hutter and G. Williams (eds), *Controlling Women: The Normal and the Deviant* (London: Croom Helm, 1981): 83, referring to Broverman *et al.* (1970).

34. Extract from trial transcript, reproduced in *The Times*, 13 September, 1923: 7.

35. *The Times*, 15 September, 1923: 5.

36. See, for example, B. Ehrenreich and D. English, *For Her Own Good* (London: Pluto, 1979), esp. chapter 4. Moreover, we may assume

that all jury members were at least lower middle-class since, in 1923, juries were still drawn exclusively from the propertied classes.

37. Extract from trial transcript reproduced in *The Times*, 15 September, 1923: 5.

38. Oakley, 'Normal Motherhood': 84.

39. E. Green, S. Hebron and D. Woodward, 'Women, Leisure and Social Control', in J. Hanmer and M. Maynard (eds), *Women, Violence and Social Control* (Basingstoke: Macmillan, 1987): 84.

40. CRIM 1/247 21629, Public Record Office, Chancery Lane, London; Jones, *Murderous Women*: 92.

41. Percival Clarke, as quoted in Jones, *Murderous Women*: 88.

42. E. Marjoribanks, *Famous Trials of Marshall Hall* (Harmondsworth: Penguin, 1950): 377.

43. Marjoribanks, *Marshall Hall*: 364

44. Marshall Hall, as quoted in Marjoribanks, *Marshall Hall*: 373.

45. Marshall Hall, as quoted in Marjoribanks, *Marshall Hall*: 370.

46. Marshall Hall, as quoted in Marjoribanks, *Marshall Hall*: 374.

47. Marshall Hall, as quoted in Marjoribanks, *Marshall Hall*: 374, 375.

48. D. Garland, 'The Punitive Society', *11th Annual Centre Lecture & Inaugural Lecture of the Chair of Penology*, University of Edinburgh, 24 May, 1995: 4.

49. Garland, 'Punitive Society': 4

50. See, for example, Marjoribanks, *Marshall Hall*: 363–80.

51. *The Times*, 17 September, 1923: 18.

52. See, for example, V. Ware, *Beyond the Pale* (London: Verso, 1992), especially her discussion of white women as victims: 4–11.

53. (a) Beattie stated in his testimony of 21 July, 1923 that he 'saw the deceased bending and whistling and snapping his fingers to a puppy' in the corridor. Between '5 to 10 seconds after' he heard three shots in rapid succession. It seems strange that Fahmy should be preoccupied with his dog in the middle of an attack upon his wife. Yet, Marie Fahmy claimed that he was about to attack her in her bedroom, and to frighten him she fired her pistol out of a bedroom window; the following three shots went off by accident, according to her statement. The possibility that the gun could go off accidentally once, never mind three times, was challenged by gun-maker Robert Churchill, who appeared as a trial witness and explained that 'the action is not automatic firing, the trigger must be pulled for each shot … At the back

of the pistol is a safety grip to prevent accidental discharge, it requires pressure before firing ... It is not likely to go off accidentally.' (CRIM 1/247 21629 PRO, Chancery Lane, London). (b) *The Times*, 23 July, 1923. Furthermore, Dr Maurice Newfield, who carried out the post-mortem, stated that the pistol would have been 'within a yard' of the deceased's temple when he was shot, and that 'the effect of that shot would be to cause the person receiving it, to fall down instantly.' Even Madame Fahmy's own doctor, Dr Gordon, conceded that it would be impossible for somebody who had been shot through the brain to reel more than '2 or 3 feet'. Yet both PC Percy Attersoll, investigating officer on the murder scene, and Beattie, agreed that Fahmy was lying 'about 30 feet away from his own door' (in the corridor), and Sergeant George Hall confirmed that he 'found no trace of blood [in the prisoner's bedroom]'. Yet Madame Fahmy stated that she had fired the pistol out of her bedroom window, and when Fahmy 'still advanced towards her ... she pointed at him and pulled the trigger' (CRIM 1/247 21629, PRO, Chancery Lane, London). (c) Part of Judge Swift's summing up speech, reproduced in *The Times*, 15 September, 1923: 7.

54. L. Marks and T. Van den Bergh, *Ruth Ellis: A Case of Diminished Responsibility?* (Harmondsworth: Penguin, 1990): 16–24.

55. When asked about her divorce while on the witness stand, Ruth replied: 'I decided not to claim any maintenance or defend myself in any way and also to give up my daughter.' (Goodman and Pringle, *Ruth Ellis*: 109).

56. B. Bardsley, *Flowers in Hell* (London: Pandora, 1987): 139.

57. See, for example, T. Healey, *The World's Greatest Crimes of Passion* (London: Hamlyn, 1990): 34.

58. Healey, *Crimes of Passion*: 34.

59. Ruth Ellis confirmed this shift in the power balance between herself and David Blakely when she gave evidence during her trial: 'I was obviously jealous of him now. I mean the tables had been turned. I was jealous of him whereas he, before, had been jealous of me. I had now given up my business – what he had wanted me to do – left all my friends behind connected with clubs and things, and it was my turn to be jealous of him.' (Transcript in Goodman and Pringle, *Ruth Ellis*: 111).

60. Transcript reproduced in Goodman and Pringle, *Ruth Ellis*: 114.

61. D. Farran, *The Trial of Ruth Ellis* (working paper included in the *Studies in Sexual Politics* series edited by Liz Stanley and Sue Scott, Sociology Department, University of Manchester, 1988): 10.

62. See, for example, *The Daily Mail*, 29 April, 1955; *Daily Express*, 15 April, 1983; *The Daily Mail*, 3 March, 1984. See also Robert Hancock, who was commissioned to write the Ruth Ellis Story for *Woman's Sunday Mirror* in 1955, and who in his book *Ruth Ellis* (London: Weidenfeld, 1989) refers to Ellis as 'the blonde' no less than three times on one page alone (page 6); H. Birch, 'If Looks Could Kill' in *idem, Moving Targets*: 52.

63. See, for example, *The Times*, 29 April, 1955; 21 and 22 June, 1955.

64. *News of the World*, 8 October, 1972: 10.

65. *The Sunday People*, 2 December, 1973.

66. J. Rose, *Why War?* (Oxford: Basil Blackwell, 1993): 51.

67. Bardsley, *Flowers*: 140.

68. Goodman and Pringle, *Ruth Ellis*: 50.

69. Marks and Van den Bergh, *Diminished Responsibility*: 134.

70. H. Birch, 'Twice Unnatural Creatures', *New Statesman,* 18 March, 1988: 25. Justice Havers eventually ruled that a defence of provocation could not be put before the jury. Instead he instructed the jury to approach the case 'without any thought of sympathy either for the deceased man or … for the accused … whom you may think was a young woman badly treated by the deceased man. No consideration of that should enter into your deliberations.' (Trial Transcript of Ruth Ellis DPP2/2430 23271).

71. Hancock, *Ruth Ellis*: 14

72. *Liverpool Daily Post*, 2 March, 1971.

73. Mrs Elizabeth Nielson being interviewed by Godfrey Winn in *Sunday Dispatch*, 26 June, 1955.

74. Trial transcript and Ellis's statement following her arrest, reproduced in Goodman and Pringle, *Ruth Ellis*: 114, 117, 103, 102.

75. *Daily Telegraph* editorial, 14 July, 1955.

76. *News of the World*, 8 October, 1972.

77. Goodman and Pringle, *Ruth Ellis*: 42.

78. Farran, *Trial*: 32.

79. *Liverpool Daily Post*, 2 March, 1971.

80. Police statement in Goodman and Pringle, *Ruth Ellis*: 104.

81. L. Webb, who attended the trial, quoted in Rose, *Why War?*: 62.

82. *The Sun*, 21 September, 1972.

83. Marks and Van den Bergh, *Diminished Responsibility*: 163.

84. Goodman and Pringle, *Ruth Ellis*: 106, 107.

85. Transcript reproduced in Goodman and Pringle, *Ruth Ellis*: 106–7.

86. Hancock had this to say on Ruth Ellis and motherhood: 'In times of upset and disaster a mother's immediate thoughts go to her children. It was only while her statement was being taken down that this woman casually disclosed that she had a son. Inspector Davies at first thought that this indifference meant that she had killed him before she left home ... Just before dawn a very relieved police-woman found ten-year-old Andria asleep on a camp bed in the rented furnished bed-sitting room that his mother had left the previous night when she set off to murder David Blakely' (Hancock, *Ruth Ellis*: 14).

87. Transcript reproduced in Goodman and Pringle, *Ruth Ellis*: 119.

88. Marks and Van den Bergh, *Diminished Responsibility*: 148.

89. Inspector Davies, as quoted in Goodman and Pringle, *Ruth Ellis*: 45.

90. Chris Auty, as quoted in Bardsley, *Flowers*: 140.

91. C. Smart, 'Law and the Control of Women's Sexuality: The Case of the 1950s', in Hutter and Williams, *Controlling Women*: 50.

92. Healey, *Crimes of Passion*: 40; Bardsley, *Flowers*: 140–1.

93. See, for example, the case of Mrs Maybrick, who in 1889 stood trial for the murder of her husband James Maybrick. He, as well as being married with two children, also had an entire unacknowledged and 'parallel' family consisting of a mistress and five children. Three of these children had been born prior to his relationship with Florence Maybrick (Bernard Ryan with The Rt Hon Lord Havers, *The Poisoned Life of Mrs Maybrick* (Harmondsworth: Penguin, 1989): 28.

94. Jones, *Murderous Women*: 26.

95. *The Daily Mail*, 22 April, 1955, as quoted in Bardsley, *Flowers*: 140.

96. Chris Auty, as quoted in Bardsley, *Flowers*: 143.

97. Rose, *Why War?*: 50.

98. Transcript reproduced in Goodman and Pringle, *Ruth Ellis*: 91. My emphasis.

99. Transcript reproduced in Goodman and Pringle, *Ruth Ellis*: 94. My emphasis.

100. Farran, *Trial*: 87.

101. Ellis was still under the care of Dr Rees at the time of the murder, being treated with tranquillizers for 'intense emotional distress' (Marks and Van den Bergh, *Diminished Responsibility*: 157).

102. Marks and Van den Bergh, *Diminished Responsibility*: 26.

103. Goodman and Pringle, *Ruth Ellis*: 121.

104. According to one jury member, 'while we were discussing whether or not she meant to kill him, the thing that sticks out in my mind was that the others were going backwards and forwards to the toilet. I reckon that of the 23 minutes we were out, only about 13 were spent actually discussing the case' (Marks and Van den Bergh, *Diminished Responsibility*: 162).

105. Farran, *Flowers*: 19.

106. Rose, *Why War?*: 50. See also Birch, 'Twice Unnatural': 25.

107. Worrall, *Offending Women*: 10.

108. See, for example, Smart's discussion on the body as a site of cultural production: '… women's bodies are constituted as the archetypal site of irrationality. The female body, as constructed in legal discourse, is seen to have failed the test of subordinating desire to reason, and emotionality to rationality' (C. Smart, *Law, Crime and Sexuality* [London: Sage, 1995]: 227).

109. This female category of the 'cold, calculating, vengeful killer' was of particular relevance in the Ellis case because of the time lapse between the last time Blakely had provoked her and the killing. Forty years later, feminist activists are still struggling (with some success) to have the male definition of provocation changed from so-called 'heat of the moment' retaliation to one which includes women's experience of accumulative provocation and delayed retaliation, 'not because they are any less provoked, or less eager to retaliate immediately, but because that is the only time when self-defensive action is likely to succeed' (S. Edwards, *Policing 'Domestic' Violence* (London: Sage, 1989): 184). The case of Sara Thornton, discussed below, provides a recent example of this struggle.

110. See, for example, J. Ritchie, *Myra Hindley*: 103, 108, 114. See also J. Goodman, *The Moors Murders: The Trial of Myra Hindley & Ian Brady* (Newton Abbot: David and Charles, 1986): 15, where in response to a neighbour's pregnancy, Hindley is reported to have said: 'Why don't you do something to shift it?' She was further reported to have 'sneered at marriage, dubbing it "conventional hypocrisy"'.

111. Ritchie, *Myra Hindley*: 114; R. Wilson, *Devil's Disciples* (Poole: Javelin, 1986): 96. See also page 117: 'Her face showed no emotion.'

112. F. Harrison, *Brady & Hindley: Genesis of the Moors Murders* (London: HarperCollins, 1994): 191.

113. Letter to *The Guardian*, 4 October, 1995.

114. Letter to *The Guardian*, 7 October, 1995.

115. Myra Hindley as quoted in Birch, *Moving Targets*: 59.

116. Helen Birch has written that 'While there is little doubt that for Myra Hindley, to have continued access to therapy would have been of considerable benefit both to her and to our understanding of why people commit crimes like these, public feeling, exacerbated by the tabloids, runs much deeper than logic or reason will allow' (Birch, *Moving Targets*: 60).

117. Kirsta, *Deadlier*: 107–12.

118. Carlen, *Criminal Women*: 156–8.

119. O'Dwyer, as quoted in Kirsta, *Deadlier*: 109.

120. O'Dwyer, as quoted in Carlen, *Criminal Women*: 158.

121. Birch, *Moving Targets*: 61.

122. *The Guardian*, 11 October, 1995.

123. For example, O'Dwyer had also 'stabbed a probation officer with a paper knife' (*The Guardian*, 11 October, 1995) and put a prison officer in hospital for three days after 'our heads collided' (Carlen, *Criminal Women*: 156) as well as 'seriously disabl[ing] a man sexually recently when he was trying it on with me' (O'Dwyer, as quoted in Kirsta, *Deadlier*: 112).

124. A. Jones, *Women Who Kill* (London: Gollancz, 1991): 304.

125. A. Jones, *Women Who Kill*: 307.

126. Letter to Master McKenzie, dated 23 May, 1991, as quoted in J. Nadel, *Sara Thornton: The Story of a Woman Who Killed* (London: Gollancz, 1993): 193–4. My emphasis. For a summary of Thornton's case, see Hargreaves, this volume, p.47.

127. Yvonne Roberts in *The Guardian*, 7 December, 1995. See also A. Jones' discussion of 'uppity women' in *Women Who Kill*: 350.

128. *The Observer*, 30 July, 1995.

129. *The Guardian*, 8 July, 1995.

130. Yvonne Roberts in *The Guardian*, 7 December, 1995.

Partners in Crime – French

1. Myriam Miedzian, *Boys Will Be Boys: Breaking the Link Between Masculinity and Violence* (London: Virago, 1992).

2. An article by Nick Davies in *The Guardian* (8 February, 1996) cited the case of Geri Andrews (not her real name), who was fined £400 for non-payment of a £15 parking ticket and failure to display a £140 car tax disc. She was unable to pay the fine and was imprisoned for 14 days, during which time her two children were taken into care. Figures released by the Howard League for Penal Reform show that a third of all women in prison are there for failure to pay fines or for offences that normally wouldn't warrant a prison offence. There may be an element of prejudice against supposedly irresponsible mothers in this, but it is mainly because single mothers are likely to be in debt and magistrates are under pressure to speed up their turnover of cases. Whatever the cause, the result is a system that is loaded against women. (The magistrates' action is, incidentally, illegal: Nick Davies interviewed a solicitor who, during 1995, had acted for 135 fine defaulters and 161 poll-tax defaulters who had received custodial sentences from magistrates: he secured release for them all.) A British Government White Paper on the disparity in sentencing is said to be imminent.

3. *The Guardian*, 18 December, 1995.

4. *The Guardian*, 21 December, 1995.

Books referred to in this essay:

Terry Manners, *Deadlier than the Male: Stories of Female Serial Killers* (Pan, 1995).

Estella V. Welldon, *Mother, Madonna, Whore: The Idealization and Denigration of Motherhood* (1988; Guilford Press edition, 1992).

There are many books about the Moors Murders, offering varying versions and interpretations. I was only concerned with the undisputed aspects of the case, which are much the same in all versions. The books I drew on were:

Frank Jones, *Murderous Women* (Headline, 1991)

Emlyn Williams, *Beyond Belief* (Hamish Hamilton, 1967)

Colin Wilson, *A Plague of Murder* (Robinson, 1995).

The most detailed book about the Hedda Nussbaum trial is Joyce Johnson's *What Lisa Knew: The Truth and Lies of the Steinberg Case* (1990).

Many details of the Karla Homolka/Paul Bernardo murders and trial remain obscure because of Canadian privacy laws. I relied on the account in Manners, above, and on contemporary press reports. For the Rosemary West trial, I drew on the detailed press coverage.

Trying the *Brookside* Two – Hargreaves

1. A 1990 survey commissioned by Granada TV's *World in Action* showed that one in four women in Britain between the ages of 18 and 54 had been raped by husbands, boyfriends, acquaintances or strangers, and that one in seven women had been raped by their husbands.
2. Sean Day Lewis, *Sunday Telegraph Review*, 7 May, 1995.
3. Lady Olga Maitland, *The Daily Mail*, 18 May, 1995.
4. *The Guardian*, 17 May, 1995.
5. Allison Pearson, *The Independent*, 21 May, 1995.
6. Christine Geraghty, *Women and Soap Opera: A Study of Prime-Time Soaps* (Cambridge: Polity Press, 1991): 5.
7. Phil Redmond, *The Guardian*, 18 May, 1995.
8. Ibid.
9. Sandra Maitland, as quoted in *The Independent*, interview with Jamie Lawrence, 8 May, 1995.
10. See Jane Thynne, *Daily Telegraph*, 17 May, 1995 and Alison Boshoff, *The Daily Mail*, 18 May, 1995.
11. *Today*, 4 February, 1995.
12. *The Guardian Law Reports*, cited in *The Guardian*, 31 July, 1991.
13. *The Guardian Law Reports*, the case of *Regina v Thornton*, 29 July, 1991, cited in *The Guardian*, 31 July, 1991.
14. *The Guardian*, 23 July, 1992.
15. *The Times*, 16 August, 1991.
16. Sara Thornton, cited in *The Times*, 23 August, 1991.
17. Phil Redmond, as quoted in *The Daily Telegraph*, 17 May, 1995.
18. *Beth Jordache: The New Journals* (Boxtree, 1995): 150.
19. In 1993, Nicholas Hall was put on probation for strangling his unfaithful wife in an argument over the custody of their children.
20. Sally Weale, quoting Horley in an article in *The Guardian*, 18 May, 1995.
21. Sandra Maitland, as quoted in *The Observer*, 13 March, 1994.
22. See *The Guardian*, 20 February, 1991.

23. Phil Redmond, 'Why I had to find Mandy and Beth guilty', *The Guardian*, 18 May, 1995.
24. *The Guardian*, 30 January, 1992.
25. Hilary Kingsley, *Today*, 5 August, 1995.
26. Hilary Kingsley, *Today*, 9 September, 1995.
27. Richard Morrison, *The Times*, 3 December, 1994.
28. Jamie Lawrence, *The Independent*, 8 May, 1995; Tapehead, *The Guardian Magazine*, 28 January, 1995.
29. Stuart Jefferies, *The Guardian*, 13 May, 1995; Brian Viner, *Mail on Sunday*, 14 May, 1995.
30. Stuart Jefferies, *The Guardian*, 13 May, 1995.
31. Allison Pearson, *Evening Standard*, 16 May, 1995.
32. Ibid.
33. Tania Modleski, *Loving with a Vengeance: Mass-produced Fantasies for Women* (London: Methuen, 1984): 13.
34. Modleski, *Loving with a Vengeance*: 77.
35. Moyra Friend, cited in the *The Guardian*, 8 April, 1992.
36. Modleski, *Loving with a Vengeance*: 93.
37. Modleski, *Loving with a Vengeance*: 108.
38. Modleski, *Loving with a Vengeance*: 111.
39. Modleski, *Loving with a Vengeance*: 75.
40. Geraghty, *Women and Soap*: 4.
41. Geraghty, *Women and Soap*: 49.
42. Jamie Lawrence, *The Independent*, 8 May, 1995.
43. Alex Bellos, 'Close to the Edge', *Observer Magazine*, 13 March, 1994.
44. *The Daily Mail*, 19 July, 1995.

Retelling the Tale – Stanko and Scully

1. Personal communication, Home Office Research and Planning Unit, 1996.
2. S. Gavigan, 'Petit Treason in Eighteenth-Century England: Women's Inequality before the Law', *Canadian Journal of Women and the Law* 3.2 (1990): 335–51.
3. *R v Ahluwalia* (1993); *R v Thornton* (1996).
4. Justice for Women, 55 Rathcoole Gardens, London N8 9NE, UK.
5. *R v Humphreys*, 1995, Transcript of Court of Appeal, Criminal Division, (No. 86/0202/D3: 2–5).

6. Frances Heidensohn, *Women and Crime* (London: Macmillan, 1985).
7. Liz Kelly, *Surviving Sexual Violence* (Cambridge: Polity Press, 1988); Elizabeth A. Stanko, *Intimate Intrusions* (London: Routledge, 1985).
8. R. E. Dobash and R. P. Dobash, *Women, Violence and Social Change* (London: Routledge, 1992).
9. Indeed, it is not only women who are directly affected by domestic violence. Kim Crenshaw recently cites a US statistic which even brought chills to our hearts: it is estimated that 63 per cent of young men between the ages of 11 and 20 who are imprisoned for homicide have killed their mothers' batterers. See Crenshaw, 'Mapping the Margins: Intersectionality, Identity Politics, and Violence Against Women of Color' in M. Fineman and R. Mykitiuk, *The Public Nature of Private Violence* (London: Routledge, 1994).
10. Mary Gilfus, 'From Victims to Survivors to Offenders: Women's Routes of Entry and Immersion into Street Crime', *Women and Criminal Justice* 4.1 (1992): 63–90; Kathleen Daly, *Gender, Crime and Punishment* (New Haven: Yale University Press, 1994).
11. Lenore Walker, *The Battered Woman Syndrome* (New York: Springer Publishers, 1984).
12. Wendy Chan, *The (un)Making of an Aberration: Women who Kill their Partners in England and Wales* (unpublished Ph.D. thesis, University of Cambridge); and Holly Maguigan, 'Battered Women and Self-defense: Myths and Misconceptions in Current Reform Proposals', *University of Pennsylvania Law Review* 140 (1991): 379–486.
13. See, for example, in the USA, Maguigan, 'Battered Women', and Cynthia Gillespie, *Justifiable Homicide* (Columbus, Ohio: University of Ohio Press, 1989); in England, Donald Nicolson, 'Telling Tales: Gender Discrimination, Gender Construction and Battered Women who Kill', *Feminist Legal Studies* 3.2 (1995): 185–206.
14. Gillespie, *Justifiable Homicide*; Elizabeth Schneider, 'Particularity and Generality: Challenges of Feminist Theory and Practice in Work on Woman-Abuse', *New York University Law Review* 67 (June, 1992) 520–68.
15. *R v Ahluwalia* [1992] 4 All E.R. 889.
16. See also Dee Dee Glass, *All My Fault* (London: Virago, 1995).

17. See also Alison Young and Peter Rush, 'The Law of Victimage in Urbane Realism: Thinking through Inscriptions of Violence', in David Nelkin (ed.), *The Futures of Criminology* (London: Sage, 1994).
18. See, in particular, Nicolson, 'Telling Tales'.
19. See Anne Worrall, *Offending Women* (London: Routledge, 1990).
20. We are indebted to Dee Dee Glass' research on self-harm for this perspective.
21. Sue Bandalli, 'Provocation – A Cautionary Note', *Journal of Law and Society* 22 (September, 1995): 398–409.
22. The rules of statutory interpretation dictate that statutory provisions should be given their literal meaning. However, where there is ambiguity of meaning, the provision may be interpreted either by reading it in the context of the statute as a whole, or by looking to the purpose of Parliament in passing the statute.
23. See also *R. v Morhall* 98 Cr App R 108. This case concerned a defendant who sniffed glue. Glue-sniffing is self-inflicted and thus a characteristic repugnant to the reasonable [wo]man.
24. The direction on the reasonable man was given following the classic statement in *DPP v Camplin* [1978, 67 Cr App R 14] in which the defendant's own characteristics were deemed to be of limited relevance.
25. Court of Appeal Judgment in *R. v Humphreys*.: 5
26. This judgment is especially interesting for the judge's elimination of 'attention-seeking behaviour' from the definition of what is repugnant to the concept of the reasonable 'person'. See page 24 of the judgment.
27. Carol Smart, *Feminism and the Power of Law* (London: Routledge, 1989): 86.
28. See Gillespie, *Justifiable Homicide*; also Jill Radford and Liz Kelly, 'Self-preservation: Feminist Activism and Feminist Jurisprudence', in M. Maynard and J. Purvis (eds), *(Hetero)Sexual Politics* (London: Taylor & Francis, 1995): 186–99.

Fighting for Freedom – Hamer

1. John Stuart Mill presented the case for women's suffrage in Parliament in 1867.
2. Usually attributed as Nurse Smith and Edith New outside Downing Street, 17 January, 1908.
3. Included, for instance, in the Museum of London's 1992–3 exhibition, *Purple, White and Green, Suffragettes in London 1906–1914*.
4. Sylvia Pankhurst, *The Suffragette Movement* (London: Virago, 1977; first published 1931): 214.
5. Pankhurst, *Suffragette Movement*: 223.
6. Ibid.
7. Pankhurst, *Suffragette Movement*: 275.
8. Pankhurst, *Suffragette Movement*: 314.
9. Pankhurst, *Suffragette Movement*: 307; this slogan was taken from the 1869 Bill of Rights.
10. Pankhurst, *Suffragette Movement*: 402–3.
11. Few suffragettes served the full term of their sentences; in this case Mary Leigh and Gladys Evans only actually served nine weeks.
12. Caroline Morrell, *'Black Friday': Violence against Women in the Suffragette Movement* (London: Women's Research and Resources Centre Publications, 1981): 54.
13. Antonia Raeburn, *The Militant Suffragettes* (London: Michael Joseph, 1973): 248.
14. Morrell, *'Black Friday'*: 56.
15. Naomi Jacob, *Me: A Chronicle about Other People* (London: Hutchinson, 1933): 193.
16. *Daily Mirror*, 18 April, 1914: 3.
17. Pankhurst, *Suffragette Movement*: 544.
18. Leah Leneman, *Martyrs in Our Midst: Dundee, Perth and the Forcible Feeding of Suffragettes* (Dundee: Abertay Historical Society Publication No. 33, 1993): 15.
19. *Daily Mirror*, 11 May, 1914: 20.
20. Pankhurst, *Suffragette Movement*: 561.
21. Raeburn, *Militant Suffragettes*: 230.
22. Leneman, *Martyrs in Our Midst*: 29.
23. Roger Fulford, *Votes for Women* (London: White Lion Publishers, 1976): 290.

24. Leneman, *Martyrs in Our Midst*: 31. Frances Parker went under the name 'Janet Arthur'.
25. *Daily Mirror*, 10 May, 1914: 3.
26. *Daily Mirror*, 5 May, 1914: 4.
27. *The Times*, 13 January, 1912: 9.
28. *The Times, Standard* and *Daily Mirror*, 19 November, 1910; *Daily Express*, 23 November, 1910.
29. Pankhurst, *Suffragette Movement*: 229.
30. *Daily Mirror*, 22 May, 1914: 3.
31. *Daily Mirror*, 22 May, 1914: 4.
32. *Daily Mirror* (22 May, 1914) stated 1,000, *The Times* (23 May, 1914) stated 1,500.
33. Pankhurst, *Suffragette Movement*: 380.
34. In this period Irish nationalists held in gaol were, for instance, classified as political prisoners.
35. Pankhurst, *Suffragette Movement*: 317.
36. Maud Ellman, *The Hunger Artists: Starving, Writing and Imprisonment* (London: Virago, 1993): 33–4.
37. Leneman, *Martyrs in Our Midst*; the two women were Frances Gordon and Frances Parker ('Janet Arthur').
38. Leneman, *Martyrs in Our Midst*: 27.
39. Raeburn, *Militant Suffragettes*: 113.
40. Pankhurst, *Suffragette Movement*: 229.
41. Leneman, *Martyrs in Our Midst*.
42. Pankhurst, *Suffragette Movement*: 559–61.
43. Pankhurst, *Suffragette Movement*: 231 and 232.
44. Pankhurst, *Suffragette Movement*: 228.
45. Pankhurst, *Suffragette Movement*: 342–5.
46. In Marie Mulvey Roberts and Tamae Mizuta (eds), *The Militants: Suffragette Activism* (London: Routledge, 1994).
47. Morrell, *'Black Friday'*: 6.
48. *The Times*, 11 January, 1912: 2; the article covers her trial for arson on letter boxes with kerosene.
49. *The Times*, 25 May, 1914: 34.
50. Ibid.
51. Ibid.
52. Mary Sophia Allen, *The Pioneer Policewoman* (London: Chatto & Windus, 1925): 13.

All Too Familiar – Holmes

1. *The Guardian*, *The Daily Telegraph*, and *The Times*, 19 March, 1996.
2. Nelson Rolihlahla Mandela, *Long Walk to Freedom* (London: Abacus, 1995): 711.
3. *The Times*, 19 March, 1996.
4. *The Guardian*, 21 March, 1996.
5. Nelson Mandela requested that this powerful group of community leaders convene to deal with the crisis emerging as a result of the burning down of Winnie Mandela's house in July, 1988. Initially thought to be the work of the government, it rapidly emerged that the house and all its contents had been burned down by students from the Daliwonga High School as a counter-strike in an escalating dispute between members of the school and the MUFC. Local residents did nothing to help stop the fire. When Nelson Mandela was given details of the events, he requested from prison that the students responsible should not have charges brought against them. Instead, he instructed the convening of the Crisis Committee, whose first move was to request the disbanding of the 'football team'. Winnie Mandela refused this request.
6. Winnie Mandela, as quoted in the *Cape Times*, 31 January, 1989.
7. Winnie Mandela, *Cape Times*, 22 February, 1989.
8. Winnie Mandela to *Tribute* magazine, cited in Emma Gilbey, *The Lady: The Life and Times of Winnie Mandela* (London: Vintage, 1994): 270.
9. For an introduction to the importance to the South African lesbian and gay movement of the homophobic defence case in the 1991 Winnie Mandela trial, see Mark Gevisser and Edwin Cameron (eds), *Defiant Desire: Gay and Lesbian Lives in South Africa* (London: Routledge, 1995).
10. Mandela, *Long Walk*: 576.
11. The armed wing of the ANC, whose name meant 'Spear of the Nation', commonly referred to as 'MK'.
12. Apart from being implicated in the murder of Stompie Moeketsi Seipei and Dr Abu-Baker Asvat, the reign of terror of the MUFC was linked to the murder of 13-year-old Finkie Marcia Msomi, shot in the head in a reprisal killing after the death of Max Madonda, a former Mandela bodyguard. The group was also involved in a battery-acid

assault case. For fuller details of the forms of violence undertaken by the MUFC in Soweto, see Gilbey, *The Lady* and Paul Trewhela, 'Mrs Mandela: "Enemy Agents!" … and the ANC Women's League', *Searchlight South Africa* 11 (October, 1993): 17–22.

13. SA Pressclips, *Winnie Affair* (Tamboerskloof: 1989): 12.

14. Mandela, *Long Walk*: 194.

15. Variously quoted; see *Washington Times*, 16 February, 1989; Gilbey, *The Lady*: 145. A necklace is a petrol-soaked tyre, placed around someone's neck and set alight.

16. Mark Gevisser, *The Guardian*, 7 December, 1993.

17. Ibid.

18. Ibid.

19. See *Daily Dispatch*, 16 May, 1991; *The Independent on Sunday*, 19 April, 1992; *Weekend Guardian*, 25 April, 1992.

20. John Carlin, *The Independent on Sunday*, 19 May, 1992.

21. Elleke Boehmer, 'Stories of Women and Mothers', in Susheila Nasta (ed.), *Motherlands: Black Women's Writing from Africa, the Caribbean and South Asia* (London: Women's Press, 1991): 6.

22. Anne McClintock, *Imperial Leather: Race, Gender and Sexuality in the Colonial Contest* (London: Routledge, 1995): 352.

23. Mandela, *Long Walk*: 252.

24. Anne McClintock, '"No Longer in a Future Heaven": Women and Nationalism in South Africa', *Transition* 54 (1991): 104–23; p. 117.

25. Winnie Mandela, as quoted in *Mandela: From Prisoner to President*, Mark Galloway documentary (Yorkshire Television, 1994).

Phallocentric Slicing – Priest, Jenefsky, and Swenson

1. *Vanity Fair* editors used this phrase on p. 16 in an introductory note for a feature article on the Bobbitts: Kim Masters, 'Sex, Lies, and an 8-inch Carving Knife', *Vanity Fair* (November 1993): 207–12; David Kaplan, 'Bobbitt Fever', *Newsweek*, 24 January, 1994: 55; *American Journal*, January 10, 1994.

2. 'Beyond Belief' was written by Tom Jarriel and produced by Barbara Baylor. As reported in *Broadcasting and Cable* on 4 October, 1993, Nielsen ratings for *20/20* on 24 September, 1993 were 18.3, with a 33 share.

3. Helen Benedict, *Virgin or Vamp: How the Press Covers Sex Crimes* (New York: Oxford University Press, 1992): 13–24. For more on rape

myths, see also Marian Meyers, 'News of Battering', *Journal of Communication* 44 (Spring, 1994): 47–63; Carol Smart and Barry Smart, *Women, Sexuality, and Social Control* (London: Routledge and Kegan Paul, 1978).

4. Benedict, *Virgin or Vamp*: 251.

5. Meyers, 'News of Battering', 52 and 48, respectively. Lisa Cuklanz's analysis of the Rideout rape case (the first nationally covered trial in the US of a rape within marriage) echoes Benedict's and Meyers' findings. She notes the media's 'emphasis on dramatic and personalized content and a reluctance to explain systems of law, logic or belief' surrounding the case ('Truth in Transition: Discursive Constructions of Character in the Rideout Rape in Marriage Case', *Women's Studies in Communication* 16 (Spring, 1993): 80. Similarly, Keith Soothill and Sylvia Walby describe the British press' preoccupation with the individual character of the rapist, a tactic used to enhance the dramatic quality of news stories at the expense of delineating a larger social context in which the drama occurs (*Sex Crime in the News* (London: Routledge, 1991)).

6. Barbara Johnson, 'A Dangerous Pattern: A Study of Media Coverage of Violence Against Women in the *San Francisco Chronicle* and *San Francisco Examiner*', March, 1994 (unpublished material, available from Barbara Johnson, 3891 26th St., San Francisco, CA 94131): 19.

7. Marian Meyers, *Engendering Blame: News Coverage of Violence Against Women* (Thousand Oaks, CA: Sage, 1996). For studies that compare police reports with newspaper accounts, see Marlyss Schwengels and James Lemert, 'Fair Warning: A Comparison of Police and Newspaper Reports about Rape', *Newspaper Research Journal* 7 (Spring, 1986): 35–42; Linda Heath, Margaret Gordon and Robert LeBailly, 'What Newspapers Tell Us (And Don't Tell Us) about Rape', *Newspaper Research Journal* 2 (July, 1981): 48–55.

8. See Sarah Kozloff's work entitled 'Narrative Theory and Television' for a fuller description of framing and embedded narratives, in Robert Allen (ed.), *Channels of Discourse Reassembled*, Chapel Hill, NC: University of North Carolina, 1992: 42–73.

9. The Bobbitt story was the second of three segments on that evening's programme.

10. Andrea Dworkin, *Pornography: Men Possessing Women* (New York: Dutton, 1989): 67.

11. This technique also surfaces in print versions of the story. A sidebar accompanying an article by Anne Gearan in *The Athens* [Georgia] *Daily News* of 2 January, 1994, for example, shows a chronology of events which collapses John and Lorena's history and lists only one mention of prior abuse. This listing was meager, too, because it merely involved Lorena's complaints about spousal abuse to a neighbour on the eve of the maiming; more substantive evidence such as the dates police responded to 911 calls at their home could have been noted ('Lorena Bobbitt Found Innocent by Virginia Jury': A12).

12. See Michael Schudson, 'Deadlines, Datelines, and History', in Robert Manoff and Michael Schudson (eds), *Reading the News* (New York: Pantheon, 1987): 79–108.

13. Feminist writer Melanie Kaye/Kantrowitz discusses this phenomenon in her chapter, 'Women, Violence, and Resistance, Naming It War', in idem, *The Issue Is Power: Essays on Women, Jews, Violence, and Resistance* (San Francisco: Aunt Lute Books, 1992): 7–74.

14. John abstained from public interviews at this point, so his lawyer speaks for him on the program.

15. At Jarriel's prompting during the interview, Lorena provides a step-by-step account of the series of events on that one night leading up to the penis severance: beginning with the rape, to spotting the knife in the kitchen, to cutting off John's penis, to fleeing the apartment, to tossing the penis out the window of her car. Alternating with close-up shots of her and Jarriel speaking are dramatic visual shots conveying an excited sense of movement paralleling Lorena's descriptions. As she describes fleeing the apartment, for instance, the camera 'takes the viewer' down the stairs of the apartment complex. We then hear a car motor start and see headlights light up. As she mentions discovering the severed penis in her hand while driving, the viewer is given a passenger's-eye-view from a moving car of the 'grassy knoll' where she threw the organ.

16. For example, his actions are briefly recreated only in a 10-second reenactment of his reckless driving the night he first punched Lorena – an incident which, while cruel, was one of the least serious of his criminal actions.

17. See Benedict, *Virgin or Vamp*; Meyers, *Engendering Blame*.

18. Cuklanz, 'Truth in Transition': 82.

19. Federal Bureau of Investigation's *Uniform Crime Reports* (Department of Justice, Washington, DC, 1993): 14, 20. Figures in various studies vary dramatically depending on age group, definitions used, and other factors (see Linda Brookover Bourque, *Defining Rape* [Durham, NC: Duke University Press, 1989]), but the average hovers around 25 per cent.

20. See also Ann Jones' book about wife battery, which discusses news writers' widespread use of words such as 'lover's quarrel' which trivialize the gravity of the violence and create the impression of mutuality in domestic violence incidents (*Next Time, She'll Be Dead* [Boston: Beacon, 1994]).

21. For a more expanded discussion of this cultural sense of entitlement, see Diana Russell, *Rape in Marriage* (2nd edn; Bloomington: Indiana University, 1990).

22. Timothy Beneke, *Men on Rape* (New York: Oxford University Press, 1982): 56.

23. *Jenny Jones*, 23 December, 1993.

24. Mike Royko, 'She Took the Law into Her Own Hands', *Chicago Tribune*, 22 January, 1993: 3.

25. This view hints at different stances generally adopted by male and female readers of rape scenarios. Women seem to read news reports of rape and often think, 'That could have been me.' Men rarely position themselves as the potential victim of a rape report; there may be a sense of sympathy and horror, but not a grim terror. The differentiation between terror and horror is described in works of literary criticism of gothic writing which discuss male authors' tendency to place females in dire, sickening jeopardy. The positioning of the male reader includes a distance from the terror. Terry Heller writes: 'Terror is fear for oneself, horror is fear on account of someone else' (*The Delights of Terror: An Aesthetics of the Tale of Terror* [Urbana, IL: University of Illinois Press, 1987]: 19). Men pick up the truncated version of the Bobbitt rape story hatcheted by the press and seem to respond by situating themselves in John's place, as victim. Men also position themselves as victims in news reports of rape when they worry that they will be falsely accused, but they seem seldom, if ever, to empathize fully with the usual victim of the story, the woman raped.

26. Beneke, *Men on Rape*: 112.

27. For analysis of the media's coverage of this marital rape case, see Benedict, *Virgin or Vamp*; Cuklanz, 'Truth in Transition'.

28. For further discussion of this point, see, for instance, Mildred Pagelow, *Woman-Battering: Victims and their Experiences* (Beverly Hills, CA: Sage, 1981); John Stoltenberg, *Refusing to Be A Man* (New York: Penguin, 1989).

29. For research on the dangers to women of machismo, see Sarah McCarthy, 'Pornography, Rape, and the Cult of Macho', *The Humanist* (September/October, 1980): 11–20; Peggy Reeves Sanday, 'The Socio-cultural Context of Rape: A Cross-cultural Study', *Journal of Social Issues* 37 (October, 1981): 5–27. See M. Thompson, 'The Living Room War', *Time*, 23 May, 1994: 48–51 for recent statistics on violence in military families.

30. Cartoon by Gamble, printed in the *Athens* [Georgia] *Banner Herald*, 31 January, 1994.

31. Kathleen Lawrence, 'Bobbitt Spouse Abuse/Assault Case', (paper delivered at the Eightieth Annual Meeting of the Speech Communication Association, New Orleans, Louisiana, November, 1994); Kaye/Kantrowitz, *The Issue is Power*, 10.

32. Magazine programs such as *20/20* have been criticized in the last few years for increasingly lurid and lax journalism (see, for example, Teresa Keller, 'Trash TV', *Journal of Popular Culture* 26 [Spring, 1993]: 195–206). However, as noted previously, the sensational language in the *20/20* report directs attention to Lorena's actions and not her abuser's.

33. Michael Ross, 'Jury Acquits Bobbitt, Rules She Was Insane', *Atlanta Journal and Constitution*, 22 January, 1994: A1; Elizabeth Gleick, Rochelle Jones, Mary Huzinec and Jane Sugden, 'Severance Pay', *People*, 13 December 1993: 92–96; David Margolick, 'Witnesses Say Mutilated Man Often Hit Wife', *The New York Times*, 12 January, 1994: A10.

34. Brian Johnson, 'The Male Myth', *MacLean's*, 31 January, 1994: 39.

35. See, for example, Bill Miller and Marylou Tousignant, 'Bobbitt Acquitted in Attack on Husband', *The Washington Post*, 22 January, 1994. An Associated Press report by Anne Gearan describes how even Lorena's prosecuting attorney admitted in closing arguments that John had forced sex on Lorena their last night together ('Lorena

Bobbitt Found Innocent': 12). Although John was not convicted, we none the less refer throughout this chapter to his actions as rape and battery because we, too, believe he was guilty.

36. *Jenny Jones*, 23 December, 1993.

37. See Suzanne Garment, 'Can the Media be Reformed?' *Commentary* (August, 1987): 37–43; Tom Goldstein, *The News at Any Cost: How Journalists Compromise Their Ethics to Shape the News* (New York: Simon and Schuster, 1985); Edward Herman, *Beyond Hypocrisy: Decoding the News in an Age of Propaganda* (Montreal: Black Rose Books, 1992); Carlin Romano, 'The Grisly Truth about the Bare Facts', in Robert Manoff and Michael Schudson (eds), *Reading the News* (New York: Pantheon, 1987); and Gaye Tuchman, *Making News: A Study in the Construction of Reality* (New York: Free Press, 1978).

38. Herbert Gans, *Deciding What's News* (New York: Random House, 1980).

Women Who Kill – Savage

1. A portion of an earlier version of this paper was originally presented at the Console-ing Passions conference, Los Angeles, 1993.

2. Lisa Priest, *Women Who Killed: Stories of Canadian Female Murderers* (Toronto: M & S, 1992): 9–10.

3. Deborah Starr Seibel, 'Caged Fury', *TV Guide* (31 October, 1992): 18.

4. Mark Harris, 'Dangerous Women', *Entertainment Weekly* (24 April, 1992): 39.

5. Wanda Holloway hired an assassin to remove her daughter's competition for the local high school cheerleading team; former police officer Bambi Bembenek was found guilty of murdering her ex-husband's second wife, but suspicion around the impartiality of the investigation into the crime made her very sympathetic to the public and 'Run, Bambi, Run' T-shirts appeared when she broke out of prison and fled to Canada; taken up as 'America's first female serial killer', Aileen Wuornos was a lesbian drifter who killed several men, she alleges in self-defence while they were raping her; 16-year-old Amy Fisher, known as the 'Long Island Lolita', shot her older lover's wife in the head (the wife survived).

6. Elaine Rapping, *The Movie of the Week: Private Stories, Public Events* (Minneapolis: University of Minnesota Press, 1992): xxxi–xlii.

7. *Los Angeles Times*, 11 March, 1990.
8. The phrase 'Hell hath no fury like a woman scorned' can be traced back to Congreve's play *The Mourning Bride* (1697): 'Heav'n has no Rage, like Love to Hatred turn'd/ Nor Hell a Fury, like a Woman scorn'd' (III.i.457). The original quotation refers to the Furies, Greek goddesses of retributive justice who pursued wrongdoers, especially those guilty of matricide. The goddesses responsible for seeking revenge upon mother-killers and punishing arrogant men seem right at home in the context of the Broderick murders. The way it circulates today, however, this phrase hardly brings to mind valiant goddess-warriors.
9. *Los Angeles Times*, 28 March, 1990.
10. *Los Angeles Times*, 29 February, 1992.
11. Broderick herself contends that, unbeknownst to her, Wallace was in contact with the producers of the show, Patchett Kaufman Entertainment, while conducting the interviews. I have not been able to verify this.
12. Amy Wallace, 'Divorce Most Foul', *TV Guide* (29 February, 1992): 7–8.
13. *Los Angeles Times*, 29 February, 1992.
14. Bryna Taubman, *Hell Hath No Fury* (New York: St. Martin's Press, 1992): 270.
15. In response to my question asking whether or not she had attempted to contact Steve Kelley for her article or *A Woman Scorned*, Wallace replied in a letter dated 22 July, 1992, 'I have talked to Steve Kelley, but not for my "Betty"-coverage. I don't believe that [television production company] Patchett-Kaufman contacted him.'
16. Kathleen Neumeyer, 'Hell Hath No Fury', *Ladies Home Journal* (March, 1991): 220.
17. Amy Wallace, 'Till Murder Do Us Part', *Los Angeles Times Magazine* (3 June, 1990): 15.
18. Wallace, 'Till Murder': 34.
19. Neumeyer, 'No Fury': 218.
20. Wallace, 'Till Murder': 17.
21. Neumeyer, 'No Fury': 221.
22. Kathryn Casey, 'The Devil Inside', *Ladies Home Journal* (June, 1992): 82.

23. *Mirabella* targets a more mature, better educated audience, declining to use young 'supermodels' in fashion layouts and featuring more articles on aging, women in the workforce, and politics.

24. Susan Lehman, 'A Woman Scorned', *Mirabella* (September, 1991): 12; Ray Finch, *Crimes of Passion* (Boca Raton, FL: Globe, 1992): 39.

25. Finch, *Crimes of Passion*: 36.

26. Unfortunately, I was unable to obtain copies of the *20/20* and *Hard Copy* television programs that featured stories on Broderick. They would have been an interesting counterpoint to my other print sources, and to television discourse aimed primarily at women (for example, *The Oprah Winfrey Show*).

27. One exception to this occurred on *The Oprah Winfrey Show*. Robin Tu'ua, a former governess employed by Dan Broderick after his divorce, echoes Wallace's tone: 'You know, what I can't get over is this woman was getting $16,000 a month alimony. Some people, some families, do not even make that in a year. And this was not enough money for her' (3 November, 1992). Neither Winfrey nor any audience or panel member attempts to contextualize this figure in the light of Dan's salary, or Betty's contribution to his education. While *Oprah* is marketed towards women, I would account for this take on Betty's alimony by suggesting that its relation to TV discourse in general may at times be stronger than its relation to trans-media networks of women's discourse.

28. Susan Ohmer, 'Female Spectatorship and Women's Magazines: Hollywood, Good Housekeeping, and World War II', *The Velvet Light Trap* 25 (1990): 54.

29. Taubman, *No Fury*: 267.

30. If I were willing to posit a 'true' text, I would defer to Broderick's own *What's a Nice Girl to Do? White Collar Domestic Violence in America*, an autobiography written throughout the period of her divorce. I have tried repeatedly to get this document from Broderick's lawyer, Jack Earley, but his staff has allegedly not been able to locate it (Broderick does not have a copy in her possession). Patchett Kaufman Entertainment did not contact Broderick about putting the movie together, and Broderick claims Earley ignored her request to try to get an injunction against CBS to keep them from using her name in the title. On the day we spoke, Broderick described Earley

as 'a cheap buy-off, not a classy guy', and suggested that CBS may even have paid Earley not to act.

31. This includes geographical area. Obviously, the impact of the trial in the San Diego area would have been considerably different than in other places in terms of the amount of newspaper coverage, for example. Broderick also appeared on *Court TV*, interrupting daytime soap operas where this station operates.

32. The children's names have been changed in the movie. Rhett, the youngest son, has been named Grant, which diffuses Dan's fascination with *Gone With the Wind* and its hero, Rhett Butler. It's one thing to assert that *Gone With the Wind* is your favorite movie, and allude to the film in conversation (two details that appear in *A Woman Scorned*), but naming your child Rhett adds a somewhat fanatical edge to these more mundane behaviors, an observation most of the magazine articles do not overlook.

33. Neumeyer, 'No Fury': 218; Taubman, *No Fury*: 45; *Los Angeles Times*, 31 October, 1990.

34. Taubman, *No Fury*: 27.

35. Taubman, *No Fury*: 11.

36. Rapping, *Movie*: 34.

37. Taubman, *No Fury*: 104–6.

38. Ironically, in the media Betty Broderick is constructed as not even having the 'job' of mother and wife. Time after time, Broderick is labeled a 'socialite', eliminating the whole notion of motherhood from her persona. Socialite, with its connotations of a silver-spoon upbringing, lack of purpose, and full-time staff of nannies, cooks and drivers, suggests that motherhood is a middle-class institution not available to women in high-income families. Betty Broderick is described as 'the 42-year-old mother of four' in the very first Wallace newspaper article, but by the time she is back in the headlines the following year, at the commencement of her trial, boldface letters proclaim: 'Trial of La Jolla Socialite in 2 Slayings Begins' (*The Los Angeles Times*, 23 October, 1990). Betty keeps this label of socialite to this day, despite her protests that, '[she] was never a socialite... [she] was a housewife' (*Oprah Winfrey Show*, 2 November, 1992).

39. Burrelle's Information Services, *The Oprah Winfrey Show: Betty Broderick's Children Speak Out* (Chicago: Harpo, 1992): 19.

40. Burrelle's, *Oprah*: 19.

41. Lehman, 'A Woman Scorned': 122.
42. Rapping, *Movie*: xli.
43. Elaine Rapping, 'TV Movies: The Domestication of Social Issues', *Cineaste* 19.3 (1988): 33.
44. Ibid.

Victimless Crimes – Yeates

1. For a discussion of the stereotyped woman-as-victim, see Jocelynne Scutt, *Women and the Law* (North Ryde: The Law Book Company, 1990) and Keith Soothill and Sylvia Walby, *Sex Crime in the News* (London: Routledge, 1991); for the woman as deviant perpetrator, see Ann Lloyd, *Doubly Deviant, Doubly Damned: Society's Treatment of Violent Women* (Harmondsworth: Penguin, 1995), and Candice Skrapec, 'The Female Serial Killer: An Evolving Criminality', in Helen Birch (ed.), *Moving Targets: Women, Murder and Representation* (London: Virago, 1993): 241–68.
2. Jennifer Craik examines this issue in particular relation to the cultural myths surrounding infanticide and the transgressive mother, in 'The Azaria Chamberlain Case and Questions of Infanticide', *Australian Journal of Cultural Studies* 4.2 (1987): 122–6, while Briar Wood gives a more recent overview of the way Chamberlain was used as a cultural scapegoat in 'The Trials of Motherhood: the Case of Azaria and Lindy Chamberlain', in Birch, *Moving Targets*: 62–94.
3. *The Courier-Mail*, the Queensland (Australia) morning broadsheet, 19 December, 1991.
4. *The Courier-Mail*, 17 June, 1992
5. *The Courier-Mail*, 25 August, 1992
6. *New Idea*, 9 May, 1992. One of the leading women's magazines (according to sales figures) in Australia, *New Idea* has evolved from a homespun family-recipes-and-knitting magazine to a relatively downmarket gossip-and-stars magazine.
7. *The Courier-Mail*, 23 September, 1992.
8. For a discussion of the different popular discourses of motherhood such as reactionary, resistant and liberatory, see E. Ann Kaplan, *Motherhood and Representation: The Mother in Popular Culture and Melodrama* (London: Routledge, 1992).
9. For a discussion on gendered television, see John Fiske, *Television Culture* (London: Methuen, 1987) and Mary Ellen Brown (ed.),

Television and Women's Culture: The Politics of the Popular (Sydney: Currency Press, 1990).

10. In her own state, Queensland, there have been an alarming number of unsolved female kidnap-murder crimes in recent times, such as the Sharron Phillips case, where a girl was abducted when her car broke down on a highway. Her body has never been found, and a grim roadside memorial has been built for her, clearly visible when driving on the highway.

11. See Scutt, *Women and the Law*: 490.

12. Grenside, as it turned out, happened to be working at the Gold Coast, Australia, both at the same place and at the same time that Fairlie Arrow staged her 'kidnap'.

13. *The Courier-Mail*, 23 December, 1992.

14. Caren J. Deming discusses the fictional nature of current affairs programmes and the way they create gendered narratives of conflict and desire in 'For Television-Centred Television Criticism: Lessons from Feminism', in Brown (ed.), *Television and Women's Culture*: 37–60.

15. Mary J. Russo, *The Female Grotesque: Risk, Excess and Modernity* (New York: Routledge, 1995), shows us feminist ways of reading unruly masquerades as ultimately celebratory and carnivalesque, or as merely grotesque and deeply conflicting.

16. For a discussion of the controversial forensic evidence, see Helen Yeates (with David Gidley), 'Which is More Persuasive, Media or Forensics?' *Australasian Science* (Summer, 1994): 50–2.

17. See John Bryson, *Evil Angels* (Victoria: Penguin, 1985); Jocelynne Scutt, 'Schemers, Dragons and Witches: Criminal "Justice" and the Fair Sex', in Barbara Garlick *et al.* (eds), *Stereotypes of Women in Power: Historical Perspectives and Revisionist Views* (New York: Greenwood Press, 1992): 181–208; and Wood, 'Trials of Motherhood': 62–94.

18. For a decade of academic wrestling with the meaning of Chamberlain in modern Western culture, see Christine Higgins, 'Naturalising "Horror" Stories: Australian Crime News as Popular Culture', in Ian Craven *et al.* (eds), *Australian Popular Culture* (Cambridge: Cambridge University Press, 1994): 135–48; Wood, 'Trials of Motherhood': 62–94; Noel Sanders, 'Azaria Chamberlain and Popular Culture', in John Frow and Meaghan Morris (eds), *Australian*

Cultural Studies: A Reader (St Leonards: Allen and Unwin, 1993):
86–94; Craik, 'The Azaria Chamberlain Case'; Dianne Johnson,
'From Fairy to Witch: Imagery and Myth in the Azaria Case',
Australian Journal of Cultural Studies 2.2 (1984): 96–101.

19. The title *Evil Angels* was changed to *A Cry in the Dark* for overseas
    release because, it was reported, *Evil Angels* may have given people
    the mistaken idea that this was a biker film about Hell's Angels. It
    seems the distributors were worried that incensed bikers might
    wreck cinemas because of the title's perceived misrepresentation.

20. *Woman's Day*, 15 June, 1992. This is a leading Australian women's
    magazine which, like *New Idea*, deals mainly with celebrities and
    gossip, targeting a broad audience of mainly middle-class readers. It
    is not as glossy as the American *Woman's Day*.

21. *Woman's Day*, 11 January, 1993

22. *Sixty Minutes*, 31 May, 1992. This current affairs programme is a
    direct copy of the American programme of the same name.

23. For a more detailed discussion of this issue, see Helen Yeates
    'Victimless Crimes and Crimeless Victims: the Media, Fairlie Arrow
    and Lindy Chamberlain', *Criminology Australia* 4.3 (January/Febru-
    ary 1993): 22–5; Kerryn Goldsworthy's review of Bryson's book *Evil
    Angels*, in *The Age*, 6 February, 1986; and E. Ann Kaplan's argument
    about Lindy as mother in *Cry in the Dark*, in 'Discourses of the
    Mother in Postmodern Film and Culture', *Westerly* 34.4 (December,
    1989): 24–34. These writers critique the contradictions inherent in
    the private, resistant motherhood discourse presented, somewhat
    unproblematically, in both book and film. Goldsworthy argues that
    the construction of Lindy in private as a 'perfect' mother presents a
    problem: 'he [Bryson] makes constant, approving references to her
    motherliness', and '[he] seems to imply that Lindy Chamberlain's
    obsessively self-sacrificing care and attention in the role of mother
    proves beyond doubt that she could not have murdered her baby.'
    Therefore, Bryson gives as many worthy examples of Lindy's
    motherliness as he can in order to counter the public condemnation.
    Goldsworthy argues strongly that this idealization of Lindy as mother
    coyly denies her sexuality:

    Sexy woman or good mother? In our society it is difficult to play
    both roles convincingly at the same time: for what we call a 'good

*mother' is a figure who, in playing that role, affirms and reinforces
the structure of society; she is defined, limited and kept under
control by a patriarchal social order, and her reward is society's
approval. But female sexuality ... potentially or actually threatens
that order: something for which, sooner or later, one will be
punished ... motherhood is good and female sexuality is not good
and never the twain shall meet.*

Bryson fails to negotiate or even acknowledge these contradictions,
especially, for instance, when he applauds Lindy's 'girlish' figure ten
weeks after the birth of Azaria. Moreover, the book and subsequent
film may therefore be seen as apologetic reconstructions of Lindy as
an ideal traditional mother, the mother the media and the community did not see, while the traditional notion of ideal motherhood *itself*
is never really challenged. As Yeates argues, the defence of Lindy as
mother in both the film and the book downplays her womanly
sexuality, even though her pregnant state at the trial attests both to
her sexuality and her maternity. This image of the pregnant Lindy on
trial suggests to the public that a woman interested in her appearance when pregnant must be a bad woman, for there is a deeply
ingrained patriarchal prejudice against so-called bad women being
mothers.

24. *Woman's Day*, 11 January, 1993
25. *Woman's Day*, 4 July, 1994.
26. *The Weekend Australian*, 16–17 December, 1995.
27. Larry Grossberg, *We Gotta Get Out of This Place: Popular Conser-
    vatism and Postmodern Culture* (New York: Routledge, 1992): 206.
28. For analyses of the female credibility issue in the Anita Hill case, see
    for instance, Toni Morrison (ed.), *Race-ing Justice, En-gendering
    Power: Essays on Anita Hill, Clarence Thomas, and the Construction
    of Social Reality* (London: Chatto & Windus, 1993); and Timothy M.
    Phelps and Helen Winternitz, *Capitol Games: the Inside Story of
    Clarence Thomas, Anita Hill, and a Supreme Court Nomination*
    (New York: HarperPerennial, 1993).

Re-Membering John Bobbitt – Grindstaff and McCaughey

1. Portions of this essay were originally published in 'Feminism, Psychoanalysis, and (Male) Hysteria over John Bobbitt's Missing Manhood', *masculinities: Interdisciplinary Studies on Gender* 4.1 (forthcoming). Reprinted with permission.

2. Jean-Joseph Goux, 'The Phallus: Masculine Identity and the "Exchange of Women'", *Differences: A Journal of Feminist Cultural Studies* 4.1 (1992): 40–75. Quoted from p. 41.

3. Goux, 'The Phallus': 41.

4. Some feminist critics have tended to view Freudian psychoanalysis as a theory that justifies and perpetuates gender inequality on biological grounds, but we do not view psychoanalysis in this way. Because psychoanalysis is a product of our heterocentric, patriarchal culture, the classic psychoanalytic framework can serve as a useful tool for interrogating the boundaries of sexual identity and desire – and, more importantly, for revealing the fragility and instability of those boundaries. For a feminist defense of Freud, see Jacqueline Rose, 'Femininity and Its Discontents', in *idem*, *Sexuality in the Field of Vision* (London: Verso, 1986). For a review of feminist revisions of Freudian psychoanalysis, see chapter three in Luce Irigaray's *This Sex Which Is Not One* (trans. Catherine Porter with Carolyn Burke; Ithaca, NY: Cornell University Press, 1985).

5. Rose, 'Femininity': 86.

6. Rose, 'Femininity': 90–1.

7. Rose, 'Femininity': 91.

8. David Kaplan, 'Bobbitt Fever: Why America Can't Seem to Get Enough', *Newsweek* 123.4 (24 January, 1994): 52.

9. Rudy Abramson, 'Has the Bobbitt Case Escalated the War Between the Sexes?' *Los Angeles Times*, 22 November, 1993: E1.

10. Rush Limbaugh, 'No Tears For Lorena', *Newsweek* 123.4 (24 January, 1994): 56.

11. David Shaw, 'Classic Example of "the Cult of the Average Person'", *Los Angeles Times* (17 February, 1994): A18.

12. Katie Roiphe, *The Morning After: Sex, Fear, and Feminism on Campus* (Boston, MA: Little, Brown, 1993).

13. Katie Roiphe, 'All the Rage', *New York Times*, 29 November, 1993: A13(N), A17(L).

14. Katha Pollitt, 'Subject to Debate', *The Nation* 258.7 (21 February, 1994): 224.

15. Mim Udovich, 'The Cutting Edge', *The Village Voice*, 30 November, 1993: 16.

16. Robin Abcarian, 'Let's Not Make Lorena Bobbitt Into a Feminist Poster Child', *Los Angeles Times*, 5 December, 1993: E1.

17. Cynthia Heimel, 'Sure, Women Are Angry', *Newsweek* 123.4 (24 January, 1994): 58.

18. Robert Keith Smith, Letter to the Editor, *People Magazine* (10 January, 1994): 13.

19. As quoted in Abramson, 'War Between the Sexes?': E1.

20. *The Maury Povich Show* on the Bobbitt case, aired on 4 November, 1993. The failure to see the Bobbitt conflict within a larger context characterized by systemic male domination was also revealed in several articles concerned about women's vigilantism. See Susan Estrich, 'Vigilante Justice: the Real Meaning of the Menendez and Bobbitt cases', *Los Angeles Times*, 16 January, 1994: M1. See also Limbaugh, 'No Tears For Lorena'.

21. As quoted in Heimel, 'Sure, Women Are Angry': 58.

22. Ann Jones, *Women Who Kill* (New York: Ballantine, 1980).

23. Sigmund Freud, *Three Essays on the Theory of Sexuality* (trans. and revised, James Strachey; New York: Basic Books, 1962).

24. Barbara Ehrenreich, 'Feminism Confronts Bobbittry', *Time* 143.4 (24 January, 1994): 74.

25. See Naomi Wolf, *Fire with Fire: The New Female Power and How It Will Change the 21st Century* (New York: Random House, 1994); Wendy Kaminer, *I'm Dysfunctional, You're Dysfunctional: The Recovery Movement and Other Self-help Fashions* (New York: Addison-Wesley, 1992).

26. Sabine Reichel, 'Some Women Nurture Misery', *Los Angeles Times*, 20 January, 1994: B11.

27. Pollitt, 'Subject to Debate', op cit.

28. See Cynthia K. Gillespie, *Justifiable Homicide: Battered Women, Self-defense, and the Law* (Columbus, OH: Ohio State University Press, 1989); Jones, *Women Who Kill*; Minouche Kandel, 'Women Who Kill Their Batterers Are Getting Battered in Court', *Ms* July/August, 1993: 88–9; Lenore Walker, *Terrifying Love: Why Battered Women Kill and How Society Responds* (New York: Harper & Row, 1989).

29. Ehrenreich, op cit.
30. Ibid. This conclusion is highly appealing; after all, what feminist *wouldn't* want to believe that her public image suffers from too little militancy rather than too much, or from behaviors deemed too dainty and accommodating rather than too aggressive and overbearing? However, our own experiences as feminists, as well as our analysis of the media discourse on the Bobbitt conflict, contradict this observation. Instead, the feminist who emerges in media representations both now and in the past more closely resembles the 'straw feminist' Ellen Goodman describes, that mythical figure who burns her bra, hates men, has an abortion as casually as getting a tooth pulled, is hostile to family life, wants all children warehoused in government-run daycare, and wants to drive all women out of their happy homes and into the workforce. Not only is this creature helpful for discrediting real feminists, says Goodman, but she is handy for scaring potential supporters away. See Ellen Goodman, 'The Straw Man Begets the Straw Feminist', *Los Angeles Times*, 26 January, 1994): B7.
31. Jacques Lacan, *Ecrits* (Paris: Seuil, 1966).
32. See Jacques Lacan, 'The Signification of the Phallus', in *idem, Ecrits: A Selection* (trans. Alan Sheridan; New York: Norton, 1977).
33. Kaja Silverman, 'The Lacanian Phallus', *Differences: A Journal of Feminist Cultural Studies* 4.1 (1992): 84–115. Quoted from p. 99. See also Jane Gallop, 'Phallus/Penis: Same Difference', in *idem, Thinking Through the Body* (New York: Columbia University Press, 1988): 124–32; and Jacqueline Rose, 'The Meaning of the Phallus', in Juliet Mitchell and Jacqueline Rose (eds), *Feminine Sexuality: Jacques Lacan and the Ecole Freudienne* (trans. Jacqueline Rose; New York: Norton, 1985).
34. Frank Krutnik, 'Masculinity and Its Discontents', in *idem, In A Lonely Street: Film Noir, Genre, Masculinity* (London: Routledge, 1991): 75–91. Quoted from pp. 82–3.
35. Vince Passaro, 'Stand by Your Manhood', *Elle* (October, 1993): 94.
36. Sigmund Freud, 'Some Psychological Consequences of the Anatomical Distinction Between the Sexes', in *idem, Sexuality and the Psychology of Love* (trans. James Strachey; ed. Philip Rieff; New York: Collier Books, 1963): 183–93. First published in 1925.

37. See Horney in Irigaray, *This Sex Which Is Not One*; see also Maria Torok, 'The Meaning of "Penis Envy" in Women', *Differences: A Journal of Feminist Cultural Studies* 4.1 (1992): 1–39.
38. *Jenny Jones*, parts 1 and 2, with John Wayne Bobbitt, aired on 11 and 12 January, 1994.
39. Kim Masters, 'Sex, Lies, and an Eight-Inch Carving Knife', *Vanity Fair* (November, 1993): 168–72, 207–12.
40. As quoted in Masters, 'Sex, Lies': 170.
41. Krutnik, 'Masculinity': 85.
42. Charles Bernheimer, 'Penile Reference in Phallic Theory', *Differences: A Journal of Feminist Cultural Studies* 4.1 (1992): 116–32.
43. Ehrenreich, op cit.
44. The fact that 'masculating' does not appear in the dictionary illustrates well the cultural assumption that masculinity is 'natural' and effortless rather than requiring constant re-articulation; within this framework a man can only be e-masculated, that is, stripped of something he already, 'naturally', has.
45. *Rolanda*, featuring John Bobbitt and his new fiancée, aired on 23 May, 1994.
46. Significantly, while Lorena did give a couple of interviews (one on ABC's *20/20* newsmagazine, and one in the November 1993 issue of *Vanity Fair*), she remained largely silent about the ordeal, refusing to discuss on the talk show circuit either severing her husband's penis or the sexual abuse which she said had lead up to it.
47. *John Wayne Bobbitt: Uncut*, XXX-rated video starring John Bobbitt and directed by Ron Jeremy, 1994.
48. The *Geraldo* episode mentioned here aired on 27 September, 1994.

SELECTED
BIBLIOGRAPHY

Allen, H. *Justice Unbalanced,* (Milton Keynes: Open University Press, 1987)

Allen, Mary Sophia, *The Pioneer Policewoman* (London: Chatto & Windus, 1925)

Bandalli, Sue, 'Provocation – A Cautionary Note', *Journal of Law and Society* 22 (September, 1995): 398–409

Bardsley, B., *Flowers in Hell* (London: Pandora, 1987)

Benedict, Helen, *Virgin or Vamp: How the Press Covers Sex Crimes* (New York: Oxford University Press, 1992)

Beneke, Timothy, *Men on Rape* (New York: Oxford University Press, 1982)

Bernheimer, Charles, 'Penile Reference in Phallic Theory', *Differences: A Journal of Feminist Cultural Studies* 4.1 (1992): 116–32

Birch, Helen, 'Twice Unnatural Creatures', *New Statesman,* 18 March, 1988

— (ed.), *Moving Targets: Women, Murder and Representation* (London: Virago, 1993)

Bourque, Linda Brookover, *Defining Rape* (Durham, NC: Duke University Press, 1989)

Bryson, John, *Evil Angels* (Victoria: Penguin, 1985)

Carlen, P. *et al., Criminal Women* (Cambridge: Polity Press, 1985)

Chan, Wendy, *The (un)Making of an Aberration: Women who Kill their Partners in England and Wales* (unpublished Ph.D. thesis, University of Cambridge)

Craik, Jennifer, 'The Azaria Chamberlain Case and Questions of Infanticide', *Australian Journal of Cultural Studies* 4.2 (1987): 122–6

Crenshaw, Kim, 'Mapping the Margins: Intersectionality, Identity Politics, and Violence Against Women of Color', in Fineman, M. and Mykitiuk, R. (eds), *The Public Nature of Private Violence* (London: Routledge, 1994)

Cuklanz, Lisa, 'Truth in Transition: Discursive Constructions of Character in the Rideout Rape in Marriage Case', *Women's Studies in Communication* 16 (Spring, 1993): 80

Daly, Kathleen, *Gender, Crime and Punishment* (New Haven: Yale University Press, 1994)

Deming, Caren J., 'For Television-Centred Television Criticism: Lessons from Feminism', in Brown, Mary Ellen (ed.), *Television and Women's Culture: The Politics of the Popular* (Sydney: Currency Press, 1990)

Dobash, R. E. and Dobash, R. P., *Women, Violence and Social Change* (London: Routledge, 1992)

Dworkin, Andrea, *Pornography: Men Possessing Women* (New York: Dutton, 1989)

Eastlea, B., *Science and Sexual Oppression* (London: Weidenfeld and Nicolson, 1981)

Edwards, S., *Policing 'Domestic' Violence* (London: Sage, 1989)

Ehrenreich, B. and English, D., *For Her Own Good* (London: Pluto, 1979)

Ellman, Maud, *The Hunger Artists: Starving, Writing and Imprisonment* (London: Virago, 1993)

Farran, D., *The Trial of Ruth Ellis* (working paper included in the *Studies in Sexual Politics* series edited by Stanley, L. and Scott, S., Sociology Department, University of Manchester, 1988)

Fiske, John, *Television Culture* (London: Methuen, 1987)

Freud, Sigmund, *Three Essays on the Theory of Sexuality* (trans. and revised, James Strachey; New York: Basic Books, 1962)

—, 'Some Psychological Consequences of the Anatomical Distinction Between the Sexes', in *idem, Sexuality and the Psychology of Love* (trans. James Strachey; ed. Philip Rieff; New York: Collier Books, 1963)

Fulford, Roger, *Votes for Women*, (London: White Lion Publishers, 1976)

Gallop, Jane, 'Phallus/Penis: Same Difference', in *idem, Thinking Through the Body* (New York: Columbia University Press, 1988)

Gans, Herbert, *Deciding What's News* (New York: Random House, 1980)

Garment, Suzanne, 'Can the Media be Reformed?', *Commentary,* August, 1987: 37–43

Gavigan, S., 'Petit Treason in Eighteenth-Century England: Women's Inequality before the Law', *Canadian Journal of Women and the Law* 3.2 (1990): 335–74

Geraghty, Christine, *Women and Soap Opera: A Study of Prime-Time Soaps* (Cambridge: Polity Press, 1991)

Gilfus, Mary, 'From Victims to Survivors to Offenders: Women's Routes of Entry and Immersion into Street Crime', *Women and Criminal Justice* 4.1 (1992): 63–90

Gillespie, Cynthia, *Justifiable Homicide: Battered Women, Self-defense, and the Law* (Columbus, OH: Ohio State University Press, 1989)

Glass, Dee Dee, *All My Fault* (London: Virago, 1995)

Goldstein, Tom, *The News at Any Cost: How Journalists Compromise Their Ethics to Shape the News* (New York: Simon and Schuster, 1985)

Goldsworthy, Kerryn, 'Martyr to Her Sex', *The Age,* 6 February, 1986: 19–20

Goodman, J. (ed.), *The Moors Murderers* (Newton Abbot: David and Charles, 1986)

Goodman, J. and Pringle, P. (eds), *The Trial of Ruth Ellis* (Newton Abbot: David and Charles, 1974)

Goux, Jean-Joseph, 'The Phallus: Masculine Identity and the "Exchange of Women"', *Differences: A Journal of Feminist Cultural Studies* 4.1 (1992): 40–75

Grossberg, Larry, *We Gotta Get Out of This Place: Popular Conservatism and Postmodern Culture* (New York: Routledge, 1992)

Hall, S. and Gieben, B. (eds), *Formations of Modernity* (Cambridge: Polity, 1992)

Hancock, R., *Ruth Ellis: The Last Woman to be Hanged* (London: Weidenfeld Paperbacks, 1989)

Hanmer, J. and Maynard, M. (eds), *Women, Violence and Social Control* (British Sociological Association; Basingstoke: Macmillan, 1987)

Harrison, F., *Brady and Hindley* (London: HarperCollins, 1987)

Hart, L., *Fatal Women: Lesbian Sexuality and the Mark of Aggression* (London: Routledge, 1994)

Healey, T., *The World's Greatest Crimes of Passion* (London: Hamlyn, 1990)

Heath, Linda, Gordon, Margaret, and LeBailly, Robert, 'What Newspapers Tell Us (And Don't Tell Us) about Rape', *Newspaper Research Journal* 2 (July, 1981): 48–55

Heidensohn, Frances, *Women and Crime* (London: Macmillan, 1985)

Heller, Terry, *The Delights of Terror: An Aesthetics of the Tale of Terror* (Urbana, IL: University of Illinois Press, 1987)

Herman, Edward, *Beyond Hypocrisy: Decoding the News in an Age of Propaganda* (Montreal: Black Rose Books, 1992)

Higgins, Christine, 'Naturalising "Horror" Stories: Australian Crime News as Popular Culture', in Craven, Ian *et al.* (eds), *Australian Popular Culture* (Cambridge: Cambridge University Press, 1994)

Hutter, B. and Williams, G. (eds), *Controlling Women: The Normal and the Deviant* (London: Croom Helm, 1981)

Irigaray, Luce, *This Sex Which Is Not One* (trans. Catherine Porter with Carolyn Burke; Ithaca, NY: Cornell University Press, 1985)

Jacob, Naomi, *Me: A Chronicle about Other People* (London: Hutchinson, 1933)

Johnson, Barbara, 'A Dangerous Pattern: A Study of Media Coverage of Violence Against Women in the *San Francisco Chronicle* and *San Francisco Examiner*', March 1994 (unpublished material available from Barbara Johnson, 3891 26th St., San Francisco CA 94131)

Johnson, Dianne, 'From Fairy to Witch: Imagery and Myth in the Azaria Case', *Australian Journal of Cultural Studies* 2.2 (1984): 96–101

Jones, Ann, *Women Who Kill* (London: Gollancz, 1991)

—, *Next Time, She'll Be Dead* (Boston, MA: Beacon, 1994)

Jones, F., *Murderous Women* (London: Headline, 1991)

Kaminer, Wendy, *I'm Dysfunctional, You're Dysfunctional: The Recovery Movement and Other Self-help Fashions* (New York: Addison-Wesley, 1992)

Kandel, Minouche, 'Women Who Kill Their Batterers Are Getting Battered in Court', *Ms* July/August, 1993: 88–9

Kaplan, E. Ann, 'Discourses of the Mother in Postmodern Film and Culture', *Westerly* 34.4 (December, 1989): 24–34

—, *Motherhood and Representation: The Mother in Popular Culture and Melodrama* (London: Routledge, 1992)

Kaye/Kantrowitz, Melanie, 'Women, Violence, and Resistance, Naming It War', in *idem, The Issue Is Power: Essays on Women, Jews, Violence, and Resistance* (San Francisco: Aunt Lute Books, 1992): 7–74

Keller, Teresa, 'Trash TV', *Journal of Popular Culture* 26 (Spring, 1993): 195–206

Kelly, Liz, *Surviving Sexual Violence* (Cambridge: Polity Press, 1988)

Kennedy, Helena, *Eve Was Framed: Women and British Justice* (London: Vintage, 1992)

Kingsley, H. and Tibballs, G., *No Way Out* (London: Headline, 1994)

Kirsta, A., *Deadlier than the Male* (London: HarperCollins, 1994)

Kozloff, Sarah, 'Narrative Theory and Television', in Allen, Robert (ed.), *Channels of Discourse Reassembled* (Chapel Hill, NC: University of North Carolina, 1992)

Krutnik, Frank, 'Masculinity and Its Discontents', in *idem, In A Lonely Street: Film Noir, Genre, Masculinity* (London: Routledge, 1991)

Lacan, Jacques, *Ecrits* (Paris: Seuil, 1966)

—, 'The Signification of the Phallus', in *idem, Ecrits: A Selection* (trans. Alan Sheridan; New York: Norton, 1977)

Lawrence, Kathleen, 'Bobbitt Spouse Abuse/Assault Case' (paper delivered at the Eightieth Annual Meeting of the Speech Communication Association; New Orleans, Louisiana, November, 1994)

Leneman, Leah, *Martyrs in Our Midst: Dundee, Perth and the Forcible Feeding of Suffragettes* (Dundee: Abertay Historical Society Publication No. 33, 1993)

Lloyd, A., *Doubly Deviant, Doubly Damned: Society's Treatment of Violent Women* (Harmondsworth: Penguin, 1995)

Lock, Joan, *The British Policewoman: Her Story* (London: Robert Hale, 1979)

McCarthy, Sarah, 'Pornography, Rape, and the Cult of Macho', *The Humanist,* September/October 1980: 11–20

Maguigan, Holly, 'Battered Women and Self-defense: Myths and Misconceptions in Current Reform Proposals', *University of Pennsylvania Law Review* 140 (1991): 379–486

Marjoribanks, E., *Famous Trials of Marshall Hall* (Harmondsworth: Penguin, 1950)

Marks, L. and Van den Bergh, T. *Ruth Ellis: A Case of Diminished Responsibility?* (Harmondsworth: Penguin, 1990)

Meyers, Marian, 'News of Battering', *Journal of Communication* 44 (Spring, 1994): 47–63

—, *Engendering Blame: News Coverage of Violence Against Women* (Thousand Oaks, CA: Sage, 1996)

Modleski, Tania, *Loving with a Vengeance: Mass-produced Fantasies for Women* (London: Methuen, 1984)

Morrell, Caroline, *'Black Friday': Violence against Women in the Suffragette Movement* (London: Women's Research and Resources Centre Publications, 1981)

Morrison, Toni (ed.), *Race-ing Justice, En-gendering Power: Essays on Anita Hill, Clarence Thomas, and the Construction of Social Reality* (London: Chatto & Windus, 1993)

Murray, Dr Jessie and Brailsford, H. N., *Treatment of the Women's Deputations by the Police*, in Roberts, Marie Mulvey and Mizuta, Tamae (eds), *The Militants: Suffragette Activism* (London: Routledge, 1994)

Nadel, J., *Sara Thornton: The Story of a Woman Who Killed* (London: Gollancz, 1993)

Nicolson, Donald, 'Telling Tales: Gender Discrimination, Gender Construction and Battered Women Who Kill', *Feminist Legal Studies* 3.2 (1995): 185–206

Ohmer, Susan, 'Female Spectatorship and Women's Magazines', *The Velvet Light Trap* 25 (1990)

Pagelow, Mildred, *Woman-Battering: Victims and their Experiences* (Beverly Hills, CA: Sage, 1981)

Pankhurst, Sylvia, *The Suffragette Movement* (London: Virago, 1977; first published 1931)

Phelps, Timothy M. and Winternitz, Helen, *Capitol Games: The Inside Story of Clarence Thomas, Anita Hill, and a Supreme Court Nomination* (New York: HarperPerennial, 1993)

Priest, Lisa, *Women Who Killed: Stories of Canadian Female Murderers* (Toronto: McClelland and Stewart, 1992)

Radford, Jill and Kelly, Liz, 'Self-preservation: Feminist Activism and Feminist Jurisprudence', in M. Maynard and J. Purvis (eds), *(Hetero)Sexual Politics* (London: Taylor & Francis, 1995)

Raeburn, Antonia, *The Militant Suffragettes* (London: Michael Joseph, 1973)

Rapping, Elaine, 'TV Movies: The Domestication of Social Issues', *Cineaste* 19.3 (1988)

—, *The Movie of the Week: Private Stories, Public Events* (Minneapolis: University of Minnesota Press, 1992)

Ritchie, J., *Myra Hindley: Inside the Mind of a Murderess* (London: Grafton, 1991)

Roiphe, Katie, *The Morning After: Sex, Fear, and Feminism on Campus* (Boston, MA: Little, Brown, 1993)

Romano, Carlin, 'The Grisly Truth about the Bare Facts', in Manoff, Robert and Schudson, Michael (eds), *Reading the News* (New York: Pantheon, 1987)

Rose, Jacqueline, 'The Meaning of the Phallus', in Mitchell, Juliet and Rose, Jacqueline (eds), *Feminine Sexuality: Jacques Lacan and the Ecole Freudienne* (trans. Jacqueline Rose; New York: Norton, 1985)

—, 'Femininity and Its Discontents', in *idem, Sexuality in the Field of Vision* (London: Verso, 1986)

—, *Why War?* (Oxford: Basil Blackwell, 1993)

Russell, Diana, *Rape in Marriage* (2nd ed; Bloomington: Indiana University, 1990)

Russo, Mary, *The Female Grotesque: Risk, Excess and Modernity* (New York: Routledge, 1995)

Sanday, Peggy Reeves, 'The Socio-cultural Context of Rape: A Cross-cultural Study', *Journal of Social Issues* 37 (October, 1981): 5–27

Sanders, Noel, 'Azaria Chamberlain and Popular Culture', in Frow, John and Morris, Meaghan (eds), *Australian Cultural Studies: A Reader* (St Leonards: Allen and Unwin, 1993)

Schneider, Elizabeth, 'Particularity and Generality: Challenges of Feminist Theory and Practice in Work on Woman-Abuse', *New York University Law Review* 67 (June, 1992) 520–68

Schudson, Michael, 'Deadlines, Datelines, and History', in Manoff, Robert and Schudson, Michael (eds), *Reading the News* (New York: Pantheon, 1987): 79–108

Schwengels, Marlyss and Lemert, James, 'Fair Warning: A Comparison of Police and Newspaper Reports about Rape', *Newspaper Research Journal* 7 (Spring, 1986): 35–42

Scutt, Jocelynne, *Women and the Law* (North Ryde: The Law Book Company, 1990)

—, 'Schemers, Dragons and Witches: Criminal "Justice" and the Fair Sex', in Garlick, Barbara, Dixon, Suzanne, and Allen, Pauline (eds), *Stereotypes of Women in Power: Historical Perspectives and Revisionist Views* (New York: Greenwood Press, 1992)

Silverman, Kaja, 'The Lacanian Phallus', *Differences: A Journal of Feminist Cultural Studies* 4.1 (1992): 84–115

Skrapec, Candice, 'The Female Serial Killer: An Evolving Criminality', in Birch, Helen (ed.), *Moving Targets: Women, Murder and Representation* (London: Virago, 1993)

Smart, Carol, *Feminism and the Power of Law* (London: Routledge, 1989)

—, *Law, Crime and Sexuality* (London: Sage, 1995)

Smart, Carol and Smart, Barry, *Women, Sexuality, and Social Control* (London: Routledge and Kegan Paul, 1978)

Soothill, Keith and Walby, Sylvia, *Sex Crime in the News* (London: Routledge, 1991)

Stanko, Elizabeth A., *Intimate Intrusions* (London: Routledge, 1985)

Stanley, L. (ed.), *Feminist Praxis* (London: Routledge, 1990)

Stoltenberg, John, *Refusing to be a Man* (New York: Penguin, 1989)

Taubman, Bryna, *Hell Hath No Fury* (New York: St Martin's Press, 1992)

Torok, Maria, 'The Meaning of "Penis Envy" in Women', *Differences: A Journal of Feminist Cultural Studies* 4.1 (1992): 1–39

Tuchman, Gaye, *Making News: A Study in the Construction of Reality* (New York: Free Press, 1978)

Walker, Lenore, *The Battered Woman Syndrome* (New York: Springer Publishers, 1984)

—, *Terrifying Love: Why Battered Women Kill and How Society Responds* (New York: Harper & Row, 1989)

Ware, V., *Beyond the Pale* (London: Verso, 1992)

Wilson, R., *Devil's Disciples* (Poole: Javelin, 1986)

Wolf, Naomi, *Fire with Fire: The New Female Power and How It Will Change the 21st Century* (New York: Random House, 1994)

Wood, Briar, 'The Trials of Motherhood: The Case of Azaria and Lindy Chamberlain', in Birch, Helen (ed.), *Moving Targets: Women, Murder and Representation* (London: Virago, 1993)

Worrall, Anne, *Offending Women* (London: Routledge, 1990)

Yeates, Helen, 'Victimless Crimes and Crimeless Victims: the Media, Fairlie Arrow and Lindy Chamberlain', *Criminology Australia* 4.3 (January/February, 1993): 22–5

Yeates, Helen with Gidley, David, 'Which is More Persuasive, Media or Forensics?' *Australasian Science* (Summer, 1994): 50–2

Young, Alison, and Rush, Peter, 'The Law of Victimage in Urbane Realism: Thinking through Inscriptions of Violence', in Nelkin, David (ed.), *The Futures of Criminology* (London: Sage, 1994)

INDEX

heterosexuality, 99, 143, 156
Hill, Anita, 141, 147
Hindley, Myra, 4, 23, 33–6, 38, 40–42
hoaxing, 131–6
homicide, English law of, 65–6
Homolka, Karla, 32–3, 37, 39
homosexuality, 90–91
horror, 38, 155, 182 n25
Hubbard, Shirley, 29–30, 37
Hughes, Francine, 27, 115, 124
Humphreys, Emma, xiii, 27, 51, 57–71;
    crime, 59–60; legal case, 57–8, 67–8
hunger strikes, 48, 73, 79
hysteria, xiii, 8, 16, 81, 143; male and
    female, 144–5; media, 159–60

imprisonment, of suffragettes, 74, 79
infanticide, 2, 130–31, 162 n7
insanity: as explanation of violence, 15,
    38, 63–4, 70; temporary, 27, 149
    see also diminished responsibility,
    hysteria, 'mad or bad'
irrationality, 7, 105, 118

John Wayne Bobbitt: Uncut, 159–60
jokes, 110, 135, 149
Jordache, Beth, 44–5, 48, 50, 53
Jordache, Mandy, 44–5, 50, 51–2, 54–5
Jordache, Rachel, 44–5, 55
Jordache, Trevor, 44, 49
journalism, see media, news reporting
judicial misogyny, 2, 17
Justice for Women (UK), 45, 58

Kennedy, Helena, xiv
Kenney, Annie, 74, 77
kidnapping, 86, 87
Kilbride, John, 33, 34
Kipling, Rudyard, 39

Lacan, Jacques, 152
language: and the body, 125–6, 159; in
    news reporting, 101, 104–5, 108, 111
law: application of, 64–9; English
    homicide, 65–6; and medicine,

68–9; and press, 111; reasonable
    man, 66–7; on television, 127; and
    women, 50, 70, 130
    see also defences, manslaughter,
    murder, provocation
lesbianism, 50
Line, Elizabeth, 51

'mad or bad', xiii, 1, 24–5, 68, 70
    see also diminished responsibility,
    hysteria, insanity
Mahaffy, Leslie, 32, 33
Maitland, Sandra, 46, 49
male privilege, 103, 143–5, 152–3,
    156–60
male-bashing, 148–9
Mandela, Nelson, 92, 94–6, relationship
    with Winnie, 85–7, 98–9
Mandela, Nomzano Winifred (Winnie),
    85–100; as symbolic mother, 89,
    90–91, 93, 94, 95, 97–100; and
    assaults, 86–91; political career,
    91–3, 99
Mandela United Football Club (MUFC),
    87–91, 178 n12
manslaughter, 63, 116, 123
    see also homicide, murder
marriage, 106, 116, 118–19
Marshall Hall, Sir Edward, 6, 9–11
masculinity, 142–60, and violence, 150
    see also gender difference
McGrail, Joseph, 48
media, 112, 121, 128; and Arrow,
    Fairlie, 131, 132–3, 135–6; and
    Bobbitts, 101–12, 142–60; and
    Broderick, Betty, 115, 117–20; and
    Chamberlain, Lindy, 137–40; failure
    to provide context, 103, 107, 110,
    112; and Mandela, Winnie, 88, 98;
    and suffragettes, 78, 79, 83; and
    West, Rosemary, trial, xii; and
    women, 130–31, 136, 140–41
    see also news reporting, public
    opinion, sympathy, television
melodrama, 51, 52